TWICE
AS FAST

TWICE AS FAST

THE FOOD PROCESSOR/ MICROWAVE COOKBOOK

BY SUE SPITLER

Contemporary Books, Inc.
Chicago

Library of Congress Cataloging in Publication Data

Spitler, Sue.
    Twice as fast.

    Includes index.
    1. Food processor cookery.   2. Microwave
cookery.   I. Title.
TX840.F6S64   1982   641.5′89   82-45439
ISBN 0-8092-5636-3
ISBN 0-8092-5635-5 (pbk.)

Copyright © 1982 by Nao Hauser and Carolyn Sue Spitler
All rights reserved
Published by Contemporary Books, Inc.
180 North Michigan Avenue, Chicago, Illinois 60601
Manufactured in the United States of America
Library of Congress Catalog Card Number: 82-45439
International Standard Book Number: 0-8092-5636-3 (cloth)
                                            0-8092-5635-5 (paper)

Published simultaneously in Canada by
Beaverbooks, Ltd.
150 Lesmill Road
Don Mills, Ontario M3B 2T5
Canada

Contents

1 Cooking Twice As Fast

Chances are that you acquired your food processor and microwave oven separately, with different hopes and plans for each. One appliance would perform chopping, slicing, shredding, mixing, and kneading tasks; the other could defrost foods quickly and cut cooking times by more than half. Because of their distinct functions, the two "kitchen whizzes" came to be celebrated in diverse contexts—the microwave oven for quick, simple meals, and the food processor for recipes that otherwise would have required tedious hand labor.

As technological achievements, each appliance merits praise and discussion in its own right. But from a cook's standpoint, it is much more exciting to consider the two together. Separately, the food processor and microwave oven represent two dimensions of speed and convenience. Together, they define a different way of cooking.

You'll find this new approach to food preparation, based on coordinated use of the food processor and microwave oven, detailed in *Twice As Fast: The Food Processor/Microwave Cookbook*. Designed as a resource book for everyone who wants to take advantage of the latest in kitchen technology, *Twice As Fast* contains more than 200 recipes for all kinds of meals and cooking occasions. Browse through and you'll discover a sampling of the possibilities—everything from quick snacks to elegant pâtés and terrines, from hearty stews to Oriental stir-fried entrées, from potato salad to pasta primavera, from chocolate desserts to whole-grain breads. Even at a glance, you'll notice something unusual about all of these recipes: they take much less time to prepare than they would without the food processor and microwave oven. And for this reason alone, they can open up a world of good eating.

The proof of the technology lies, of course, in the tasting. But once you start cooking, you'll recognize other benefits as well. For one thing, food processor/microwave cooking is exceptionally clean. Because most of the preparation is done in the food processor workbowl, there are fewer utensils to wash. Since you can microwave and serve food (and refrigerate and reheat leftovers) in the same dish, separate cookware cleanup and pot-

scrubbing are eliminated. Moreover, the microwave oven wipes clean with a damp sponge. So when you prepare *Twice As Fast* recipes, you can look forward to relaxed meals—without dreading the sight of the kitchen afterwards.

Other advantages can be traced to the fact that the functions of the food processor and microwave oven coordinate beautifully. You'll notice this while you're cooking: there is a very comfortable rhythm to the recipe steps. The time required for ingredient preparation and processing dovetails with microwave cooking time; so multistep procedures can be accomplished in an efficient sequence, without wasting time between steps.

It shouldn't take you long to get used to the incomparable precision of the appliances. The food processor chops, minces, purees, slices, shreds, blends, mixes, and kneads almost instantly, with much more reliable results than you could achieve by hand. The microwave oven heats foods more uniformly than a conventional stove can, so there is much less danger of overcooking or scorching. No doubt you'll have to try a few recipes before you can break the habit of watchful worrying. But then you'll come to realize that predictability is an essential component of kitchen technology. Like all appliances, the food processor and microwave oven can be counted on to perform the same tasks repeatedly, in precisely the same way.

The speed and precision of the appliances add up to freedom for the cook. You can fill a shopping cart with nothing but fresh ingredients—and not worry about having packaged provisions on hand for extra-busy days. You can watch both your diet and your budget more easily, since there is less temptation to buy processed foods or to eat out in restaurants. You can vary menus just by trying different recipes, since all recipes call for the same basic techniques. You can easily substitute ingredients, since the appliances process and cook all foods within certain categories, such as leafy vegetables or boneless meats, in virtually the same way.

You'll probably most appreciate the convenience of *Twice As Fast* cooking in the routine of everyday meals. Used together, the food processor and microwave oven make it incredibly easy to serve wholesome, interesting, family-style dinners in less than an hour. And you can plan menus according to appetite rather than cooking schedule, for the appliances make it possible to prepare chili, Chinese-style beef, a chicken casserole, or a favorite Mexican dish, for example, within the same time framework. For this reason, *Twice As Fast* cooking can save money, too. You don't have to invest much labor to make cheaper cuts of meat or inexpensive vegetables quite tantalizing. In fact, it takes no more time to prepare poultry, fish, or meatless entrées than it does to broil burgers or steaks conventionally—and the results can prove calorie- and cholesterol-wise as well as delicious.

If the versatility of *Twice As Fast* cooking recommends it for everyday meals, the sheer speed can prove equally valuable for special occasions and dinner parties. You may decide to surprise guests with specialties you wouldn't have attempted before—such as a delicate vegetable terrine or a French-style fruit tart— just because it is so easy to do. *Twice As Fast* recipes can tempt and taunt you with all kinds of culinary ambitions, since you never have to worry about getting bogged down in hours of complex preparations. You can serve a

complete Chinese dinner, if you wish, or indulge a passion for chocolate mousse pie. You can plan to feature a flawless hollandaise sauce or loaves of homemade bread—without fear of failure. In short, you can have a lot of fun—and take a great deal of pride—in *Twice As Fast* cooking.

To make the most of *Twice As Fast*, you should note a few things about the organization of this book. Before you start cooking, read through the chapters on "Twice As Fast Techniques" and "Shopping and Serving Shortcuts"; these will clarify recipe directions and can answer many questions before they arise.

In addition to recipe chapters devoted to meal courses, from appetizers through breads and desserts, *Twice As Fast* also contains special chapters on sauces and do-ahead mixes, calorie-counted entrées, and candies and food gifts. Many recipes, however, don't fit neatly into a single category. So do consult the Index for the widest choice of possibilities. If you look under "Appetizers" or "Vegetables," for example, you'll find some recipes that have been included under other chapter headings. Also check the Index if you have a question about an unfamiliar ingredient or procedure, since you are likely to discover an explanation elsewhere in the book.

2 Twice As Fast Techniques

All *Twice As Fast* recipes have been kitchen-tested in standard-size food processors fitted with a Steel Knife, a Medium Slicing Disc, and a Medium Shredding Disc, and in variable-power, 650- to 700-watt microwave ovens. Your appliances may have extra features, such as an expanded feed tube or a microwave oven temperature probe, that can make *Twice As Fast* recipes even faster and easier; so you should read the manufacturer's directions carefully. To use your food processor and microwave oven safely and most efficiently, it is important that you follow the safety, handling, and usage procedures outlined in the appliance manufacturers' manuals.

Here is a guide to *Twice As Fast* cooking terms and the techniques needed to prepare recipes accurately and successfully. Explanations are listed according to recipe directions, so that you can find whatever information you may need as quickly as possible. For example, if a recipe says "Process (Steel Knife) until chopped," check under "Process (Steel Knife)" for the appropriate explanation. If you have some food processor and microwave cooking experience, you probably will not have to refer to this guide very often; if not, you should study both these guidelines and those outlined in your appliance manuals before you start to cook.

USING PREPARATION AND MICROWAVE TIMES

Each *Twice As Fast* recipe is accompanied by separate preparation and microwave times. The preparation time has been calculated from the time when you assemble the recipe ingredients, through the cooking process and standing time, to the finished dish; it assumes that some steps will be done simultaneously, such as processing one ingredient while another is cooking in the microwave oven. It includes whatever time is required to prepare ingredients, such as paring potatoes or cutting up meat. It also includes any time needed to make a sauce, pastry, or other important part of the finished dish. (Only optional ingredients are excluded from the time calculations; see Chapter 14, "Sauces and Do-Ahead Mixes," for additional information.) Each preparation time

is necessarily approximate; it might take you slightly more or less time to accomplish each step in the recipe.

The purpose of the preparation time is to let you know about how much time you need to allow before a dish can be served. This information can be especially helpful, for example, when you want to choose a recipe that can be served for dinner within half an hour or an hour. You might also want to check the preparation time when you are entertaining, so that you'll know how long in advance of serving time or guests' arrival you should begin to cook. You should note, however, that preparation time is not always the same as "work" time; very often, foods need time to cook, stand, or chill but require little attention during that period. A soup or stew, for example, may need to cook as long as an hour, but you can use that time to do other things. So check the preparation time for scheduling purposes, but also read the recipe to determine how much "time off" it actually allows.

Microwave oven time is both included in the preparation time and listed separately. By letting you know how much time your oven will be in use, the separate microwave time can help you schedule the preparation of several recipes. It is usually inefficient to microwave more than one dish at a time, since length of cooking is directly related to the amount of food in the microwave oven. If you are planning to serve several *Twice As Fast* dishes, you should be aware of how much oven time each requires, so that you can coordinate the cooking sequence. For more detailed information on scheduling *Twice As Fast* menus, see Chapter 3, "Shopping and Serving Shortcuts."

For several reasons, microwave oven times can only be approximate. Not only do various oven models perform at different speeds, but any two identical ovens are also likely to give varying results. Just a few of the factors that influence timing are the amount of electrical power delivered to your home or geographic area; the time of day, as it affects the amount of electricity being used in the area; and the number of other appliances, if any, that share an electrical circuit with your microwave oven (ideally, the oven should have its own circuit).

In *Twice As Fast*, you will usually find a range of microwave times given, along with a specific way to tell if the food is done. For more detailed information on timing, see the Microwave Oven Techniques section of this chapter.

PREPARING THE INGREDIENTS

Quantities of ingredients are specified in volume, weight, or size, according to the easiest form of measurement. When volume measurement would be impractical, weights are specified; so you should use a kitchen scale to ensure accuracy. Precise volume measurements are critical to baking success. Be sure to measure liquids into a clear measuring cup set at eye level; dip or lightly spoon flour and other dry ingredients (except brown sugar which should be packed) into dry measuring cups and level the top with the straight edge of a knife or spatula.

Because small quantities of fresh parsley, coriander, and dill are difficult to measure, amounts are designated in sprigs. A sprig is the small bunch of leaves you can conveniently cut (with kitchen shears or a paring knife) from one small stem. To process fresh herbs effectively with the Steel Knife, you must remove large stems. It is also essential that the herbs be dry; so towel-dry fresh herbs after you wash them.

Prepare *Twice As Fast* ingredients as directed in the recipes, referring to these explanations as needed.

- *Cut into 1-inch pieces.* This description applies to foods that will be chopped, minced, or pureed with the Steel Knife. Cutting foods into small, uniform-size pieces ensures consistent chopped or minced texture. If you start with pieces that are too large or not uniform in size, the results will be uneven. A mix of large and small cubes of beef, for example, cannot be processed to desired meat loaf texture; the smaller pieces will become minced before the larger pieces are properly chopped.
- *Cut into halves or cut into quarters.* This description applies to small foods, such as

hard-cooked eggs, that will be processed with the Steel Knife. Dividing these foods, as directed, into equal pieces ensures consistent chopped or minced texture.

- *Cut to fit feed tube.* This description applies to foods that will be sliced with the Slicing Disc or shredded with the Shredding Disc. Use the feed tube pusher as a convenient guide to the length and width of foods that will fit into the tube. Trim potatoes, lemons, and other medium-size foods to fit the feed tube, or cut them lengthwise into halves. Cut larger foods, such as eggplant or iceberg lettuce, into wedges to fit the feed tube. Cut meat and cheese into the largest size pieces that will fit into the feed tube. To fit a seeded, cored green pepper into the feed tube, slit it lengthwise and roll it tightly before inserting it into the tube.

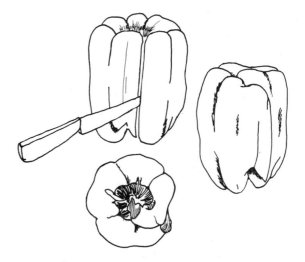

Because the bottom of the feed tube is slightly wider than the top, you may find that you can insert some foods, such as a whole lemon or rolled-up green pepper, through the bottom even though they won't fit through the top. For neatest slices and most efficient shredding, trim ends of rounded fruits and vegetables so that they will rest securely between the Slicing or Shredding Disc and the feed tube pusher.

- *Chilled or cold.* When applicable, chilling is specified so that ingredients will be firm enough for effective processing. All firm cheeses should be chilled before processing with the Shredding or Slicing Disc. Moist, pliable Parmesan cheese should be chilled before processing with the Steel Knife; dry, aged Parmesan is firm enough to process at room temperature. (Do not attempt to process Parmesan cheese or any other food that is too hard to pierce easily with the tip of a knife blade.) Unless a recipe specifies otherwise, assume that all ingredients are at normal storage temperature; vegetable oil, for example, should be at room temperature, and meat should be at refrigerated temperature.

- *Softened.* When a recipe calls for softened butter, margarine, or cream cheese, microwave the ingredient to the proper consistency. Remove any aluminum foil wrapping, place the butter or cream cheese on a glass plate or in a glass measuring cup, and microwave at High just until soft enough to spread easily. The time will vary according to quantity and oven. The butter or cream cheese should not lose its shape; so watch carefully, and begin checking at 30 seconds.
- *Room temperature.* When egg yolks are used to bind butter or oil with vinegar, lemon juice, or another acidic liquid, as in mayonnaise or hollandaise-type sauces, the yolks should be brought to room temperature before processing. To bring yolks to room temperature, place eggs in a bowl of warm (about 105° F) water and let stand at least 5 minutes before separating them.
- *Seeded.* There are two reasons to seed tomatoes or cucumbers before processing. First, the seeded vegetable will yield firmer, more attractive chopped pieces or slices. Second, the vegetable won't contribute excess juices to the finished dish. The latter reason is especially important in microwave cooking, because the speed of the process does not allow time for excess moisture to evaporate. To seed a tomato, cut it horizontally into halves and squeeze each half gently until the seeds pop out; if you do this over a strainer or colander placed in a bowl, you can save the juice and substitute it for an equal amount of the water called for in a recipe. To seed a cucumber, cut it

lengthwise into halves and scrape out the pulp with a spoon or remove it in strips with a small paring knife.

To remove seeds from jalapeño and other chili peppers, slit the pepper lengthwise and rinse under cold water; remove the veins with a paring knife, if you wish. Most of the heat in chili peppers comes from the seeds and veins; so the flavor will be milder if you remove both. Always be careful not to touch your eyes when you are handling chilies; the volatile oils in the juices can cause irritation. You may want to wear rubber gloves to protect your skin from the oils also.

FOLLOWING THE RECIPE

The sequence of steps in each *Twice As Fast* recipe has been designed for maximum speed and convenience. So when you read through a recipe you'll find that the steps follow these general principles:

1. Foods that require a clean, dry workbowl are always processed first, even though they may not be used until later in the recipe. This sequence ensures that you will rarely have to wipe out or wash the workbowl before you are finished cooking.
2. Foods that should remain separate from the rest of the ingredients, such as garnishes, are processed in a sequence that prevents them from mingling in the workbowl. If you remove each of these ingredients carefully, using a rubber spatula to scrape the side of the bowl and the blade or disc, you will not have to wipe out the workbowl with paper toweling.
3. You should empty the workbowl each time you change the blade or disc. But you can process two or more ingredients using the same blade or disc without emptying the workbowl. If the ingredients should be kept separate, the recipe will specify that they be processed separately, even if the same blade or disc is used.
4. In each recipe, the sequence of food processor steps is coordinated with the sequence of microwave cooking. Usually you can be preparing one part of the

recipe in the food processor while another part is in the microwave oven. So read ahead in the recipe to make best use of your cooking time.

FOOD PROCESSOR TECHNIQUES

Twice As Fast recipes call for a few very simple food processor techniques. These are the directions you will find in the recipes, with explanations of how to proceed. Please note that the blade or disc to be used is always indicated in parentheses following the food processor procedure.

Process (Steel Knife) until blended, mixed, or smooth. This is the most fundamental food processor technique. Position the Steel Knife securely in the workbowl. Add food to the workbowl. Let the machine run until the food has been processed as indicated. Stop the machine and scrape down the side of the bowl at least once during processing to ensure smooth and consistent results.

Process (Steel Knife) using on/off technique until coarsely chopped, chopped, finely chopped, minced, mixed, or blended. This is the key to controlling food processor action. Position the Steel Knife securely in the workbowl. Add food to the workbowl. Turn the machine on and off until food has been processed as indicated; use the pulse or on/off switch on your machine or rotate the cover, according to manufacturer's instructions. Check the food after 1 or 2 on/off turns for desired texture; continue processing with on/off turns as necessary. Scrape down the side of the bowl with a rubber spatula at least once.

The on/off technique ensures that foods will not be overprocessed. Be especially careful to use the on/off technique, as directed in the recipe, when mixing batters, doughs, and pastries for baking, since overprocessing can cause toughness.

With machine running (Steel Knife), drop or add through feed tube; process or process using on/off technique. This technique ensures that a small food, such as a clove of garlic, will be processed thoroughly, and that a liquid will be thoroughly incorporated into foods already in the workbowl. Be sure that the Steel Knife is positioned securely in the workbowl. Start the machine. Add food through the feed tube and process as indicated in the recipe.

Slice (Slicing Disc). The standard, Medium Slicing Disc that comes with all food processors is used in *Twice As Fast* recipes. To slice foods with the Slicing Disc, position the disc securely in the workbowl and place food upright in the feed tube. Use the pusher to guide food through the feed tube.

Efficient use of the Slicing Disc depends on how the food is positioned in the feed tube and how much pressure is applied to the feed tube pusher. Whenever possible, pack the feed tube so that food is held tightly in place. Sometimes you will be able to pack long foods, such as carrots, more securely if you cut them crosswise into halves. You may be able to slice two carrots more efficiently, for example, if you cut them into halves and wedge the four pieces into the feed tube (inserting them through the bottom, if necessary). To slice a single food, such as one carrot, position it against one side of the feed tube, opposite the cutting edge of the oncoming disc.

To slice small round foods, such as olives or cherry tomatoes, layer them in the feed tube, filling the width of the tube. Mushrooms can be arranged the same way or they can be stacked sideways with caps placed against alternate sides of the feed tube.

To slice leafy vegetables, such as spinach, arrange the leaves in a neat stack; roll up the stack of leaves and insert the roll vertically into the feed tube. Slice with light pressure on the pusher.

When raw meat is to be sliced, the recipe will direct you to freeze the meat until slightly frozen; the meat should be frozen only until firm—not until it is too hard to pierce with the tip of a sharp knife. Slice with firm pressure on the pusher. Some *Twice As Fast* sandwich and salad recipes call for cooked roast beef, which can be either leftover or purchased at a deli. If you wish to slice leftover beef with the food processor, be sure that it is well chilled (not frozen); then cut it to fit the feed tube and slice with firm pressure on the pusher. Pieces of raw or cooked meat should be cut with the grain and inserted with the grain parallel to the feed tube, so that the Slicing Disc will cut across the grain.

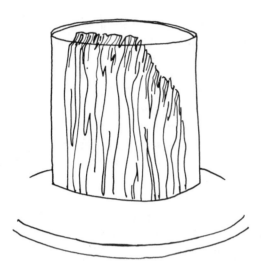

Apply pressure to the feed tube pusher according to the texture of the food. Press firmly on hard foods, such as potatoes, and lightly on delicate foods, such as mushrooms. Always use light pressure with cheese.

Most *Twice As Fast* recipes do not require perfectly even slices; so don't worry if yours aren't. Cut up any scraps that remain on the disc and add them to the food in the workbowl. If a scrap of food gets caught in the disc, stop the machine immediately and carefully remove the scrap from the disc before you continue processing.

Slice (Slicing Disc), arranging food horizontally in the feed tube. Some foods, such as carrots and zucchini, can be positioned upright or sideways in the feed tube for slicing. If you position the food sideways, you will get longer slices. Long slices of fresh vegetables are especially useful when the vegetables will be served with dips. Green beans are arranged horizontally for slicing when French-cut beans are desired. Snow peas are sliced horizontally to yield long, delicate strips in Chinese-style entrées.

Shred (Shredding Disc). To shred foods with the Shredding Disc, position the disc securely in the workbowl and place food upright in the feed tube. Use the pusher to guide food through the feed tube. To use the Shredding Disc efficiently, position food in the feed tube and apply pressure on the feed tube pusher as directed above under *Slice (Slicing Disc)*.

Some foods can be positioned upright or sideways in the feed tube. Upright positioning yields short shreds; sideways, long shreds. Ingredients specified in *Twice As Fast* recipes should be positioned upright for shredding. Firm blocks of sweet or semisweet chocolate can be shredded to garnish desserts; arrange chocolate in feed tube whichever way it fits most securely and apply firm pressure on the feed tube pusher.

Using the food processor workbowl. *Twice As Fast* cooking adds another dimension to the versatility of the food processor. In some *Twice As Fast* recipes, the workbowl is used as a cooking utensil. By microwaving some of the recipe ingredients right in the food processor workbowl, you often can avoid the inconvenience of transferring ingredients back and forth from the food processor to a cooking container. You'll find this procedure used for melting chocolate and letting yeast dough rise, as well as for cooking vegetables, eggs, hollandaise sauce, and Béarnaise sauce. This procedure is not used when prolonged contact with hot foods might damage the bowl. It is also avoided when microwave use of the bowl would interfere with other food processor steps in the recipe. Since there are occasions when you could be microwaving one ingredient in the workbowl while processing another ingredient in a second workbowl, you might wish to purchase a second bowl; however, the recipes in this book assume that you have only one bowl.

Be sure to take these precautions when using the food processor workbowl in the microwave oven:

1. Remove the Steel Knife (or appropriate disc) before you place the bowl in the oven. You can reinsert the Steel Knife and continue processing after the bowl has been removed from the oven. Be very careful when handling the Steel Knife; grasp it by the handle, never by the blade.

2. Check your manufacturer's manual to make sure that your food processor workbowl is dishwasher-safe. If it isn't, don't put it in the microwave oven; transfer the food to an appropriate-size glass casserole or glass measuring cup.

MICROWAVE OVEN TECHNIQUES

Twice As Fast microwave techniques do not require any special cookware or oven accessories. But they do require you to know these facts about your oven:

1. *Oven watts. Twice As Fast* recipes were developed and tested in 650- to 700-watt microwave ovens. If you have an older model oven, it may be only 400 to 600 watts. If it is 400 to 500 watts, you will have to increase *Twice As Fast* recipe cooking times by about 35 percent. If it is 500 to 600 watts, you will have to increase *Twice As Fast* cooking times by about 20 percent.
2. *Power settings.* For maximum speed advantage, *Twice As Fast* recipes are cooked at High, or full power, whenever possible. Lower power settings are used to cook some foods, such as large pieces of meat, more evenly and to prevent delicate ingredients, such as cheese or eggs, from overcooking. The lowest power setting is always used for yeast doughs left to rise in the microwave oven.

The power settings in *Twice As Fast* are designated High; 70% (Medium High); 50% (Medium); 30% (Medium Low); and 10% (Low). High indicates 100% power. Check your manufacturer's manual to see which settings correspond to the other power percentages. If you cannot find this information in the manual, you may wish to obtain a copy of the Microwave Oven Power Level Setting Guide; to do so, send $1.00 to Microwave Cooking Library, 5700 Green Circle Drive, Minnetonka, Minnesota 55343. The chart lists power percentages and corresponding settings for a wide variety of oven makes and models.

If your oven only has one setting, High or full power, you can still prepare the recipes in this book. But you will have to adjust both cooking and standing times. When cooking times are short, reduce them according to the power percentage designated. If the recipe specifies 50% (Medium) for 10 minutes, for example, you could microwave at High for 5 minutes and let the food stand 5 minutes. For longer cooking times, you should alternate cooking and standing times until the food is done. If the recipe specifies 50% (Medium) for 30 minutes, for example, you could microwave at High for 10 minutes, let stand for 10 minutes, and then microwave in 5-minute intervals and let stand until done. Be very cautious with delicate sauces; these should be stirred at least twice as often as specified in the recipe if you are cooking them at High. If you do not have variable-power settings, do not attempt to let yeast dough rise in the oven; you are likely to kill the yeast if you subject it to High power.

Here are explanations of the microwave terms used in *Twice As Fast* recipes:

Glass casseroles and glass baking dish. *Twice As Fast* recipes specify glass casseroles ranging in capacity from 1 to 4 quarts and a 12″ × 8″ glass baking dish. These utensils are all you need to prepare most of the recipes. The glass must be heatproof; you can substitute ceramic dishes that do not have metal trim or a metallic glaze. (Do not place any metal utensil in the microwave oven unless it is specially designed for microwave use.) If you don't have the size specified, you can use a larger dish. However, the food may cook faster when it is spread in a larger container, so check for doneness a few minutes before the time specified.

An important point to remember when buying dishes for microwave use is that you can cook and serve foods in the same containers. So you may decide it is worthwhile to invest in the most attractive microwave-safe casseroles and dishes.

Be careful when removing all dishes from the microwave oven. Although not heated by microwaves, the dishes will hold heat transferred from the food, so use hot pads.

Glass measuring cups. A set of heatproof glass measuring cups is extremely useful for microwave cooking. These allow you to measure, cook, and conveniently stir ingredients in a single utensil. *Twice As Fast* recipes specify 1-cup, 2-cup, 4-cup, and 8-cup measures. Other containers, including heatproof glass or ceramic mugs and casseroles, can be substituted in the microwave oven, but you will have to use additional measuring utensils.

Other cooking utensils. Whenever a food, such as an appetizer or a pastry, can be heated and served on the same plate, the recipe will specify a glass plate, but any heatproof (not necessarily ovenproof) ceramic dish, without metal trim, can be used.

Some *Twice As Fast* meat and poultry recipes specify a microwave meat rack or a clay pot. A heatproof plate inverted in a glass baking dish can be substituted for the meat rack; be sure to remove the plate when you take the meat out of the oven, because a vacuum can form as the dish cools. Substitutions for the clay pot are indicated in tips following the recipes.

Several recipes specify glass loaf pans; other glass dishes can be substituted, but you should check timing carefully if using a dish with a larger capacity or surface area, as the food will cook slightly faster. A few recipes specify glass custard cups or a glass quiche dish. Small, heatproof ceramic bowls, without metal trim, usually can be substituted for the custard cups; a glass pie plate can be used instead of the quiche dish. In both types of recipes, however, the presentation will be best if you use the container specified; if you use a larger dish, be sure to check timing carefully, as the food will cook slightly faster. Substitutions for specially designed plastic microwave cake and muffin pans are given, whenever possible, in tips following the recipe.

Arranging food in the cooking dish. Always arrange foods for microwave cooking so that thicker pieces or parts are positioned toward the outside of the dish. Because food placed around the edge of a dish cooks more quickly than the food in the center, thick and thin parts of chicken or meat, for example, will cook in the same amount of time if arranged as directed in *Twice As Fast* recipes. When appropriate, recipes will direct you to fold under thin ends of meat or fish fillets to ensure even doneness.

Covered or uncovered. Every *Twice As Fast* recipe specifies whether dishes should be covered before placing them in the microwave oven or left uncovered. Dish coverings are designated in these ways:

- *Covered.* When the dish used is a casserole, the directions will just say "covered," without any other description. You can use the appropriate casserole lid or plastic wrap. If you use plastic wrap, cover the dish tightly, but leave one corner open to allow some steam to escape. By "venting" the plastic wrap, you can avoid any buildup of steam that might cause a burn when the wrap is removed.

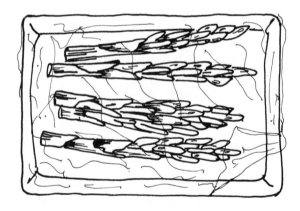

- *Covered with plastic wrap.* For oblong baking dishes, glass measuring cups, the food processor workbowl, and other containers that don't usually come with a tight-fitting lid, plastic wrap is specified when a tight cover is needed. Be sure to vent one corner of the plastic wrap to avoid possible steam burns.
- *Covered with waxed paper.* When it is desirable to hold heat near the surface of the food but not to trap too much moisture, the recipe will specify that a dish be

covered with waxed paper. Lay a sheet of waxed paper loosely over the dish.

- *Covered with paper toweling.* Occasionally, paper toweling is laid over foods to absorb excess moisture or fat. Sandwiches, breads, and other baked goods can be wrapped in paper toweling rather than placed in a dish for microwave cooking; the toweling helps to keep the food crisp.

Arrangement of dishes. When appropriate, *Twice As Fast* recipes will tell you how to place dishes in the microwave oven. This direction applies when you are microwaving more than one dish at a time; it will tell you to arrange the dishes in a circle or in a triangle pattern. These patterns speed microwave cooking by ensuring that microwaves can reach foods from all directions at the same time. You should rearrange the dishes, in the same pattern, during the cooking time to compensate for any unevenness of microwave distribution in the oven. Arrange foods cooked without dishes, such as potatoes, similarly, but place smaller items in the center of the circle or triangle.

Microwave power settings. *Twice As Fast* recipes will direct you to microwave at a specific power setting. Except for High, which is always full power, the settings are given in two ways. The percentage of power, such as 50% or 70%, will be followed, in parentheses, by the most frequently used label for that power level, such as Medium or Medium High. Please note that the power level settings on your oven may not correspond to the same percentages of power. It is quite possible, for example, that 50% power corresponds to the Low, Simmer, Slo-Cook, or Defrost setting on your oven, rather than to Medium. So be sure that the power setting you choose corresponds to the percentage specified in the recipe.

The microwave industry hopes to standardize power settings within the next five years; the settings indicated in parentheses in *Twice As Fast* recipes correspond to those proposed by the industry. For ovens made up until now, however, the power percentages are the only completely accurate guide.

You will notice that some microwave dishes begin cooking at one power setting and are finished at another. It is not necessary to remove the dish from the oven when you change the power setting, unless the food needs to be stirred or rearranged.

Microwave times. Most *Twice As Fast* recipes give a range of cooking times or an approximate cooking time, along with a way to tell if the food is done. Because of differences in ovens and amount of electrical power delivered to an area at various times of the day, cooking times cannot be absolutely specific. Start checking for the degree of doneness indicated at the end of the minimum amount of time given; continue cooking as necessary.

It is important to take into account your own oven and tastes. If you have a very fast, 700-watt oven, or if you like vegetables very crisp, you should start checking for doneness about a minute before the time given; you can always cook longer, but you cannot retrieve overcooked delicate foods, such as fish, eggs, sauces, or vegetables. Recipes do not specify microwave times for boiling water or melting butter. Times for these procedures will differ according to quantity and temperature and are best judged just by looking at the water or butter.

Remember that there is no substitute for a reliable meat thermometer when you are roasting whole meat or poultry. The only way to be sure that meat is cooked the way you prefer is to test it with a thermometer. Never leave a conventional thermometer in the microwave oven. Use a special microwave meat thermometer in the oven, or remove the meat to check doneness with an instant-register or conventional meat thermometer.

Stirring. Food near the sides and top of a dish will begin cooking, due to friction generated by microwaves, almost as soon as the oven is turned on; the rest of the food in the dish will cook only as fast as the microwave-generated heat is conducted inward. Therefore, stirring is important in microwave cooking, both to speed the cooking process and to ensure even doneness. Always stir from the outside of the dish inward, with a circular motion. Use a wire whisk to stir sauces thoroughly. Other foods can be stirred effectively with a plastic or wooden spoon, a wooden spatula, or a rubber spatula. You can leave a nonmetallic stirrer in the dish for short periods of microwave time, if you wish.

Rotating dishes. Virtually every microwave oven cooks somewhat unevenly. Foods heat faster in the oven's "hot spots" and slower in other areas of the oven. All recipes that aren't stirred should be rotated at least once during cooking to ensure even doneness.

Shielding. When you are microwaving large, unevenly shaped pieces of meat or poultry, or baking in a rectangular pan, the thinnest parts, or corners, can become overcooked before the rest of the food is done. To avoid this problem, a few *Twice As Fast* recipes will tell you to shield the thinnest parts with small pieces of aluminum foil before the total cooking time is completed. The foil will prevent further cooking, since microwaves cannot penetrate the metal.

Standing time. Dense foods and large quantities of food will continue cooking in their own heat after they have been removed from the microwave oven. The internal temperature of meats and poultry will rise 10 to 20 degrees during standing. Baked goods will dry to desirable texture. Therefore, many *Twice As Fast* recipes specify a standing time. This amount of time is considered a critical cooking step and is included in the total preparation time. Recipes for meats and other dense foods often will tell you to let the food stand covered with aluminum foil (it doesn't matter which side of the foil faces the food). Recipes for baked foods will sometimes tell you to let the food stand directly on the countertop, rather than on a rack. Both these directions are designed to maximize heat and moisture retention, so that the center of the food will reach a uniform degree of doneness during the standing time.

TWICE AS FAST RECIPES

The best way to master all *Twice As Fast* techniques is to start cooking. If, after reading the above guidelines, you still feel uncertain of your skills, begin with recipes that will succeed even if you make a few mistakes. A dip, for example, will taste good even if the ingredients are overcooked or overprocessed a little. If you are new to food processor slicing, practice with a soup or stew recipe—nobody will notice a few uneven slices. Similarly, you can test the timing on your microwave oven with a soup or stew; if the food is completely cooked in the minimum amount of time or not quite done in the maximum amount of time, you'll know that your oven is faster or slower than average. You can then use that information to adjust timing on foods where precision is more important, such as fish, vegetables, or sauces. If you keep on cooking, you'll soon lose any uncertainty you have about using the food processor and microwave oven. In fact, you'll begin to wonder how you ever cooked without them.

3 Shopping and Serving Shortcuts

The food processor and microwave oven provide incomparable shopping, serving, and storage flexibility. So the following guide to *Twice As Fast* ingredients, preparation scheduling, and storage possibilities is designed not only to answer questions about the recipes but also to maximize their convenience in your kitchen.

SHOPPING FOR INGREDIENTS

Freshness is the flavor key to *Twice As Fast* recipes. Use of the food processor and microwave oven make it easy to enjoy the taste of fresh ingredients and save the expense of processed foods. But that's no reason to go out to eat if you don't have all the ingredients specified in a recipe! Nor is it any reason to pay a premium price for one ingredient when a suitable alternative is on sale in the supermarket. This alphabetized "shopping list" can help you to make appropriate substitutions as well as to choose ingredients that will yield the most pleasing results. You'll find more detailed directions for ingredient substitutions in the tips following the recipes.

Bouillon and broth. Most *Twice As Fast* recipes call for chicken- and beef-flavor instant bouillon and water when broth is required. The proportion of instant bouillon to water given in the recipe is somewhat higher than that specified on most packages: 1½ teaspoons of bouillon to 1 cup of water. This formula ensures good flavor in the finished dish, and you also can use it when a recipe calls for broth. However, the only reason the recipes specify instant bouillon is that most cooks have it available. If you have homemade broth in the refrigerator or freezer, by all means use it—the flavor will be better. You can also use canned broth or broth made from concentrated stock base. In all cases, substitute an equal amount of broth for the water in the recipe and omit the bouillon. Taste the food before adding any more salt, as the substituted broth may be saltier or less salty than the bouillon.

Bread, bread crumbs, and croutons. Although bread is a routine purchase, it's worth remembering to buy an extra loaf when it's on sale. Use it to make supplies of Bread Crumbs and Croutons (see Index). You can make dried, plain, or seasoned bread crumbs and croutons from any kind of bread and store them for months. Unless a recipe specifies otherwise, you can use either homemade or commercial bread crumbs.

Browning and seasoning sauce. Many foods cook too quickly to brown in the microwave oven. So browning and seasoning sauce is called for in the few recipes where deeper color is desirable for attractive presentation. The sauce can be omitted, or you can substitute other ingredients that would add color, such as Worcestershire sauce, soy sauce, or paprika.

Browning is very rarely needed in *Twice As Fast* recipes, but you can always choose to brown meat or poultry conventionally in a skillet or under the broiler and finish cooking recipes in the microwave oven; you'll still save some time and the food will remain moister than if completed conventionally.

Butter and margarine. *Twice As Fast* recipes were developed and tested with unsalted butter. Margarine can be substituted in almost all cases. If you use salted butter or margarine, taste foods, especially sauces, before adding salt. For the best-tasting butter and seasoned butters, see the Index for Food Processor Butter and Variations. The homemade butter can be stored as commercial butter is, in the refrigerator or freezer.

Cheese. The world of firm cheeses is wide open to substitutions. In a pinch, you can always exchange one mild, nonimported cheese for another; brick, Swiss, mild Cheddar, Muenster, mozzarella, Edam, Monterey Jack, and Colby all fall into this category. Do exercise caution, though, when substituting more assertively flavored, imported cheeses— they will smell much stronger when melted! You may find it convenient to shred a whole block of cheese at one time and keep it refrigerated in a tightly covered container. One ounce of a firm cheese equals slightly more than ¼ cup of shredded cheese.

When Parmesan cheese is specified in a recipe, use whichever kind you prefer. The best grade of Parmesan imported from Italy is stamped Parmigiano Reggiano on the rind; it has a marvelous, slightly nutty flavor. Other imported Parmesan, called *grana*, may come from either Italy or Argentina. The important thing to remember about imported Parmesan is that it can be too hard to process effectively if cold; so bring it to room temperature. (Never attempt to process any food that you cannot pierce with the tip of a knife.) By contrast, some brands of domestic Parmesan are so soft that they cannot be processed to grated texture at room temperature; so be sure that soft Parmesan is well chilled. Do not substitute Romano or another hard cheese for Parmesan unless you are sure you want a much stronger, and often harsher, flavor.

Do not attempt to substitute any cheese for ricotta; when ricotta is specified, its consistency is essential to the recipe.

Cream. If cream is to be whipped, you must use whipping cream. When cream is used for flavor, you can substitute half-and-half or even whole milk, if necessary. But always use the type of cream specified in dessert and candy recipes for proper consistency. Food processor whipped cream will be dense and have less volume than cream whipped with a mixer or a whisk, but it doesn't make any difference in *Twice As Fast* recipes. Cream will whip faster if the food processor workbowl and Steel Knife are chilled, so you may wish to place these in the refrigerator or freezer before processing. However, be careful not to process cream to the point of butter—unless you intend to!

Eggs. Twice As Fast recipes were developed and tested with USDA Grade A large eggs. If you wish to substitute medium eggs in recipes where volume of eggs is important, such as cakes and soufflés, use 3 medium eggs for every 2 eggs specified in the recipe; if only 1 egg is specified, you can just substitute directly.

Fish and seafood. Since the market supply of fresh fish varies almost daily, possible substitutions are specified in virtually every *Twice As Fast* fish recipe. An exception is made for trout, since farm-raised trout usually are available; however, another mild-flavored freshwater fish, such as whitefish or walleye pike, can be substituted for the trout. You can always substitute an equal weight of fish steaks for fillets and vice versa, using the type of fish specified. It's a good idea to choose thick, evenly shaped fillets, since these will microwave more evenly and are less likely to overcook.

You can substitute frozen fish for fresh. The taste and texture will be inferior to those of good-quality fresh fish, but they may be better than those of poor-quality fresh fish. These signs of quality apply to all fish, whether fresh or frozen, whole or filleted: there should not be any strong, fishy odor, and no part of the fish should look dried-out or discolored. Do not buy any fresh fish and do not use any frozen fish that doesn't meet these standards. Defrost frozen fish by microwaving it according to the manufacturer's manual. Do not overdefrost; the fish should still be cold and firm. Rinse off the last remaining ice crystals under cold running water, if necessary. All fish should be rinsed and patted dry with paper toweling before cooking.

The question of fresh versus frozen is almost irrelevant to shrimp. In most parts of the country (the Gulf Coast being a possible exception), almost all the shrimp sold as fresh has been frozen at some point. So look for the best value, according to the size of the shrimp, before you pay more for fresh. Microwave frozen shrimp to defrost them, according to the manufacturer's manual; do not overdefrost. Shrimp cook so fast, whether in the microwave oven or conventionally, that you have to be very careful not to overcook. It's wise to start checking for doneness after 1 minute for each pound of shrimp; you can always microwave them another minute or two, but you cannot save toughened, overcooked shrimp.

Flour. Use all-purpose flour, unbleached or bleached, in *Twice As Fast* recipes unless the recipe specifies whole wheat or rye. You don't ever have to sift, but you do need to measure accurately. Dip measuring spoon or cup into flour, or spoon flour lightly into cup, and level off the measure with a spatula or the flat edge of a knife.

Fruits. Because fresh fruit is one of the changing pleasures of the seasons, *Twice As Fast* recipes suggest substitutions for all types except citrus and avocados. Avocado can be omitted when used as a garnish. Since most avocados are sold at less than peak ripeness, you should remember to purchase them a few days before you plan to use them; avocados will ripen at room temperature and should be used quickly or refrigerated once they are ripe. Lemons can be substituted for limes, if necessary. To get maximum juice from any citrus fruit, microwave the fruit at High 15 seconds before cutting. When recipes specify green or tart cooking apples, you can use other types and reduce any sugar in the recipe to taste; for applesauce or fruit cobbler, a combination of several kinds of apples will yield optimum flavor.

The food processor allows two easy tricks with fruit. First, you can puree any type of fresh or thawed, frozen berries or peaches to make an instant fruit sauce for ice cream, plain cake, or sliced, fresh fruit; add sugar to taste and a teaspoon or two of a fruit liqueur, if you wish. Pureed raspberries are delicious spooned over peach or strawberry ice cream.

Second, you can keep a supply of shredded or grated fresh coconut on hand, if you wish. Puncture eyes of coconut with an ice pick or screwdriver; drain milk and discard. Microwave coconut at High 5 minutes; crack coconut open with a hammer. Pare brown skin from coconut and cut into pieces to fit feed tube for shredding or small chunks for grating. Shred with Shredding Disc for long shreds appropriate for toppings and garnishes; or, with machine running (Steel Knife), drop chunks through feed tube to grate. Coconut can be frozen in a tightly covered container up to 3 months.

Herbs and spices. Fresh herbs can always be substituted for the dried herbs specified in *Twice As Fast* recipes; use twice the amount or more, to taste, and process with the parsley, garlic, or another ingredient chopped in the recipe. Substitute 3 to 4 sprigs fresh dill for 1 teaspoon dried dillweed and 3 to 4 fresh basil leaves for 1 teaspoon dried. Food processor chopping power might encourage you to cultivate basil and other fresh herbs on a sunny windowsill if you don't have a garden; the fresh herbs will reward you with incomparable flavor.

Fresh herbs that are widely available, including parsley, dill, and coriander are specified in *Twice As Fast* recipes. Dried can be substituted, if necessary. You can chop a quantity of any fresh herb and keep it refrigerated or frozen in a tightly covered container. Substitute about ½ teaspoon chopped fresh herb for each sprig specified in a recipe. Substitute half the quantity of dried for fresh herbs.

Don't substitute dried, powdered ginger for gingerroot; omit gingerroot if not available. There's no need to pare slices of gingerroot before processing. To refrigerate gingerroot longer than a week, place it in a jar, add dry sherry to cover, and cover the jar tightly.

There shouldn't be any need to substitute powdered dried garlic for whole cloves, but if there is, substitute ⅛ teaspoon powder for each clove. You can chop a quantity of garlic, place it in a jar, add olive or vegetable oil to cover, and store it tightly covered at room temperature. Substitute ½ teaspoon drained chopped garlic for each whole clove specified in a recipe.

Mayonnaise. Unless a recipe specifies otherwise, you can use either commercial or homemade mayonnaise (see Index for Food Processor Mayonnaise and Variations) in *Twice As Fast* recipes. The homemade product tastes infinitely better and can be refrigerated, tightly covered, up to 10 days.

Meats. Shop supermarket beef sales to build greatest economy into *Twice As Fast* recipes. You can buy beef pot roasts or steaks and freeze them. Then partially defrost, according to microwave manufacturer's manual, and cut them as needed into 1-inch pieces to chop in the food processor for meat loaf, hamburgers, or meatballs; larger cubes for stew; or strips for beef casseroles. It is easier to cut up meat by hand if the meat is partially frozen; it is essential that raw meat be partially frozen for food processor slicing. Cuts of beef round, chuck, and sirloin can be used interchangeably in chopped beef and stew-type recipes. Chuck is fattier and therefore more tender than round; sirloin is the most flavorful. For chopped beef, the fat content should be about 10 percent.

When flank steak or a certain type of beef for roasting is specified, do not make substitutions. These cuts have certain flavors and textures that are important to the success of the recipe.

Any cut of boneless pork, such as shoulder, butt, or chops, can be used in recipes that require boneless pork. Large cuts of both pork and ham can be frozen and cut up as needed for food processor chopping and casseroles, so you may want to stock up at supermarket sales.

If you find it more convenient to cut up meat or chop it prior to freezing, you can do so. But the larger the piece of meat, the longer it can be kept frozen.

Mexican cooking ingredients. The tastes of tortillas, chilies, and all things Mexican have become so popular that most large supermarkets stock the ingredients you'll need for *Twice As Fast* Mexican-style recipes. If you can't get fresh chilies, use canned ones, preferably those packed in water rather than brine; rinse and dry canned chilies thoroughly. If you can't get fresh coriander, you may want to substitute parsley rather than dried coriander leaves, which don't have much flavor. Fresh coriander, sometimes called cilantro or Chinese parsley, often can be found in Oriental supermarkets. Tortillas, chili peppers, and chopped fresh coriander all can be frozen. To seed chili peppers, see Chapter 2, "Twice As Fast Techniques," for instructions given under Preparing the Ingredients.

Mushrooms. Look for fresh, unblemished white or brown mushrooms with tightly closed caps. Don't soak fresh mushrooms; clean them with damp paper toweling or rinse them quickly and dry thoroughly. If you must, you can substitute drained canned mushrooms in recipes that call for chopped texture.

When a recipe calls for dried mushrooms, it is because these contribute a deeper, more woodsy flavor than fresh mushrooms. Fresh mushrooms can be substituted but the taste won't be the same.

You can use imported Chinese or European dried mushrooms interchangeably, except in Chinese-style recipes, where you will want the unique flavor of dried Chinese black mushrooms. Soak dried mushrooms before using as directed in the recipes.

Mustard. Many *Twice As Fast* recipes specify Dijon-style mustard because a little bit of this type of mustard can go a long way when a tangy highlight is desired. You can substitute other mustards, but you should adjust the amount according to the strength of the mustard you are using; Dijon-style is stronger than bright yellow, salad-style mustard but milder than most German-style mustards. You might want to substitute one of the flavored mustards available, such as tarragon or white wine.

Nuts. Since the food processor takes the effort out of chopping nuts, you can buy nuts in the most economical form available, whether whole or in pieces. When sliced almonds are specified in a recipe, you can chop whole almonds and use them instead. Purchase hazelnuts blanched for maximum convenience. To toast nuts, spread them in a glass baking dish and microwave uncovered at High 2 to 3 minutes, rotating dish every minute.

Onions. One of the most important seasoning ingredients, onions are also one of the most diverse. They vary enormously in flavor and flavoring potency. So you will see several different kinds of onions specified in *Twice As Fast* recipes, including fresh green onions and leeks; pearl onions for mildness and small, appealing size; large Spanish onions for mild, sweet taste; and red onions for sweetest, least assertive taste. Common yellow-skinned onions can be substituted for all but the pearl onions;

you can substitute a quarter of a small yellow onion for a green onion that will be chopped. Green onion used for garnish can be omitted. Six green onions can be substituted for 1 medium leek.

If the recipe doesn't specify the type of onion, any dried onion can be used; if the onion is very strong and tear-provoking, you may wish to reduce the quantity. Try white-skinned dried onions in Mexican-style recipes and you'll discover why Mexican cooks count on this variety for inimitable sweet piquancy.

The food processor can give you instant access to this fresh-tasting seasoning mix for tossed green salads: Process (Steel Knife) 1 green onion and top, cut into 1-inch pieces, with 4 sprigs parsley until minced; sprinkle over salad greens before tossing with dressing. If you have 2 fresh basil leaves or 2 sprigs of fresh dill, you may wish to process them with the onion and parsley—the fragrance is wonderful!

Oriental cooking ingredients. You'll find soy sauce, sesame oil, won ton wrappers, 5-spice powder, rice wine vinegar, bean sprouts, and snow peas in a large supermarket or an Oriental grocery store. You can use any type of soy sauce sold in the supermarket in *Twice As Fast* recipes; choose a light or medium, rather than dark, soy sauce if you're shopping in an Oriental grocery store. Sesame oil has a very distinctive, nutty flavor; vegetable oil can be substituted. Rice wine vinegar has about half the acidity of other vinegars, so substitute lemon juice. There are no substitutes for won ton or egg roll wrappers, which can be kept frozen, or 5-spice powder.

Fresh bean sprouts and snow peas taste much better than canned or frozen products, but the latter can be substituted in cooked dishes. Drain canned bean sprouts and refresh them in ice water for at least 10 minutes. Rinse frozen snow peas under cold running water to separate them and proceed with the recipe; do not attempt to slice snow peas that have been frozen.

Poultry. An equal weight of chicken breasts, thighs, or drumsticks can be substituted for a cut-up chicken, and vice versa, in any *Twice As Fast* recipe. Whole and boneless chicken breasts can be used interchangeably unless the boneless breast has to be cut into strips. You can easily bone a chicken breast by inserting the tip of a paring or boning knife through the membrane around the breastbone, cutting the large breastbone from the meat, and inserting your fingers under the small rib bones to release them. So buy chicken according to the best price or your taste and convenience preferences. Cut-up chicken or parts can be frozen, securely wrapped, up to 1 month. Freeze boneless chicken breasts individually wrapped, so that you can easily remove as many as you want. Be very careful to wash all surfaces and utensils that come into contact with raw chicken, as there is the possibility of salmonella contamination.

When you want boneless cooked chicken for salads, casseroles, and sandwiches, microwave chicken parts and remove the meat from the bones. Arrange chicken in a glass baking dish with meatier portions toward the outside of the dish; microwave covered with plastic wrap at High until juices run clear when chicken is pierced with a fork, 7 to 9 minutes a pound. One pound of mixed chicken parts will yield about 6 ounces of cooked meat; a 1-pound chicken breast will yield about 12 ounces of cooked meat.

Cooked turkey breast offers an economical alternative to cooked boneless chicken in salads and casseroles. To microwave turkey breast, see the Index for Turkey Breast with Honey-Mustard Sauce. Turkey breast and duckling can be purchased fresh or frozen; defrost according to manufacturer's manual. To microwave duckling, see the Index for Roast Duckling with Sweet and Sour Cabbage. If you microwave duckling for use in your own recipes and then broil the duckling conventionally about 10 minutes, you can enjoy the best of both worlds—fast, moist cooking and crisp, tantalizing skin.

Rice. Long-grain, converted, and brown rice can be used interchangeably in *Twice As Fast* recipes. Microwave whichever kind you want to use as directed in recipes for Rice and

Seasoned Variations or Sherried Brown Rice with Mushrooms and Pork (see Index); then proceed with any recipe that calls for cooked rice. The microwave oven does not offer much timesaving over conventional rice cookery, but it does have cleanup advantages.

Tomatoes. Twice As Fast recipes display an odd ambivalence toward tomatoes. When full, ripe tomato flavor is needed, the recipe will specify canned tomatoes; a tip at the end of the recipe will give the amount of fresh tomatoes that can be substituted when they are ripe and full-flavored. Ideally, all tomatoes used should be fresh and ripe, but it is difficult to find good tomatoes during most of the year; so the canned tomatoes make year-round, flavorful tomato sauces possible. Fresh tomatoes are specified when texture is an important as taste. You can ripen tomatoes at room temperature, stem ends down, away from direct sunlight—but you cannot instill fullest flavor. When good-quality fresh tomatoes are abundant, you might want to chop and freeze a supply for sauces. Microwave tomatoes at High just long enough to loosen skins, about 15 seconds for each tomato. Let tomatoes stand 1 minute; then peel and core. Cut tomatoes into eighths; process (Steel Knife) just until chopped. Freeze tomatoes in a tightly covered container.

Vegetable oils. Although some *Twice As Fast* recipes specify olive or nut oils, you can always substitute your favorite kind of vegetable oil. Olive oil can be delightfully light and fruity or heavy and overwhelming, depending on its source and how long it has been standing around. Don't use a heavy, intensely flavored olive oil full strength; mix it with plain vegetable oil. Fragrant nut oils, such as walnut or sesame, are used only for flavoring, not for all-purpose cooking; so they are almost always combined with vegetable oil in recipes.

Vegetables. Pick whatever vegetables look freshest and best—and most enticingly priced—in the market. Then check the Index for appropriate *Twice As Fast* recipes. It's smarter to shop this way than to select an expensive or less-than-fresh vegetable just because it fits a specific recipe. If you don't find a suitable recipe, you can always microwave the vegetable, either whole or sliced, and serve it with a *Twice As Fast* sauce or seasoned butter. You will find dozens of sauces that can be made in minutes, including such favorites as Hollandaise and Butter Sauce. Microwave green and yellow vegetables covered at High until crisp-tender, about 5 to 6 minutes a pound.

If you wish to serve frozen vegetables, you can microwave them right in the package; remove the paper wrapper, cut 1 or 2 slits in the box, and microwave at High about 5 minutes. Among the few frozen vegetables specified in *Twice As Fast* recipes are lima beans, which usually are difficult to buy fresh, and chopped spinach, which can provide convenience without sacrifice of flavor when used in a sauce.

Vinegars. Few ingredients can highlight seasonings as easily and effectively as vinegar. Keep several varieties on hand, including red wine, tarragon, white wine, distilled white, and cider vinegars. You can substitute one for another in *Twice As Fast* recipes, but flavor will be better if you use the type specified.

If you would like to make your own herb vinegars, microwave white or red wine vinegar in a glass measure, uncovered, just until boiling. Pour the vinegar over chopped fresh herbs in a jar; cover tightly and let stand at least 10 days. Use 1 tablespoon of herbs for each cup of vinegar, or more to taste.

Wine. When a recipe calls for dry white wine, you can use any appropriate type, such as an American Chablis or Chardonnay, a French white Bordeaux or Muscadet, or an Italian Soave. Remember that the flavor of the wine will come through in the finished dish; so don't use a wine that you wouldn't enjoy drinking.

Yeast. Twice As Fast yeast breads call for active dry yeast. Check the date on the package before you use the yeast to make sure it isn't too old to be effective. Proofing yeast enables you to tell if it is still active. Dissolve the yeast in warm (110° F)—never hot or cold—liquid, as directed in the recipe. If the mixture doesn't begin to foam in about 5 minutes, throw it out and start over with fresh yeast.

SCHEDULING PREPARATIONS

The *Total Preparation Time* listed with each recipe has been calculated as honestly as possible, with time allowances made for measuring ingredients, paring vegetables, cutting up meat, making the sauce or the pastry, and anything else that might be required. The *Total Preparation Time* indicates how many minutes will be needed from the time you take out the ingredients until the dish is ready to be served.

There are many ways to schedule preparation time so that the cooking can be done at your convenience. First, you can prepare almost any *Twice As Fast* recipe to the point of final cooking or heating up to 1 day in advance and refrigerate it; because the food will be chilled, it may require additional minutes to heat through before serving. Second, you can accomplish part of the preparations, such as cooking the chicken or making the sauce, as long as 1 day ahead of time; then refrigerate the food and finish preparations before serving. (Any food that needs to be marinated or chilled can be prepared up to that step and refrigerated overnight.) And third, you can complete most dishes that don't involve microwaving eggs or mayonnaise as long as 1 day in advance, refrigerate them, and reheat just before serving. You will find more detailed directions, when appropriate, in the tips following the recipes. Leftovers can be refrigerated and reheated in the cooking dish.

Soups, poultry entrées, meat casseroles, and breads freeze well. As with all frozen foods, it is important that the freezer be maintained at no higher than 5° F, and preferably lower, for prolonged storage. If you wish to freeze foods for longer than 1 month, be sure that the packaging is airtight. Rigid plastic containers, freezer bags, freezer paper, and heavy-duty aluminum foil are suitable packaging materials. You can store leftovers TV-dinner style, in paper or metal trays or on paper plates; overwrap the trays or plates securely with aluminum foil. It's often convenient to freeze soups, stews, and casseroles in casserole dishes lined with heavy-duty aluminum foil. Once the food is frozen, remove it from the casserole, overwrap it with another sheet of foil, and put it back in the freezer. When you want to defrost and reheat it, the food can be unwrapped and fitted neatly into the casserole dish. Defrost foods in the microwave oven according to the manufacturer's manual.

SCHEDULING MICROWAVE TIMES

The *Microwave Time* that accompanies each recipe will allow you to tell at a glance whether it's possible to prepare more than one *Twice As Fast* recipe within a certain time framework. You cannot save much time by microwaving more than one recipe at a time, since cooking time increases according to the volume of food in the oven.

If you want to prepare a dinner menu of a poultry entrée, a rice dish, and a vegetable, for example, you might find that the recipes would require a total of about an hour of microwave time. So you couldn't possibly serve them together in less than an hour. You might then decide to change your menu plans or analyze the recipes for shortcuts.

You could cook the rice conventionally while the entrée was in the microwave oven. You could then let the entrée stand, covered with aluminum foil, while you microwaved the vegetable. Your total cooking time would be significantly reduced. You could also coordinate the recipes so that some ingredients for the rice dish could be cooking in the microwave oven while you were preparing entrée and vegetable ingredients in the food processor. Or you might conclude that the microwave time for all these dishes would not impose on your schedule, since you could use that time for cleanup, table setting, or relaxing.

The microwave time is the "bottom line" for each recipe. Total preparation time cannot be streamlined further than that, but you can use the microwave time to do other things, since the food will not require much attention.

Standing time is another factor to consider when you're scheduling microwave time. Many recipes finish cooking outside the microwave oven in 5 or 10 minutes of standing time. Often, it is convenient to microwave a vegetable or a dessert while the entrée is standing.

Remember that all foods can be slightly undercooked and reheated in the microwave oven without reduction in quality. Therefore, you can microwave several dishes consecutively and reheat any of them that need it just before serving.

HALVING AND DOUBLING RECIPES

Most *Twice As Fast* recipes make 4 to 6 servings. You can cut the recipe yield in half by cutting ingredient quantities in half; using a smaller casserole dish, if appropriate; and microwaving the food, as directed in the recipe, for about three-quarters of the recommended time. When cooking half-recipes of fish, vegetables, or sauces, start checking for doneness after half the recommended microwave time has elapsed.

Ten to 12 servings are about the maximum quantity of most foods that you can microwave efficiently. It is usually more time efficient to cook larger quantities conventionally. To double recipes, double the amounts of ingredients and use a suitably larger cooking dish. Microwave as directed in the recipe, increasing the time by three-quarters. Be sure to keep stirring or rotating the dish throughout the cooking time. When preparing double quantities of ingredients in the food processor, be careful not to overload the workbowl. Check the manufacturer's manual for maximum quantities that can be processed with the Steel Knife. When using the Slicing or Shredding Disc, don't let food accumulate in the bowl to the point where it is pressing against the disc. Process only single batches of batters and doughs.

THE ECONOMY OF CONVENIENCE

The food processor and microwave oven can change the meaning of leftovers by giving them new identities. If you think about all the ways you can quickly transform the texture and taste of leftovers with the food processor and microwave oven—by chopping, pureeing, slicing, shredding, combining in a salad, melting, reheating, or adding a sauce, just to name a few possibilities—you'll begin to recognize the potential for economy that is built into the appliances. The two stalks of broccoli, accumulated cheese scraps, and boring chunks of ham that seem to take up almost permanent residence in many refrigerators need not be discarded. You'll find ways to use these foods, for example, in Three-Vegetable Terrine, French-style Vegetable Puree, Continuous Cheese Crock, and Ham Salad Rolls. Look at other recipes and you'll discover enough patterns of ingredient combinations and cooking procedures to ensure new life for virtually every single leftover, right down to an abandoned piece of fruit and the last pickle spear.

Hot Deviled Eggs
Shrimp Japonaise
Party Brie Cheeses
Eggplant Dip with Pita Triangles
Hot Beef and Cheese Dip
Layered Nacho Dip
Liver Pâté with Cognac
Mixed Nut Pâté
Three-Vegetable Terrine
Four-Cheese Quiche
Steamed Dumplings
Mexican Hash in Cheese
Hot Buttered Toddies
Hot Cranberry Punch

4 Appetizers

HOT DEVILED EGGS

Heat quickly processed deviled eggs to make them taste even creamier. All ingredients can be kept on hand for an impromptu appetizer, but these shrimp-topped eggs might also highlight a brunch or lunch of cold meats and a salad.

Total Preparation Time: 12 to 13 minutes
Microwave Time: 2 to 3 minutes
Yield: 12 servings

---

1 shallot or ¼ small onion, peeled
6 hard-cooked eggs, peeled, cut lengthwise
   into halves
¼ cup mayonnaise or salad dressing
2 tablespoons sour cream
½ teaspoon Dijon-style mustard
¼ teaspoon dried or ½ to 1 teaspoon minced
   fresh dillweed
⅛ teaspoon salt
1 tablespoon drained capers
12 small cooked shrimp
Fresh dill or parsley sprigs (optional)

With machine running (Steel Knife), drop shallot through feed tube; process until minced. Add egg yolks, mayonnaise, sour cream, mustard, dillweed, and salt to bowl; process using on/off technique until smooth. Add capers to bowl; process using on/off technique until blended. Fill egg whites with yolk mixture; top eggs with shrimp. Place eggs around edge of 10-inch glass quiche pan or pie plate. Microwave uncovered at 50% (Medium) just until warm, 2 to 3 minutes. Garnish with fresh dill sprigs.

Tips: Microwave deviled eggs just until heated through; overcooking can make the yolks rubbery.

   Do not attempt to boil eggs in the microwave oven (unless you have cookware specially designed for that purpose); the buildup of steam in the shell can cause an explosion. To hard-cook eggs conventionally, cover them with water and bring to a full boil. Remove pot from heat and let stand, covered, 10 minutes. Place eggs under cold running water to prevent further cooking and to make peeling easier.

   If capers are very salty, place them in a strainer and rinse well under cold water.

   Frozen or canned salad shrimp may be used; rinse canned shrimp and drain well. Substitute salmon caviar (¼ to ½ teaspoon per egg) or small pieces of smoked salmon for the shrimp, if you wish, but don't use whitefish or lumpfish caviar, as these are dyed and will discolor the eggs. Add caviar after heating eggs; don't put caviar in the microwave oven.

SHRIMP JAPONAISE

Simplicity defines the elegance of this appetizer—nothing fussy or complex, just a mutual complement of delicate flavors and textures.

Total Preparation Time: 10 to 10½ minutes
Microwave Time: 4½ to 5½ minutes
Yield: 6 servings

---

1 pound medium to large peeled, deveined,
   uncooked shrimp
1 egg yolk, room temperature
2 teaspoons lemon juice
1 teaspoon Dijon-style mustard
1 teaspoon rice wine vinegar
¼ teaspoon salt
⅛ teaspoon white pepper
½ cup vegetable oil
1 tablespoon sesame oil
2 teaspoons soy sauce

Arrange shrimp in single layer in glass baking dish; microwave covered at High until shrimp are pink, 4 to 5 minutes, stirring after 2 minutes. Drain well. Arrange on glass serving plate. Process (Steel Knife) egg yolk, lemon juice, mustard, vinegar, salt, and pepper until smooth. With machine running, gradually add oils through feed tube, processing until very thick; add soy sauce through feed tube, processing until blended. Spoon dollop of sauce on each shrimp; microwave uncovered at 70% (Medium High) to heat sauce, 20 to 30 seconds (watch carefully as sauce can melt easily). Serve immediately.

Tips: Rice wine vinegar, sesame oil, and soy sauce can be found in the Oriental sections of large supermarkets or in Oriental grocery stores.

Because the mayonnaise-type sauce for the shrimp is made with only one egg yolk, you can process it more efficiently by tilting the food processor forward slightly. Use a book to prop up the back of the machine. The sauce may be prepared in advance and refrigerated, covered, up to 1 week.

Leave tails on shrimp, if desired, for most attractive serving. Shrimp may be cooked ahead of time and refrigerated. Heat shrimp with sauce on serving dish.

For a vegetable first course, substitute 1 pound asparagus for the shrimp. Arrange asparagus in a spoke pattern, with tips in center, on a glass plate; sprinkle with 2 tablespoons water. Microwave asparagus covered with plastic wrap at High until crisp-tender, 5 to 6 minutes.

PARTY BRIE CHEESES

A golden fruit glaze and crunchy almonds dress up warm, melting Brie for a party buffet. Cheese lovers will also adore this slightly sweetened cheese at dessert time.

Total Preparation Time: 8 to 9 minutes
Microwave Time: 6 to 7 minutes
Yield: 6 to 8 servings

¼ **cup sliced almonds**
2 **fresh or preserved kumquats, seeded**
¼ **cup apricot preserves**
⅛ **teaspoon curry powder**
2 **whole Brie cheeses (4½ ounces each), chilled**
Sliced French bread or assorted crackers

Microwave almonds in glass pie plate, uncovered, at High until toasted, about 3 minutes, stirring after 1½ minutes. Process (Steel Knife) kumquats using on/off technique until chopped. Add preserves and curry powder to bowl; process using on/off technique until mixed. Spoon mixture on top of cheeses; sprinkle with almonds. Place cheeses on glass or wood serving plate; microwave uncovered at 50% (Medium) until cheeses are softened, 3 to 4 minutes. Spread softened cheese on French bread.

Tips: The kumquats can be omitted, but you will lose the perfect balance of textures and tart-rich taste. However, peach or pineapple preserves can be substituted for the apricot.

The 4½-ounce Bries are especially well suited to heating and make an attractive presentation. You can, however, spoon the topping over 4-ounce wedges of a larger Brie; arrange the wedges on opposite sides of a plate with pointed ends in the center. Be careful not to overcook, especially if the cheese is 1 inch thick or less.

If you wish to heat one cheese at a time, reduce cooking time by 1 to 2 minutes. Cheese can be reheated at 50% (Medium) for 1 to 2 minutes. Microwave time will vary according to the temperature of the cheese.

EGGPLANT DIP WITH PITA TRIANGLES

Prepared and cooked right in the food processor bowl, this eggplant dip is not only fragrant and delicious but also incredibly convenient.

Total Preparation Time: 14 to 17 minutes
(plus chilling time)
Microwave Time: 8 to 10 minutes
Yield: about 2 cups

---

8 sprigs parsley
2 cloves garlic, peeled
1 medium eggplant (about 1 pound), pared, cut into 1-inch pieces
¼ cup water
1 teaspoon fennel seeds, crushed
1 teaspoon lemon juice
¼ cup mayonnaise or salad dressing
¼ cup sour cream or sour half-and-half
Pita breads, cut into triangles

Process (Steel Knife) parsley using on/off technique until minced. With machine running, drop garlic through feed tube; process using on/off technique until minced. Add eggplant to bowl; process using on/off technique until finely chopped. Remove Steel Knife; add water to bowl. Microwave eggplant mixture and water in food processor bowl, covered with plastic wrap, at High until eggplant is very tender, 5 to 7 minutes, stirring after 3 minutes; do not drain. Microwave fennel seeds on glass pie plate, uncovered, at High until toasted, about 3 minutes, stirring after 1½ minutes.

Insert Steel Knife. Add fennel seeds, lemon juice, mayonnaise, and sour cream to bowl; process until smooth. Spoon dip into serving bowl; refrigerate covered until chilled, about 1½ hours. Serve with pita triangles as dippers.

Tips: *Use a rubber scraper to push eggplant mixture away from the center of the bowl when reinserting Steel Knife. Be sure the Steel Knife is firmly in place.*

To heat pita bread triangles, place them in a basket or serving dish lined with cloth or paper napkins and microwave on High just until warm, about 30 seconds. Be careful not to overheat or the bread will dry out and toughen.

HOT BEEF AND CHEESE DIP

There are plenty of practical reasons to serve this hot, substantial dip—as a warm welcome on a cold evening, an appetite-appeaser at cocktail parties, or a convenient after-theater snack. But don't forget the pure pleasure, either, after a long day or on a lazy Sunday afternoon!

Total Preparation Time: 22 to 23 minutes
Microwave Time: 8 to 9 minutes
Yield: about 3 cups

---

2 carrots, pared, cut to fit feed tube horizontally
1 medium zucchini, cut to fit feed tube horizontally
1 cup walnuts
1 small clove garlic, peeled
1 small onion, peeled, cut into quarters
1 jar (2½ ounces) dried beef slices, cut into halves
2 ounces Swiss cheese, cut into 1-inch pieces
1 package (3 ounces) cream cheese, cut into 1-inch pieces
1 cup sour cream
¼ cup mayonnaise or salad dressing
½ teaspoon Worcestershire sauce
½ teaspoon dried chervil leaves
¼ teaspoon prepared horseradish
Breadsticks

Slice (Slicing Disc) carrots and zucchini, positioning vegetables in feed tube horizontally; reserve carrots and zucchini. Microwave walnuts in glass pie plate, uncovered, at High until toasted, 3 to 4 minutes, stirring after 2 minutes. With machine running (Steel Knife), drop garlic through feed tube, processing until minced. Add onion to bowl; process until coarsely chopped. Add walnuts, dried beef, and Swiss cheese to bowl; process until coarsely chopped. Add cream cheese, sour cream, mayonnaise, Worcestershire sauce, chervil, and horseradish to bowl; process using on/off technique until blended. Transfer mixture to 1½-quart glass casserole. Microwave uncovered at 70% (Medium High) until hot through, about 5 minutes, stirring after 3 minutes. Serve dip hot with carrots, zucchini, and breadsticks for dippers.

Tips: *If dried beef is very salty, blanch it in*
boiling water for 30 seconds; drain well.
Serve Hot Beef and Cheese Dip as a
fondue, if you wish. Transfer the dip to a
fondue pot and serve it with cubes of
French bread for dipping.
For buffet-style serving, microwave the
dip in an attractive, heatproof bowl and
place the bowl on a warming tray. Dip
can be processed up to 1 day in advance;
refrigerate covered and microwave just
before serving.

LAYERED NACHO DIP

The hallmarks of Mexican food—cheese, chili, avocado, and tomato—in a fast, richly flavored dip. Bright and colorful, the layers of ingredients offer a marvelous contrast of hot and cooling tastes. A pitcher of margaritas or sangría would go perfectly!

Total Preparation Time: 17 to 20 minutes
Microwave Time: 7 to 8 minutes
Yield: 6 to 8 servings

---

4 ounces Monterey Jack or Cheddar cheese,
    chilled, cut to fit feed tube
1 small onion, peeled, cut into 1-inch pieces
½ to 1 jalapeño pepper, seeded, cut into
    quarters
1 teaspoon butter or margarine
1 can (16 ounces) refried beans
¼ teaspoon chili powder
½ cup sour cream
1 medium tomato, seeded, cut into 1-inch
    pieces
1 medium avocado, peeled, pitted, cut into
    1-inch pieces
Tortilla chips

Shred (Shredding Disc) cheese; reserve.
Process (Steel Knife) onion and pepper using

on/off technique until finely chopped. Microwave onion mixture and butter in 1-quart glass casserole, covered, at High until onion is tender, about 3 minutes. Stir in beans and chili powder; microwave uncovered at High until beans are hot through, about 3 minutes, stirring after 1½ minutes. Spread bean mixture on 9-inch glass or wood serving plate; sprinkle with reserved cheese, leaving 1-inch border of beans at the outside of the plate. Microwave uncovered at High until cheese melts, about 45 seconds. Spoon sour cream over cheese, leaving ½-inch border of cheese. Process (Steel Knife) tomato and avocado separately, using on/off technique, until coarsely chopped; sprinkle tomato and avocado over sour cream. Serve with tortilla chips.

Tips: *Bean mixture and cheese may be*
prepared up to 1 day in advance and
refrigerated covered. Microwave and add
remaining ingredients just before serving.
A fresh jalapeño pepper contributes
unique flavor and not too much heat if you
remove the seeds; be careful not to touch
eyes when handling hot peppers, as the
juice can cause irritation. Whole fresh
jalapeño peppers can be kept frozen, in a
plastic bag, up to 3 months. Canned
jalapeño peppers, hot or mild, can be
substituted.
Homemade tortilla chips are superior
to packaged and can be easily made. Cut
each corn tortilla into 6 wedges (use
scissors to cut single tortilla or a serrated
knife to cut through a stack) and fry in ½
inch hot vegetable oil 1 to 2 minutes,
turning chips over once. Chips can be
fried in advance and reheated in the
microwave oven; place them in a napkin-
lined bowl or basket and microwave at
High 5 to 15 seconds.
You can use the above recipe ingredients
to make tostadas. Preheat a browning
dish at High 5 minutes. Butter 1 side of a
9-inch flour tortilla; place buttered side on
preheated browning dish. Microwave at
High 30 seconds. Turn tortilla over and
arrange ingredients as above. Microwave
at High 1 minute.

LIVER PÂTÉ WITH COGNAC

The food processor brought pâtés into common parlance by eliminating all the tedious chopping and grinding that used to be required. The microwave oven eliminates the mess of sautéing or simmering livers on top of the stove as well. So few appetizers are easier to prepare than this elegant, subtly seasoned blend.

Total Preparation Time: 18 to 20 minutes
(plus chilling time)
Microwave Time: 8 to 10 minutes
Yield: 1¾ cups

---

1 pound chicken livers, cleaned, cut into halves
¼ cup water
2 large sprigs parsley
¼ medium onion, peeled, cut into 1-inch pieces
2 tablespoons cognac or brandy
8 tablespoons butter or margarine, softened
½ teaspoon salt
¼ teaspoon ground allspice
⅛ teaspoon ground mace
1/16 teaspoon ground ginger
Garlic Herb Toast (optional; see Index)

Microwave livers and water in 1½-quart glass casserole, covered, at High until livers lose pink color, 8 to 10 minutes, stirring after 5 minutes. Drain. Process (Steel Knife) parsley using on/off technique until minced. Add onion to bowl; process using on/off technique until coarsely chopped. Add livers, cognac, 2 tablespoons of the butter, the salt, allspice, mace, and ginger; process until smooth, adding 6 tablespoons butter, 1 tablespoon at a time, through feed tube while machine is running. Spoon liver mixture into crock or serving bowl; refrigerate until serving time. Make Garlic-Herb Toast; serve with pâté.

Tips: Liver Pâté with Cognac can be prepared up to 4 days in advance and refrigerated covered; bring to room temperature before serving for spreading ease.

For silkiest texture, you can microwave the livers, process (Steel Knife) them with the parsley and onion until smooth, and then press the mixture through a fine sieve. Return the mixture to the food processor workbowl and proceed with the recipe. To soften butter, microwave at High just until softened, but not melted.

MIXED NUT PÂTÉ

A pâté without meat but with all the deep, rich flavor of ground pecans, walnuts, and almonds bound with yogurt and whole-grain bread.

Total Preparation Time: 22 to 26 minutes
Microwave Time: 7 to 8 minutes
Yield: 12 servings

---

3 large sprigs parsley
2 shallots or ½ small onion, peeled, cut into 1-inch pieces
1½ cups pecans
¾ cup walnuts
¼ cup blanched almonds
4 slices whole wheat bread, torn into pieces
3 medium tomatoes, seeded, cut into 1-inch pieces
2 eggs
2 tablespoons plain yogurt
1 tablespoon light brown sugar
¼ teaspoon salt
¼ teaspoon dried thyme leaves
⅛ teaspoon paprika
⅛ teaspoon white pepper
¾ cup plain yogurt
½ teaspoon dried dillweed

Process (Steel Knife) parsley using on/off technique until minced. With machine running, add shallots through feed tube, processing until minced. Add nuts and bread to bowl; process using on/off technique until very finely chopped. Add remaining ingredients except ¾ cup yogurt and the dillweed to the bowl;

process using on/off technique until thoroughly mixed.

Spoon mixture into greased 4- or 6-cup plastic ring mold. Microwave uncovered at High until set, 7 to 8 minutes, rotating mold ¼ turn every 2 minutes. Let stand on counter top, loosely covered, 5 minutes. Unmold onto serving plate. Serve warm or at room temperature; spoon ¾ cup yogurt over pâté and sprinkle with dillweed.

Tips: For a toasted nut flavor, microwave pecans, walnuts, and almonds in glass pie plate, uncovered, at High 2 minutes. Stir to redistribute nuts; microwave at High until lightly toasted, 1 to 2 minutes. Cool and process as above.

A 2-quart glass casserole, with a glass placed open end up in the center, can be substituted for the plastic ring mold.

Mixed Nut Pâté can be prepared up to 3 days in advance. Unmold and refrigerate tightly covered with plastic wrap; bring to room temperature and top with yogurt and dill before serving. This pâté makes fine picnic fare. Carry it in the mold, with a separate container of yogurt and dill. Unmold before serving and spoon yogurt over.

THREE-VEGETABLE TERRINE

Each slice of this beautiful terrine displays a tricolor of broccoli, cauliflower, and carrots. French-inspired and fashionably light, the terrine is simpler and sturdier than it appears. Serve individual portions warm as a first course, framed by Fresh Tomato or Butter Sauce (see Index) or slice the whole terrine to set out on a buffet table at room temperature with sauce on the side.

Total Preparation Time: 65 to 72 minutes
Microwave Time: 30 to 37 minutes
Yield: 8 servings

1 **ounce Parmesan cheese, cut into 1-inch pieces**
2 **ounces Swiss cheese, chilled, cut to fit feed tube**
8 **ounces broccoli, cut to fit feed tube**
8 **ounces cauliflower, cut to fit feed tube**
8 **ounces carrots, pared, cut to fit feed tube**
9 **tablespoons water**
9 **tablespoons butter or margarine**
3 **teaspoons lemon juice**
3 **eggs**
3 **egg yolks**
¼ **teaspoon ground mace**
¾ **teaspoon white pepper**
¼ **teaspoon ground nutmeg**
Watercress or parsley sprigs

Process (Steel Knife) Parmesan cheese until finely grated. Shred (Shredding Disc) Swiss cheese. Reserve cheeses. Slice (Slicing Disc) broccoli, cauliflower, and carrots separately. Place each vegetable in small glass bowl; add 3 tablespoons water to each and arrange in oven in triangle pattern. Microwave vegetables covered with plastic wrap at High until very tender, 10 to 12 minutes; drain.

Process (Steel Knife) broccoli, 3 tablespoons of the butter, the Swiss cheese, 1 teaspoon of the lemon juice, 1 egg, 1 egg yolk, the mace, and ¼ teaspoon of the pepper until smooth; spread in bottom of ungreased 1-quart glass loaf pan. Process (Steel Knife) cauliflower, 3 tablespoons of the butter, the Parmesan cheese, 1 teaspoon of the lemon juice, 1 egg, 1 egg yolk, the nutmeg, and ¼ teaspoon of the pepper until smooth; spread over broccoli mixture. Process (Steel Knife) carrots, 3 tablespoons butter, 1 teaspoon lemon juice, 1 egg, 1 egg yolk, and ¼ teaspoon pepper until smooth; spread over cauliflower mixture.

Place loaf pan in 12″ × 8″ glass baking dish; fill baking dish with ½ inch warm water. Microwave covered with plastic wrap at 50% (Medium) until bottom of terrine appears set, 20 to 25 minutes. Let stand covered on counter top 10 minutes. Loosen edges of terrine with knife; unmold onto serving platter. Serve warm or at room temperature; garnish with watercress.

(See Tip next page)

Tip: Terrine can be made 1 day in advance. To reheat individual portions, place one slice on serving plate and microwave covered with waxed paper at 50% (Medium) until warm, 1½ to 2 minutes. Terrine can also be served cold.

FOUR–CHEESE QUICHE

A fluffy quiche without a crust starts a meal on a lighter note and doubles as a lunch or brunch entreé.

Total Preparation Time: 33 to 34 minutes
Microwave Time: 19 to 20 minutes
Yield: 6 servings

---

6 slices bacon
1 medium onion, peeled, cut into 1-inch
   pieces
2 green onions and tops, cut into 1-inch
   pieces
1 to 2 tablespoons dry bread crumbs
2 ounces Swiss cheese, chilled, cut to fit feed
   tube
2 ounces Cheddar cheese, chilled, cut to fit
   feed tube
2 tablespoons flour
1 ounce Parmesan cheese, cut into 1-inch
   pieces
1 cup small curd cottage cheese
⅔ cup half-and-half
3 eggs
¼ teaspoon ground nutmeg
¼ teaspoon salt
⅛ teaspoon white pepper

Microwave bacon in glass baking dish, covered with paper toweling, at High until crisp, about 6 minutes, rotating dish ¼ turn after 3 minutes. Crumble bacon; drain all but 1 tablespoon of the drippings.

Process (Steel Knife) onions using on/off technique until chopped. Microwave onions in 1 tablespoon drippings in glass baking dish, uncovered, at High until tender, about 3 minutes.

Lightly grease 9-inch glass quiche dish; coat with bread crumbs. Shred (Shredding Disc) Swiss and Cheddar cheese; sprinkle in bottom of quiche dish. Sprinkle with onion mixture, flour, and bacon.

With machine running (Steel Knife), drop Parmesan cheese through feed tube; process until finely grated. Add remaining ingredients to bowl; process until smooth. Pour filling into quiche dish. Microwave uncovered at High until almost set, 10 to 11 minutes, rotating dish ¼ turn every 2 minutes; elevate quiche dish on an inverted saucer after 8 minutes. Let stand uncovered on counter top 5 minutes. Cut into wedges to serve.

Tip: Elevating the quiche dish on an inverted saucer or microwave meat rack for the last few minutes of cooking time will ensure that the center cooks evenly.

STEAMED DUMPLINGS

No Chinese family celebration would be complete without a generous supply of *shu mai*, or steamed dumplings. These small, juicy morsels release an inimitable gift of flavor with each bite. Serve them with predinner drinks or as part of a Chinese meal, with Lemon Chicken and Snow Peas or Chinese Pepper Beef (see Index). Or enjoy them anytime with tea, as a typically Chinese snack or light lunch.

Total Preparation Time: 28 to 32 minutes
Microwave Time: 7 to 8 minutes
Yield: 4 servings

---

1 tablespoon sesame seeds
2 large sprigs fresh coriander or ½ teaspoon
   dried coriander leaves
4 ounces uncooked boneless chicken breast,
   cut into 1-inch pieces
1 green onion and top, skinned, cut into 1-
   inch pieces
2 pitted dates

2 mushrooms
2 teaspoons soy sauce
1 teaspoon sweet-sour sauce or apricot
  preserves
1 teaspoon dry sherry
8 won ton wrappers or 2 egg roll wrappers,
  cut into quarters
Soy sauce

Microwave sesame seeds in glass pie plate uncovered at High until toasted, about 2 minutes, stirring after 1 minute. Process (Steel Knife) sesame seeds and remaining ingredients except won ton wrappers and additional soy sauce using on/off technique until finely chopped.

Divide mixture on won ton wrappers; gather sides of wrappers around filling, crimping at the top.

Place inverted saucer in bottom of 2-quart glass soufflé dish or casserole; pour in ½ inch water. Microwave at High until water is boiling. To make steaming rack, fold a sturdy paper plate into ¾-inch pleats, accordion style; cut off ends to fit into soufflé dish. Place steaming rack on saucer; place dumplings on rack. Microwave covered with plastic wrap (tops of dumplings should not touch plastic wrap) at High until dumplings are tender, about 4 minutes, rotating dish ¼ turn after 2 minutes. Let stand, covered, 5 minutes. Serve with soy sauce.

Tips: Won ton wrappers are available in
specialty sections of large supermarkets
and in Oriental groceries.
To fill and seal won ton wrappers:

To make a paper plate steaming rack:

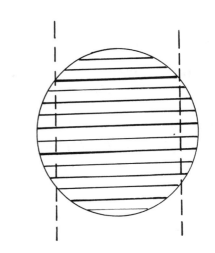

If you have a round microwave meat
rack that will fit the soufflé dish, you may
use it as a steaming rack instead of the
paper plate.

Uncooked Steamed Dumplings can be
assembled 1 day in advance. Refrigerate
tightly covered with plastic wrap.

MEXICAN HASH IN CHEESE

In traditional Mexican cuisine, this fabulous first course is accorded more than a day of preparation—and it's definitely worth it. But what a joy to savor the mingled flavors of cheese, meat, and spices in just a fraction of the time! Serve larger portions for lunch or an informal supper.

Total Preparation Time: 40 to 45 minutes
Microwave Time: 25 to 28 minutes
Yield: 6 to 8 servings

½ **pound boneless beef chuck, fat trimmed, cut into 1-inch pieces**
¼ **cup water**
½ **teaspoon beef-flavor instant bouillon**
1 **whole Edam cheese (about 1 pound)**
1 **medium potato, unpared**
1 **small clove garlic, peeled**
1 **jalapeño pepper, seeded, cut into 1-inch pieces**
½ **medium onion, peeled, cut into 1-inch pieces**
1 **sprig fresh coriander or ½ teaspoon dried coriander leaves**
½ **teaspoon chili powder**
⅛ **teaspoon ground cumin**
Pinch cayenne pepper
2 **tablespoons sour cream**
Hot Salsa (optional; see Index)
12 **to 16 corn tortillas**

Microwave beef, water, and bouillon in 1-quart glass casserole, covered with plastic wrap, at High 5 minutes; microwave at 50% (Medium) until beef is tender, about 10 minutes, rotating dish ¼ turn every 5 minutes. Let stand covered 10 minutes; drain.

Remove wax covering from cheese. Scoop out interior of cheese, leaving a ½-inch shell. (Reserve scooped-out cheese for other use; see Index for Continuous Cheese Crock recipe.)

Pierce potato in several places with fork. Microwave potato on paper toweling at High until tender, 4 to 5 minutes. Let stand 5 minutes. Cut potato into 1-inch pieces.

With machine running (Steel Knife), drop garlic and jalapeño pepper through feed tube; process until minced. Add meat, onion, coriander, chili powder, cumin, and cayenne pepper to bowl; process using on/off technique until coarsely chopped. Add potato and sour cream to bowl; process using on/off technique until potato is coarsely chopped. Microwave in 1-quart glass casserole, covered with plastic wrap, at High until hot, 4 to 5 minutes, rotating dish ¼ turn after 2 minutes.

Make Hot Salsa.

Spoon meat mixture into cheese; microwave in 1½-quart glass casserole, uncovered, at 50% (Medium) just until cheese begins to melt (begin checking after 1 minute, as cheese should not melt so much that it loses its shape). Spoon salsa over top of meat mixture. Place tortillas between paper toweling; microwave at 50% (Medium) until warm. Spoon meat mixture and cheese onto tortillas and roll up.

Tips: One-half pound of leftover cooked roast beef or pot roast can be substituted for the chuck roast; cut meat into 1-inch pieces and proceed with recipe, omitting the first step. Meat filling and Hot Salsa can be prepared 1 day in advance; refrigerate separately, covered with plastic wrap.

To scoop out interior of Edam cheese, cut a deep circle ½ inch from edge of cheese. Use a sturdy spoon and small paring knife to scoop and scrape out interior. Leftover Edam makes delicious grilled ham-and-cheese sandwiches; shred (Shredding Disc) chilled large chunks or process (Steel Knife) small pieces until chopped for easiest melting. The shredded cheese can also be used in Creamiest Potato Salad (see Index).

Fresh jalapeño peppers and coriander add immeasurably to this dish; they can be found in the produce section of a large supermarket or in a Mexican grocery store. Coriander, sometimes called cilantro or Chinese parsley, can also be found in Oriental grocery stores. Canned and dried products can be substituted. Be careful not to touch eyes when handling hot peppers, as the juice can cause irritation.

HOT BUTTERED TODDIES

A great way to warm up and relax, whether après-ski or with late-night TV. In fact, having the ice cream mixture already made and ready to go in your freezer can become a secret source of solace!

Total Preparation Time: 8 to 9 minutes
Microwave Time: 5 to 6 minutes
Yield: 8 servings (1½ cups mixture)

---

1 cup vanilla ice cream
½ cup butter or margarine
¾ cup packed light brown sugar
¼ cup honey
¼ teaspoon ground nutmeg
Dash ground cloves
Water, orange juice, pineapple juice, or apple cider
Dark rum, bourbon, or brandy
8 cinnamon sticks (optional)

Microwave ice cream in glass bowl, uncovered, at 10% (Low) until just softened, about 30 seconds. Microwave butter in glass bowl at High, uncovered, until softened. Process (Steel Knife) ice cream, butter, brown sugar, honey, nutmeg, and cloves until blended. Store in covered container in freezer.

Fill mug with ¾ cup water or desired juice; add 3 tablespoons ice cream mixture. Microwave uncovered at High until water is boiling, about 2 minutes (about 5 minutes for 4 mugs). Stir 1 ounce desired liquor into each mug; serve with cinnamon stick stirrers.

HOT CRANBERRY PUNCH

A delicious change of pace from ordinary cocktails and delightfully festive for the holiday season. Keep a pitcherful on hand and reheat or serve cold. Add vodka or bourbon, according to guests' preferences, at serving time.

Total Preparation Time: 35 to 37 minutes
Microwave Time: 25 to 27 minutes
Yield: 12 servings (about 6 ounces each)

---

12 ounces fresh cranberries
6 cups water
1 cinnamon stick
6 whole cloves
6 whole allspice
2 oranges, peeled, cut into quarters
1 lemon, peeled, cut into quarters
1 lime, peeled, cut into quarters
¾ to 1 cup sugar
Freshly grated nutmeg

Process (Steel Knife) cranberries until very finely chopped. Microwave cranberries, water, cinnamon, cloves, and allspice in 8-cup glass measure, uncovered, at High until boiling, about 15 minutes. Strain through cheesecloth or fine strainer; discard cranberries and spices. Process (Steel Knife) oranges, lemon, and lime until all juice is extracted; strain and add juice to cranberry juice mixture in 8-cup glass measure. Discard pith and seeds. Stir in sugar according to taste and sweetness of fruit. Microwave uncovered at High until boiling, 10 to 12 minutes, stirring after 5 minutes. Serve hot in mugs or Irish coffee glasses; sprinkle with nutmeg.

Tips: Frozen cranberries can be used in this recipe. Microwave in 8-cup glass measure at defrost setting until thawed, about 5 minutes. Proceed with recipe as above.

One-half ounce bourbon or vodka can be stirred into each mug.

Hot Cranberry Punch is also delicious cold. Cool to room temperature; refrigerate until chilled. Serve over ice.

5 Soups

SUMMER SQUASH SOUP

A lovely, light prelude for a dinner party, as well as an easy, nutritious soup for everyday meals. You can adapt this recipe to all-seasons economy by substituting other vegetables for the summer squash.

Total Preparation Time: 20 to 22 minutes
Microwave Time: 11 to 13 minutes
Yield: 4 servings (about ¾ cup each)

---

1 pound yellow summer squash, cut to fit feed tube
½ medium onion, peeled, cut to fit feed tube
1 cup water
3 tablespoons Twice-As-Fast Sauce Mix (see Index)
2 teaspoons chicken-flavor instant bouillon
½ cup whipping cream or half-and-half
1 tablespoon lemon juice
⅛ teaspoon ground allspice
1/16 teaspoon white pepper
1½ tablespoons port wine or 3 tablespoons plum wine (optional)

Slice (Slicing Disc) squash and onion. Microwave squash, onion, water, sauce mix, and bouillon in 2-quart glass casserole, covered, at High until squash is very tender, 5 to 7 minutes. Process (Steel Knife) squash mixture until smooth, about 2 minutes. Return mixture to casserole; stir in remaining ingredients. Microwave uncovered at 50% (Medium) until hot but not boiling, about 6 minutes.

Tips: Substitute 1 pound of broccoli, asparagus, zucchini, or carrots for the squash and follow above directions. You may also substitute two 10-ounce packages of frozen peas, without slicing. If soup is too thick, stir in equal amounts of water and cream. For broccoli or asparagus soup, you may wish to omit the wine and garnish each bowl with a thin slice of lemon; diners can then press some of the lemon juice into the soup to highlight the seasonings.

To prepare the soup in advance, microwave and puree the vegetable mixture. Refrigerate covered up to 2 days or freeze covered up to 2 months. Microwave frozen puree, covered, at 50% (Medium) until thawed, and proceed with recipe.

Garnish soup, if desired, according to the vegetable you use. Some suggestions: A thin ring of red bell pepper for the Summer Squash Soup; a sprig of fresh dill or parsley for carrot soup; fresh mint leaves for pea soup. You may wish to reserve a few uncooked slices of the vegetable you are using (or asparagus tips or broccoli flowerets) to garnish individual servings. If you wish, microwave slices in glass baking dish with a tablespoon of water, covered, at High until crisp-tender, 1 to 2 minutes.

DOUBLE MUSHROOM SOUP

Imported dried mushrooms deepen the flavor of fresh mushrooms just enough to add a note of intrigue to a favorite light soup.

Total Preparation Time: 34 to 38 minutes
Microwave Time: 14 to 18 minutes
Yield: 4 servings (1 cup each)

---

2 cups water
1 ounce Chinese or European dried mushrooms
4 ounces fresh mushrooms
4 green onions and tops, cut to fit feed tube
2 tablespoons butter or margarine
1½ cups water
1 tablespoon chicken-flavor instant bouillon
1 tablespoon Worcestershire sauce
½ teaspoon salt
¼ teaspoon dried marjoram leaves
⅛ teaspoon pepper

Microwave 2 cups water in 2-cup glass measure at High until boiling. Pour over dried mushrooms in medium bowl; let stand until mushrooms are softened, about 20 minutes. Drain and reserve liquid; if mushrooms have tough centers, cut out and discard.

Slice (Slicing Disc) fresh mushrooms and onions. Microwave fresh mushrooms and onions in butter in 1½-quart glass casserole, covered, at High 2 minutes. Process (Steel Knife) dried mushrooms using on/off technique until coarsely chopped; add to casserole with reserved liquid and remaining ingredients. Microwave uncovered at High just until boiling, 8 to 12 minutes.

Tip: Any kind of imported dried mushroom can be used in Double Mushroom Soup. Dried morels have an especially delicate flavor.

HOT GAZPACHO

A hot version of Spanish gazpacho enlivens winter tables with vegetable-garden flavor and a bright assortment of garnishes.

Total Preparation Time: 20 to 24 minutes
Microwave Time: 12 to 14 minutes
Yield: 4 servings (about 1 cup each)

---

2 carrots, pared, cut into ½-inch pieces
1 rib celery, cut into ½-inch pieces
1 ounce fresh spinach leaves, stems discarded
¼ medium green pepper, seeded, cut into 1-inch pieces
¼ cup water
1 green pepper, seeded, cut into 1-inch pieces
1 small onion, peeled, cut into 1-inch pieces
1 hard-cooked egg, cut into quarters
1 small avocado, peeled, pitted, cut into 1-inch pieces
4 cups tomato juice
2 teaspoons Worcestershire sauce

1 teaspoon beef-flavor instant bouillon
½ teaspoon dried chives
⅛ teaspoon dried tarragon leaves
⅛ to ¼ teaspoon cayenne pepper
⅛ teaspoon red pepper sauce

Microwave carrots, celery, spinach, ¼ green pepper, and the water in 2-quart glass casserole, covered, at High until very tender, 6 to 8 minutes, stirring after 4 minutes.

Process (Steel Knife) 1 green pepper, the onion, egg, and avocado separately, using on/off technique, until coarsely chopped. Place in small bowls; refrigerate.

Process (Steel Knife) carrot mixture, 1½ cups of the tomato juice, the Worcestershire sauce, bouillon, chives, tarragon, cayenne pepper, and red pepper sauce until smooth, 30 to 60 seconds. Mix carrot mixture and remaining 2½ cups tomato juice in 8-cup glass measure or casserole. Microwave covered at High until very hot, about 6 minutes, stirring after 3 minutes. Serve in shallow bowls with selection of chopped vegetables and egg.

Tips: Hot Gazpacho may be served in mugs, as a cocktail, without garnishes; stir ½ ounce vodka into each serving, if desired. It makes an attractive opener for a cold-weather brunch.

Garlic or Herb Croutons (see Index) go well with Hot Gazpacho.

SHRIMP BISQUE

The classic refinement of a smooth, pale pink bisque, with a hint of curry for excitement and a bonus of ease for the cook.

Total Preparation Time: 29 to 36 minutes
Microwave Time: 21 to 26 minutes
Yield: 6 servings (about ⅔ cup each)

Garlic Croutons (optional; see Index)
10 ounces peeled, deveined, uncooked
    shrimp
1 medium onion, peeled, cut into 1-inch
    pieces
2 tablespoons butter or margarine
3 tablespoons flour
3 tablespoons tomato paste
2½ cups chicken broth
2 teaspoons curry powder
⅛ teaspoon paprika
⅛ to ¼ teaspoon cayenne pepper
1 cup whipping cream or half-and-half
1 medium tomato, seeded, cut into 1-inch
    pieces

Make Garlic Croutons. Arrange shrimp in
single layer in glass baking dish; microwave
covered with plastic wrap at High until shrimp
turn pink, 2 to 3 minutes, stirring after 1
minute.

Process (Steel Knife) onion using on/off
technique until finely chopped. Microwave
onion and butter in 1½-quart glass casserole,
covered, at High until onion is tender, about 5
minutes. Stir in flour and tomato paste;
microwave uncovered at High 1 minute. Stir in
chicken broth, curry, paprika, and pepper.
Microwave uncovered at High until thickened,
10 to 12 minutes, stirring with whisk every 3
minutes.

Process (Steel Knife) shrimp using on/off
technique until minced. Stir shrimp and cream
into broth mixture; microwave uncovered at
High just until boiling, 4 to 5 minutes. Process
(Steel Knife) tomato until coarsely chopped.
Spoon soup into small bowls; sprinkle with
tomato and croutons.

Tips: Any size shrimp may be used. If you wish
    to use cooked shrimp, omit the
    microwaving step. Rinse frozen cooked
    shrimp to separate them; arrange in a
    single layer in a glass baking dish and
    microwave at defrost setting until thawed.

    Shrimp Bisque can be prepared to the
    point of final heating 1 day in advance;
    refrigerate covered.

FRENCH ONION SOUP

Microwave onions long enough to bring out
fullest flavor in this classic soup and you still
save hours of conventional preparation time.
Round out a French-style supper with a salad
and an omelet or sliced cold meats.

Total Preparation Time: 52 to 56 minutes
Microwave Time: 44 to 45 minutes
Yield: 4 servings (about 1
    cup each)

Parmesan Croutons (see Index)
2 ounces Swiss cheese, chilled, cut to fit feed
    tube
2 pounds Spanish onions, peeled, cut to fit
    feed tube
2 cloves garlic, peeled
¼ cup butter or margarine
1 teaspoon sugar
3 tablespoons flour
3 cups water
4 teaspoons beef-flavor instant bouillon
2 tablespoons Worcestershire sauce
¼ teaspoon dried marjoram leaves
Pinch thyme
¼ cup dry sherry (optional)

Make Parmesan Croutons. Shred (Shredding
Disc) Swiss cheese; reserve. Slice (Slicing Disc)
onions and garlic. Microwave butter in 3-quart
glass casserole at High until melted. Stir in
onions, garlic, and sugar; microwave covered
with plastic wrap at High 20 minutes, stirring
every 5 minutes. Stir in flour; microwave
uncovered 2 minutes. Stir in water, bouillon,
Worcestershire sauce, marjoram, and thyme.
Microwave covered at High 15 minutes. Stir in
sherry; spoon soup into glass bowls. Sprinkle
with croutons; sprinkle with reserved cheese.
Microwave uncovered at High until cheese is
melted, about 45 seconds. Serve immediately.

Tip: French Onion Soup can be prepared 2
    days in advance up to the addition of the
    sherry; refrigerate covered.

WON TON SOUP

Homemade won tons are incomparably better than most Chinese restaurant versions—lighter and more delicately seasoned. Your menu needn't be Chinese to start with this soup; it goes well with any simple entrée, such as roast chicken or broiled chops.

Total Preparation Time: 48 to 54 minutes
Microwave Time: 15 to 18 minutes
Yield: 6 servings (about 1¼ cups each)

2 ounces fresh watercress, stems removed
5 ounces fresh spinach, stems removed
5 ounces lean boneless pork, cut into 1-inch pieces
⅓ cup water chestnuts, cut into halves
1 small piece gingerroot (about the size of a dime)
3 teaspoons soy sauce
¼ teaspoon Chinese 5-spice powder
¼ teaspoon salt
⅛ teaspoon pepper
18 won ton wrappers, or 4 egg roll wrappers, cut into quarters
6 cups chicken broth

Slice (Slicing Disc) watercress and spinach. Remove half the spinach mixture from the bowl and reserve. Insert Steel Knife. Add pork, water chestnuts, gingerroot, 2 teaspoons of the soy sauce, the 5-spice powder, salt, and pepper to food processor bowl; process using on/off technique until mixture is finely chopped. Microwave pork mixture in 1-quart glass casserole, uncovered, at High until meat loses pink color, about 5 minutes. Remove; cool to room temperature.

Place scant 1½ teaspoons pork mixture along center of won ton wrapper; moisten edges of wrapper with water and fold in half to make rectangle, pressing edges to seal. Bring outside ends together to form a circle, sealing edges with water. Repeat with remaining filling and wrappers. Cover with towel until ready to cook.

Microwave chicken broth and remaining 1 teaspoon soy sauce in 3-quart glass bowl at High until boiling, 8 to 10 minutes. Add won tons and reserved spinach mixture; let stand covered 10 minutes, or until won tons are tender. Microwave covered at High until broth is hot, 2 to 3 minutes.

Tips: Won ton wrappers and 5-spice powder are available in specialty sections of large supermarkets or in Oriental groceries. There is no substitute for 5-spice powder.

If desired, 2 additional ounces fresh spinach can be substituted for the watercress. To slice watercress, roll up sprigs in the spinach leaves and slice the greens together.

To shape won tons:

Won tons and reserved spinach mixture can be prepared in advance and frozen up to 1 month. Freeze won tons in a single layer on a baking sheet; then transfer to a plastic bag and seal. It is not necessary to thaw won tons before adding them to the broth, but do allow extra standing and heating time. Won tons can be prepared 1 day in advance and refrigerated tightly covered with plastic wrap.

CHEESE AND CORN CHOWDER

A satisfying, whole-meal soup, rich with sausage, cheese, and the flavor of corn. Add a tossed green salad for a complete lunch or supper.

Total Preparation Time: 26 to 28 minutes
Microwave Time: 21 to 23 minutes
Yield: 6 servings (about 1½ cups each)

Savory Croutons (optional; see Index)
1 clove garlic, peeled
½ medium onion, peeled, cut into 1-inch pieces
1 medium green pepper, cut into 1-inch pieces
1 medium potato, pared, cut into 1-inch pieces
¼ cup butter or margarine
3 cups milk
2 teaspoons chicken-flavor instant bouillon
6 tablespoons Twice-As-Fast Sauce Mix (see Index)
1 pound fully cooked smoked sausage, cut into scant ½-inch chunks
1 can (16 ounces) whole-kernel corn, drained
1 can (16 ounces) cream-style corn
4 ounces Cheddar cheese, chilled, cut to fit feed tube
4 ounces Swiss cheese, chilled, cut to fit feed tube
2 medium tomatoes, cut into 1-inch pieces

Make Savory Croutons using chili powder. With machine running (Steel Knife), drop garlic through feed tube; process until minced. Add onion, green pepper, and potato to bowl; process using on/off technique until chopped. Microwave butter in 3-quart glass bowl at High until melted. Stir in garlic, onion, green pepper, and potato; microwave uncovered at High until tender, about 4 to 6 minutes. Stir milk and bouillon into vegetables. Microwave uncovered at High until boiling, 8 to 10 minutes. Stir in sauce mix; microwave uncovered until thickened, 2 to 4 minutes, stirring every minute. Stir in sausage and corn; microwave covered at High until hot through, about 4 minutes.

Shred (Shredding Disc) cheeses; remove. Process (Steel Knife) tomatoes until coarsely chopped. Stir cheeses and tomatoes into soup until cheese is melted. Microwave uncovered at 50% (Medium) 2 minutes. Serve soup in bowls; garnish with croutons.

Tip: Cheese and Corn Chowder can be prepared up to 2 days in advance; refrigerate covered.

CHICKEN–VEGETABLE CHOWDER

Whipped cream yields a glorious, satiny chowder. Reduce the number of servings and enjoy it as a main course if you wish.

Total Preparation Time: 40 to 44 minutes
Microwave Time: 26 to 30 minutes
Yield: 8 servings (about 1 cup each)

1½ pounds boneless chicken breasts, skinned, cut into 1-inch pieces
4 cups water
2 tablespoons chicken-flavor instant bouillon
4 peppercorns
3 whole cloves
½ teaspoon dried marjoram leaves
1 bay leaf
2 sprigs parsley
1 clove garlic, peeled
1 medium onion, peeled, cut to fit feed tube
1 medium green pepper, seeded, cut to fit feed tube
2 carrots, pared, cut to fit feed tube
2 medium zucchini, cut to fit feed tube
1 rib celery, cut to fit feed tube
6 tablespoons Twice-As-Fast Sauce Mix (see Index)
Salt
Pepper
1 cup whipping cream

Microwave chicken, water, bouillon, peppercorns, cloves, marjoram, bay leaf, and parsley in 3-quart glass casserole, covered, at High until chicken loses pink color and is tender, 10 to 12 minutes. Remove chicken with slotted spoon; strain broth, discarding spices and herbs.

With machine running (Steel Knife), drop garlic through feed tube, processing until minced. Slice (Slicing Disc) onion, green pepper, carrots, zucchini, and celery. Add to broth in 3-quart glass casserole; microwave, covered, at High until tender, about 10 minutes. Stir in sauce mix; microwave uncovered at High until thickened, 4 to 5 minutes, stirring every 2 minutes.

Stir chicken back into broth; microwave, uncovered, at High until hot through, 2 to 3 minutes. Season to taste with salt and pepper. Process (Steel Knife) cream until thick; stir into soup just before serving.

Tips: *Chowder can be prepared up to 2 days in advance; stir in whipped cream just before serving.*

    To slice green pepper easily, slit the cored, seeded pepper lengthwise down one side; roll up and place in feed tube, inserting from bottom of tube if necessary.

SOUTHERN GUMBO

Serve this southern favorite with Poppy Seed Biscuits or Onion Corn Bread (see Index). Twice-As-Fast Sauce Mix gives you a head start on the nut-brown roux that southern cooks swear by for best flavor.

Total Preparation Time: 40 to 45 minutes
Microwave Time: 30 to 35 minutes
Yield: 4 servings (about 1 cup each)

---

2 **tablespoons Twice-As-Fast Sauce Mix (see Index)**
2 **large sprigs parsley**
2 **cloves garlic, peeled**
1 **medium onion, peeled, cut into 1-inch pieces**
1 **medium green pepper, seeded, cut into 1-inch pieces**
2 **medium tomatoes, seeded, cut into 1-inch pieces**
3 **cups chicken broth**
⅛ **teaspoon pepper**
4 **ounces fresh okra, stems removed**
1 **tablespoon butter or margarine**
8 **ounces fully cooked smoked sausage, chilled, casing removed, cut to fit feed tube**
1 **teaspoon filé powder**

Microwave sauce mix in 2-quart glass casserole, uncovered, at High until golden brown, 6 to 8 minutes, stirring every 2 minutes. Process (Steel Knife) parsley using on/off technique until minced; reserve. With machine running, drop garlic through feed tube; process until minced. Add onion and green pepper to bowl; process using on/off technique until chopped. Stir garlic, onion, and green pepper into sauce mix; microwave covered at High until vegetables are tender, about 5 minutes. Process (Steel Knife) tomatoes using on/off technique until coarsely chopped. Stir tomatoes, chicken broth, and pepper into vegetables. Microwave uncovered at High until slightly thickened, 10 to 12 minutes, stirring every 3 minutes.

Slice (Slicing Disc) okra; sauté okra conventionally in 1 tablespoon butter in medium skillet until okra begins to brown. (See Tips.) Stir okra into casserole. Microwave covered at High until okra is tender, 5 to 8 minutes. Slice (Slicing Disc) sausage. Stir sausage, filé powder, and reserved parsley into soup; microwave covered at High until sausage is hot, about 4 minutes. Serve gumbo in shallow bowls.

Tips: *When okra is cooked in soup, it makes the broth viscous. Sautéing the okra before adding it to the soup reduces the viscosity.*

    Filé powder can be found in the spice section of the supermarket.

BLACK-EYED PEA AND LENTIL SOUP

Economical and high in protein, this soup is well worth the microwave time required to cook the dried peas. The peas don't have to be presoaked; the soup requires very little attention once it's in the oven—and the cooking fragrance is marvelous!

Total Preparation Time: 96 to 106 minutes
Microwave Time: 84 to 94 minutes
Yield: 8 servings (1¼ cups each)

12 slices bacon
3 medium carrots, pared, cut to fit feed tube
2 medium ribs celery, cut to fit feed tube
1 medium onion, peeled, cut into 1-inch pieces
12 ounces smoked ham, cut into 1-inch pieces
3 medium tomatoes, cut into 1-inch pieces
6 to 8 cups beef broth
1½ cups dried lentils
¾ cup dried black-eyed peas
¼ teaspoon dried thyme leaves
¼ teaspoon dried marjoram leaves
1 bay leaf
Salt
Pepper

Microwave bacon, 6 slices at a time, in glass baking dish, uncovered, at High until crisp, about 6 minutes. Drain bacon and crumble; reserve ¼ cup drippings.

Slice (Slicing Disc) carrots and celery; remove. Process (Steel Knife) onion, ham, and tomatoes separately, using on/off technique, until chopped. Stir carrots, celery, onion, and ham into reserved drippings in baking dish. Microwave covered with plastic wrap at High 6 minutes, stirring after 3 minutes. Drain excess drippings; transfer vegetable mixture to 4-quart glass casserole. Stir in bacon, tomatoes, 6 cups of the broth, and the remaining ingredients; microwave covered at High until boiling, about 12 minutes. Stir. Microwave covered at 50% (Medium) until peas are tender, 60 to 70 minutes, stirring every 15 minutes and adding additional broth if necessary.

Tip: *Black-eyed Pea and Lentil Soup can be refrigerated covered up to 5 days or frozen in a covered container up to 2 months. The soup will thicken, however; so stir in additional broth or water before reheating. Since the broth will dilute the seasonings, you may wish to add more thyme and marjoram or stir ½ teaspoon of Dijon-style mustard into each serving.*

6 Fish and Seafood

SOLE FILLETS WITH SPINACH PESTO

A spinach variation of pesto, the luscious Italian fresh basil sauce, blankets juicy sole fillets with appealing color contrast and rich flavor.

Total Preparation Time: 29 to 31 minutes
Microwave Time: 10 to 12 minutes
Yield: 6 servings

1 package (10 ounces) frozen spinach
4 ounces mozzarella cheese, chilled, cut to fit feed tube
2 ounces Parmesan cheese, cut into 1-inch pieces
1 small clove garlic, peeled
1 large shallot or ¼ small onion, peeled
2 tablespoons pine nuts or walnuts
⅓ cup sour cream
2 tablespoons fresh or 1 tablespoon dried basil leaves
¼ teaspoon dried marjoram leaves
¼ teaspoon salt
⅛ teaspoon white pepper
1½ pounds sole or other white fish fillets
3 tablespoons dry vermouth or white wine

Remove paper wrappers from spinach box; make 1 or 2 slashes in box. Microwave in box at High until thawed, about 4 minutes. Drain spinach very well in a strainer, pressing to remove as much moisture as possible.

Shred (Shredding Disc) mozzarella cheese; reserve. With machine running (Steel Knife), drop Parmesan cheese through feed tube; process until finely grated. Drop garlic and shallot through feed tube; process until minced. Add pine nuts to bowl; process using on/off technique until coarsely chopped. Add spinach, sour cream, basil, marjoram, salt, and pepper to bowl; process using on/off technique until blended.

Arrange fish in single layer in 12″ × 8″ glass baking dish, folding thin ends of fillets under; sprinkle with vermouth. Spoon spinach sauce over. Microwave covered with plastic wrap at High until fish is tender and flakes with a fork,

6 to 8 minutes, rotating dish ¼ turn and sprinkling with reserved mozzarella after 3 minutes.

Tips: Be careful not to overcook, as the fish should remain firm. Microwave most fish no longer than 4 to 5 minutes per pound, covered, at High.

TROUT WITH HAZELNUT STUFFING BAKED IN PARCHMENT

Parchment paper wrappers promote even cooking of whole fish, secure the stuffing, and tantalize diners at serving time. Fishermen can appreciate this fast, respectful treatment of any mild-flavored freshwater catch.

Total Preparation Time: 29 to 35 minutes
Microwave Time: 13 to 17 minutes
Yield: 4 servings

Basic Croutons and Variations (see Index)
½ cup blanched hazelnuts or almonds
1 rib celery, cut into 1-inch pieces
1 carrot, pared, cut into 1-inch pieces
½ to ⅔ cup chicken broth
2 to 4 tablespoons dry white wine
4 whole dressed trout (about 8 ounces each)
Lemon wedges

Make croutons, using variations with garlic and chervil. Process (Steel Knife) nuts, celery, and carrot using on/off technique until coarsely chopped. Combine croutons, nuts, celery, and carrot in medium bowl; add chicken broth and wine; toss. Stuff cavities of fish. Wrap each fish in piece of parchment paper; seal by folding edges of paper and crimping. Place fish packets in glass baking dish; microwave uncovered at High until fish is tender and flakes with a fork, 8 to 10 minutes, rotating baking dish ¼ turn every 4 minutes. Serve fish in parchment paper; garnish with lemon wedges.

Tips: Make croutons up to 4 weeks in advance; see recipe for storage directions.

Parchment paper can be found in large supermarkets and cookware shops. Wrap fish efficiently to fit them into the baking dish, but not too tightly. Waxed paper cannot be substituted. If parchment paper is not available, fish can be cooked in a glass baking dish tightly covered with plastic wrap.

Whole or boneless trout can be used. Recipe can be cut in half; microwave fish 4 to 5 minutes. Or stuffing can be divided between two 1-pound fish; microwave as above.

SALMON STEAKS WITH AVOCADO BUTTER

Tempt even diners who claim not to like fish with this superb balance of vinaigrette-seasoned salmon and pale green Avocado Butter.

Total Preparation Time: 29 to 30 minutes (plus marinating time)
Microwave Time: 10 to 12 minutes
Yield: 6 servings

---

2 tablespoons olive or vegetable oil
2 tablespoons water
2 tablespoons white wine vinegar
1 tablespoon lemon juice
¼ teaspoon paprika
¼ teaspoon ground cumin
Dash liquid smoke
¼ teaspoon salt
1/16 teaspoon white pepper
6 salmon steaks, ½ to ¾ inch thick (about 2½ pounds)
Avocado Butter (recipe follows)
Coriander or parsley sprigs

Mix oil, water, vinegar, lemon juice, paprika, cumin, liquid smoke, salt, and pepper in 12″ × 8″ glass baking dish. Place salmon in baking dish, turning over to coat with vinaigrette. Let stand 20 minutes.

Make Avocado Butter.

Microwave salmon, covered with plastic wrap, at High until fish is tender and flakes with a fork, 4 to 5 minutes per pound, rotating baking dish ¼ turn after 4 minutes. Arrange salmon steaks on serving platter; garnish with coriander and serve with Avocado Butter.

Tip: Coriander Rice (see Index) would go well with Salmon Steaks with Avocado Butter. Fresh coriander, also called cilantro or Chinese parsley, can be found in large supermarkets and Oriental or Mexican grocery stores.

Avocado Butter

Yield: about 1¼ cups

---

3 large sprigs parsley
½ clove garlic, peeled
4 ounces butter or margarine, softened
1 large ripe avocado, peeled, pitted, cut into 1-inch pieces
2 teaspoons lime juice
¼ teaspoon chili powder
Dash cayenne pepper

Process (Steel Knife) parsley using on/off technique until minced. With machine running, drop garlic through feed tube; process until minced. Add remaining ingredients to bowl; process until smooth, about 30 seconds, scraping side of bowl with spatula if necessary.

Tips: Avocado Butter can be made 2 days in advance; refrigerate in covered container. Salmon steaks can be cooked, refrigerated covered, and served cold with Avocado Butter for brunch, lunch, or a soothing hot-weather supper.

Halibut or swordfish steaks can be substituted for the salmon.

Liquid smoke can be found in the spice section of the supermarket.

RED SNAPPER CREOLE

This New Orleans-style recipe for a Gulf Coast fish features a robust sauce and just a hint of cayenne heat. Serve with plain rice, Onion Rice, or Pimiento Rice (see Index).

Total Preparation Time: 37 to 41 minutes
Microwave Time: 24 to 28 minutes
Yield: 6 servings

---

3 cloves garlic, peeled
½ teaspoon paprika
¼ teaspoon cayenne pepper
1½ pounds red snapper fillets
2 green onions and tops, cut into 1-inch pieces
1 medium onion, peeled, cut into 1-inch pieces
1 rib celery, cut into 1-inch pieces
1 medium green pepper, seeded, cut into 1-inch pieces
2 tablespoons butter or margarine
1 can (16 ounces) tomatoes, drained, cut into quarters
3 tablespoons tomato paste
1 teaspoon sugar
1 bay leaf

With machine running (Steel Knife), drop 2 of the garlic cloves through feed tube, processing until minced. Mix minced garlic, paprika, and cayenne pepper; rub on snapper fillets. Arrange fillets in 12″ × 8″ glass baking dish, with thickest portions toward outside of dish and thin ends folded under.

With machine running (Steel Knife), drop remaining clove of garlic through feed tube, processing until minced. Add onions, celery, and green pepper; process using on/off technique until chopped. Microwave vegetable mixture and butter in 1-quart glass casserole, covered, at High until tender, 6 to 8 minutes, stirring after 3 minutes. Process (Steel Knife) tomatoes using on/off technique until coarsely chopped. Add tomatoes, tomato paste, sugar, and bay leaf to vegetable mixture; microwave covered with waxed paper at High until thick, about 9 minutes, stirring after 4 minutes.

Microwave fish covered with waxed paper at High until fish is tender and flakes with a fork, 6 to 8 minutes, rotating dish ¼ turn after 3 minutes; drain. Spoon sauce over fish; microwave uncovered at High until hot through, about 3 minutes.

Tips: Substitute two large fresh tomatoes, cored and cut into 1-inch pieces, for the canned tomatoes, but only when tomatoes are at peak flavor.

Grouper and sea bass are worthy substitutes for snapper; haddock or halibut can also be used.

SHRIMP WITH FETA CHEESE

The flavors of seafood, ripe olives, tomatoes, herbs, and feta cheese combine to recall sunny Greek islands.

Total Preparation Time: 26 to 30 minutes
Microwave Time: 16 to 20 minutes
Yield: 4 servings

---

3 sprigs parsley
1 medium onion, peeled, cut into 1-inch pieces
1 tablespoon olive oil or vegetable oil
1 medium carrot, pared, cut into 1-inch pieces
½ cup pitted ripe olives
3 medium tomatoes, seeded, cut into 1-inch pieces
3 tablespoons dry white wine
1 tablespoon tomato paste
½ teaspoon dried oregano
¼ teaspoon dried marjoram
4 ounces feta cheese, crumbled
1 pound shelled, deveined shrimp

Process (Steel Knife) parsley using on/off technique until minced; remove half the parsley and reserve. Add onion to bowl; process using on/off technique until finely chopped. Microwave onion mixture and oil in 2-quart glass casserole, covered, at High until tender, about 3 minutes.

Process (Steel Knife) carrot, olives, and tomatoes separately, using on/off technique, until chopped; stir vegetables into onion mixture. Stir in wine, tomato paste, oregano, and marjoram; microwave covered at High until mixture boils and carrots are tender, 8 to 10 minutes, stirring after 4 minutes.

Reserve 2 tablespoons of the cheese; stir remaining cheese into vegetable mixture; microwave uncovered until cheese is melted, about 2 minutes. Stir in shrimp; microwave uncovered at High until shrimp turn pink, 3 to 5 minutes, stirring after 4 minutes. Spoon into serving dish; sprinkle with reserved parsley and cheese.

Tips: If feta cheese is very salty, soak it in cold water and squeeze it dry in several layers of cheesecloth or a dish towel. Imported feta cheese, available in large supermarkets and Middle Eastern groceries, is usually made from ewe's milk; it is tangier than domestic feta, which is made from cow's milk. Both kinds of feta are preserved in brine, resulting in varying degrees of saltiness.

Plan a large party menu of Shrimp with Feta Cheese, Greek Meatball Kebabs, and Pastitsio, with Baklava for dessert, if you wish (see Index). Serve the entrées together, either buffet-style or sit-down; the dishes will stand well, reflecting the Mediterranean custom of setting out opulent "nibbling" buffets. Add a mixed garden salad with an oregano-seasoned vinaigrette and plenty of crusty bread.

Half portions of Shrimp with Feta Cheese can be served as an appetizer with an entrée of broiled chicken or roast lamb.

CRAB-STUFFED FILLETS OF SOLE

Bright green asparagus and pink-flecked crab rolled in moist, white fillets—a very attractive choice for brunch, lunch, or dinner.

Total Preparation Time: 22 to 25 minutes
Microwave Time: 8 to 11 minutes
Yield: 4 servings

---

8 ounces fresh asparagus
¼ cup water
3 ounces crab meat
1 egg
1 tablespoon plain yogurt
1 tablespoon dry bread crumbs
1 teaspoon drained capers
1 teaspoon prepared mustard
¼ teaspoon salt
⅛ teaspoon pepper
4 sole fillets (about 1 pound)
¼ cup dry white wine
2 tablespoons Parmesan-Garlic Butter (see Index) or melted butter

Reserve 8 (2-inch) asparagus spears; cut remaining asparagus into 1-inch pieces. Microwave asparagus spears and water in 1-quart glass casserole, covered, at High until asparagus is crisp-tender, 3 to 4 minutes; drain. Process (Steel Knife) cut asparagus, the crab meat, egg, yogurt, bread crumbs, capers, mustard, salt, and pepper using on/off technique until finely chopped.

Spread crab mixture on fillets; place 2 asparagus spears on each fillet and roll up, enclosing spears. Place rolled fillets seam sides down in 8-inch square glass baking dish; add wine. Microwave covered with waxed paper at High until fish is tender and flakes with a fork, 5 to 7 minutes, rotating dish ¼ turn after 3 minutes.

Make Parmesan-Garlic Butter; spoon over fish.

Tips: Use good-quality frozen or fresh crab meat for preferred appearance; if you use canned crab meat, rinse well with cold water, drain, and remove any bits of shell.

If capers are very salty, place them in a strainer and rinse well under cold water.

Other mild-flavored fish fillets, such as haddock, flounder, or turbot, can be substituted for the sole.

MEDITERRANEAN FISH STEW

An aromatic, vermilion stew that's delicious when made with any saltwater fish fillets and exceptionally attractive when enriched with mussels. Serve with French bread and a dry white wine.

Total Preparation Time: 45 to 47 minutes
Microwave Time: 21 to 22 minutes
Yield: 6 servings

½ cup parsley sprigs
2 cloves garlic, peeled
1 medium onion, peeled, cut into 1-inch pieces
½ medium green pepper, seeded, cut to fit feed tube
½ cup pitted ripe olives
2 tablespoons olive juice
1 tablespoon olive or vegetable oil
1 teaspoon dried basil leaves
½ teaspoon dried savory leaves
¼ teaspoon fennel seeds, crushed
4 ounces mushrooms
2 large tomatoes, cored, cut into 1-inch pieces
1 can (8 ounces) tomato sauce
½ cup dry white wine
½ cup clam juice
¼ cup orange juice
¼ teaspoon grated orange rind
2 bay leaves
¼ teaspoon salt
¼ teaspoon pepper
1 pound white fish fillets, cut into 2-inch pieces
8 to 12 mussels, cleaned (optional)

Process (Steel Knife) parsley using on/off technique until minced. With machine running, drop garlic through feed tube, processing until minced. Add onion to bowl. Process using on/off technique until chopped; remove. Slice (Slicing Disc) green pepper and olives. Microwave onion mixture, pepper, olives, olive juice, olive oil, basil, savory, and fennel in 3-quart glass casserole, covered, at High 6 minutes.

Slice (Slicing Disc) mushrooms; remove. Process (Steel Knife) tomatoes using on/off technique until chopped. Stir mushrooms, tomatoes, tomato sauce, wine, clam juice, orange juice, orange rind, bay leaves, salt, and pepper into casserole. Microwave uncovered at High 10 minutes, stirring after 5 minutes.

Remove 1½ cups vegetables from casserole with slotted spoon. Process (Steel Knife) vegetables until smooth; stir back into stew. Add fish and mussels; microwave uncovered until fish is tender and flakes with a fork, about 5 minutes, stirring after 3 minutes. Serve in shallow bowls.

Tips: For even cooking, place thinner or smaller pieces of seafood in the center of the casserole. Make sure seafood is covered by the sauce to prevent dryness.

To clean mussels, scrub them with a stiff brush if they are very sandy or rub them together to remove traces of sand. If beards are attached, scrub with a stiff brush to remove them. Let mussels stand in cold, salted water 10 minutes; rinse well in cold water. Discard any mussels that are broken or opened.

SCALLOPS DE JONGHE

Microwaves make it easy to control timing, both when toasting buttered bread crumbs and "baking" scallops. So the textures of both ingredients remain delicate, and the simple combination couldn't be more pleasing. Serve half portions as an elegant first course.

Total Preparation Time: 22 to 24 minutes
Microwave Time: 7 to 9 minutes
Yield: 4 servings

Garlic-Herb Crumbs (see Index)
½ cup cold butter or margarine, cut into pieces
1 pound sea scallops, cut into halves
3 tablespoons dry white wine

Make Garlic-Herb Crumbs; add butter to bowl and process using on/off technique until mixed. Microwave crumb mixture in glass pie plate, uncovered, at High until crisp, 3 to 4 minutes, stirring after 2 minutes.

Microwave scallops and wine in 1-quart glass casserole, covered with waxed paper, at High 2 minutes; drain well. Spoon half the crumbs into 4 shell dishes or 10-ounce glass custard cups; spoon scallops over crumbs and top with remaining crumbs. Microwave uncovered at High until scallops are tender, 2 to 3 minutes. Serve immediately.

Tips: To serve Scallops de Jonghe as a first course, divide crumbs and scallops among 8 ramekins or miniature quiche pans. Microwave 4 at a time for 1½ to 2 minutes; bring the first 4 to the table while the remainder are cooking. Set each ramekin on a plate garnished with sprigs of curly or flat-leaf parsley or dill and a lemon wedge, if desired.

Shelled, deveined shrimp can be substituted for the scallops; proceed as above, microwaving until shrimp turn pink, 2 to 3 minutes.

PICKLED TROUT

The whole pickled fish makes a marvelous addition to a brunch table or party buffet. Half-size portions, served chilled with Food Processor Mayonnaise (see Index), are a superb way to start a meal.

Total Preparation Time: 28 to 32 minutes (plus cooling time)
Microwave Time: 18 to 22 minutes
Yield: 4 servings

---

1 **medium onion, peeled, cut to fit feed tube**
1 **rib celery, cut to fit feed tube**
1 **carrot, pared, cut to fit feed tube**
2 **cups dry white wine**
1¾ **cups water**
1¼ **cups white tarragon vinegar**
¼ **cup sugar**
¼ **cup whole pickling spice**
1 **tablespoon drained capers**
1 **whole dressed trout (1¾ to 2 pounds)**
1 **lemon, cut to fit feed tube**
Watercress or parsley sprigs

Slice (Slicing Disc) onion, celery, and carrot. Microwave vegetables and remaining ingredients except trout, lemon, and watercress in 12″ × 8″ glass baking dish, uncovered, at High until simmering, about 8 minutes.

Wrap trout in cheesecloth; place in wine mixture. Microwave covered with plastic wrap at High until fish is tender and flakes with a fork, 10 to 14 minutes, turning fish over every 5 minutes.

Let fish cool in wine mixture about 1½ hours, turning fish over occasionally. Remove from wine mixture; drain and remove cheesecloth. Place on serving platter. Slice (Slicing Disc) lemon; garnish trout with lemon and watercress.

Tips: If more intense pickled flavor is desired, refrigerate fish in wine mixture several hours or overnight.

You can purchase whole dressed trout, with bones intact, or boneless trout with head and tail attached. For buffet serving, remove the top skin and make 1-inch cuts along the fish to indicate servings but leave fish intact. You may wish to sprinkle the fish with chopped parsley. An equal weight of smaller trout can be substituted for the single, large trout.

Chicken Provençal
Indonesian Chicken
Chicken with Curry Sauce
Coq au Vin in Clay
Lemon Chicken with Snow Peas
Savory Chicken Rolls
Chicken and Shrimp in Fillo Shells
Mock Fried Chicken Breasts
Chicken Livers Stroganoff
Roast Cornish Hens with Fruit Pilaf
Roast Duckling with Sweet and Sour Cabbage
Turkey Breast with Honey-Mustard Sauce
Turkey Tetrazzini

7 Poultry

CHICKEN PROVENÇAL

Moist, juicy chicken in an herb-scented tomato sauce. Spinach Rice (see Index) would turn it into a feast; plain or Parmesan Rice could complete a family meal.

Total Preparation Time: 45 to 48 minutes
Microwave Time: 32 to 35 minutes
Yield: 4 servings

---

1 medium onion, peeled, cut into 1-inch pieces
2 tablespoons olive or vegetable oil
8 medium tomatoes, seeded, cut into 1-inch pieces
1 can (6 ounces) tomato paste
2 teaspoons sugar
½ teaspoon dried basil leaves
½ teaspoon dried tarragon leaves
¼ teaspoon dried oregano leaves
1/16 teaspoon ground nutmeg
Salt
Pepper
4 ounces mushrooms
10 pitted ripe olives
1 frying chicken, cut up (about 3 pounds)
Browning and seasoning sauce
2 medium zucchini, cut to fit feed tube
1 medium green pepper, seeded, cut to fit feed tube

Process (Steel Knife) onion using on/off technique until coarsely chopped. Microwave onion and oil in 2-quart glass casserole, covered, at High until tender, about 3 minutes. Process (Steel Knife) tomatoes using on/off technique until chopped. Stir tomatoes, tomato paste, sugar, basil, tarragon, oregano, nutmeg, salt, and pepper into onion. Microwave covered at High 8 minutes, stirring every 3 minutes. Slice (Slicing Disc) mushrooms and olives; stir into tomato sauce. Microwave uncovered at High 4 minutes.

Arrange chicken pieces skin sides down in 12″ × 8″ glass baking dish, placing meatier pieces toward edges of dish. Microwave uncovered at High 7 minutes. Turn pieces over; brush lightly with browning sauce. Spoon tomato sauce over chicken. Microwave covered with plastic wrap at High until chicken is done, 10 to 13 minutes, rotating dish ¼ turn after 7 minutes. Slice (Slicing Disc) zucchini and green pepper; stir into sauce during last 5 minutes of cooking time. Let stand, covered, 5 minutes.

Tips: *If you can obtain fresh herbs, substitute 1 teaspoon each of fresh basil and tarragon and ½ teaspoon fresh oregano leaves; chop them with the tomatoes. If full-flavored tomatoes are not available, 2 cans (28 ounces each) Italian-style plum tomatoes, seeded and drained, can be substituted.*

To seed tomatoes, cut them horizontally into halves. Squeeze each half gently until seeds pop out.

Provençal dishes are often seasoned with garlic. You may wish to add 1 or 2 peeled cloves of garlic to this recipe. Process (Steel Knife) the garlic until minced before you process the onion; drop garlic cloves through the feed tube with the machine running.

Chicken Provençal can be prepared 1 day in advance; refrigerate covered.

INDONESIAN CHICKEN

A showcase recipe for the food processor and microwave oven. Lusty flavor and colorful garnishes make it a good choice for entertaining. It comes together very quickly, but harried party hosts will also discover that it holds well in the refrigerator and reheats beautifully.

Total Preparation Time: 40 to 45 minutes
Microwave Time: 20 to 23 minutes
Yield: 4 servings

---

1 clove garlic, peeled
½ medium onion, peeled, cut into 1-inch pieces

2 large green onions and tops, cut into 1-
  inch pieces
1 small cucumber, pared, seeded, cut into 1-
  inch pieces
1 large tomato, seeded, cut into 1-inch
  pieces
2 tablespoons butter or margarine
1 tablespoon flour
2 cups cocktail peanuts
1½ cups chicken broth
1 teaspoon crushed dried red pepper
2½ to 3 pounds chicken pieces
Coriander or parsley sprigs
1 lime, cut into wedges

With machine running (Steel Knife), drop
garlic through feed tube, processing until
minced. Add onions to bowl; process using
on/off technique until finely chopped, and
remove. Process (Steel Knife) cucumber and
tomato separately, using on/off technique, until
coarsely chopped; reserve. Microwave butter in
1-quart glass casserole at High until melted;
stir in onion mixture. Microwave uncovered at
High 2 minutes; stir in flour. Microwave
uncovered at High 1 minute.

Process (Steel Knife) peanuts using on/off
technique until peanuts are coarsely chopped;
remove 2 tablespoons and reserve. Process
remaining peanuts until a smooth peanut
butter is formed; add broth through feed tube,
processing until blended. Add onion mixture
and red pepper to bowl; blend into peanut
mixture using on/off technique.

Arrange chicken pieces skin sides down in
12″ × 8″ glass baking dish, placing meatier
pieces toward edges of dish. Microwave loosely
covered with waxed paper at High 7 minutes.
Turn chicken pieces over; pour peanut mixture
over chicken. Microwave loosely covered at
High until chicken is tender, 10 to 13 minutes,
rotating dish ¼ turn after 7 minutes. Let stand
5 minutes.

Arrange chicken on serving platter; garnish
with reserved cucumber, tomato, chopped nuts,
the coriander, and lime.

*Tips: Turmeric Rice (see Index) is excellent with
this recipe. Make rice before cooking the*

*chicken; let stand covered while chicken is
cooking. Microwave covered at High until
hot, about 2 minutes, while chicken is
standing.*

*You can cheat some of the calories in
this rich dish by making half the amount
of sauce; cut quantities of ingredients
other than cucumber, tomato, chicken, and
lime in half and proceed as above. The
presentation will be much less lavish, but
your conscience may be assuaged!*

*To seed cucumber, cut it lengthwise into
halves and scrape out the seeds with a
spoon or cut them out in strips with a
small paring knife.*

CHICKEN WITH CURRY SAUCE

Curry powder, a seasoning shortcut blended
from many spices, adds another dimension to
speedy cooking. Its fragrance creates an
irresistible bond between a smooth sauce and
white-meat chicken. Serve with Minted or
Coriander Rice (see Index). Curry Sauce is also
good with green vegetables or lamb.

Total Preparation Time: 30 to 33 minutes
Microwave Time: 24 to 27 minutes
Yield: 6 servings

6 chicken breast halves, skinned (about 3
  pounds)
Browning and seasoning sauce
¼ cup chicken broth
Curry Sauce (recipe follows)

Brush chicken with browning sauce; arrange
pieces in 12″ × 8″ glass baking dish with
meatiest portions toward edges of dish. Add
chicken broth; microwave covered with plastic
wrap at High until chicken is done and juices
run clear when thickest pieces are pierced with
a fork, 18 to 20 minutes, turning pieces over
halfway through cooking time. Let stand,
covered, 5 minutes.

Make Curry Sauce; serve over chicken.

Curry Sauce

Yield: about 1¼ cups

---

3 tablespoons Twice-As-Fast Sauce Mix
½ clove garlic, peeled
¼ medium onion, peeled, cut into 1-inch pieces
1 cup chicken broth
¼ teaspoon curry powder
Pinch cayenne pepper
2 tablespoons plain yogurt

Microwave sauce mix in 4-cup glass measure, uncovered, at High 2 minutes. Process (Steel Knife) garlic and onion using on/off technique until minced; stir into sauce mix. Microwave uncovered at High 1 minute. Stir in chicken broth, curry, and pepper; microwave uncovered at High until mixture boils and thickens, 3 to 3½ minutes, stirring with whisk every minute. Stir in yogurt.

COQ AU VIN IN CLAY

A clay cooking pot achieves an almost miraculous blending of flavors in record time. The secret lies in the continuous release of steam from the lid and sides of the pot. For best flavor and appearance, however, you should brown chicken conventionally before combining it with other ingredients.

Total Preparation Time: 46 to 47 minutes
Microwave Time: 24 to 25 minutes
Yield: 4 servings

---

3 pounds chicken pieces
Flour
3 tablespoons vegetable oil
Salt
Pepper
3 large sprigs parsley

1 clove garlic, peeled
2 shallots or ½ small onion, peeled, cut into 1-inch pieces
½ medium leek, cleaned, or 3 green onions and tops, cut into 1-inch pieces
1 tablespoon butter or margarine
½ cup dry white wine
½ teaspoon dried basil leaves
¼ teaspoon dried marjoram leaves
¼ teaspoon dried tarragon leaves
1 can (8 ounces) pearl onions, drained
4 ounces small mushrooms
2 tablespoons cornstarch
¼ cup cold water

Soak clay pot in water 15 minutes. Coat chicken pieces with flour; sauté conventionally in oil in large skillet until browned on all sides. Sprinkle lightly with salt and pepper.

Process (Steel Knife) parsley using on/off technique until minced; reserve. With machine running (Steel Knife), drop garlic and shallots through feed tube; process until minced. Add leek to bowl; process using on/off technique until finely chopped. Remove Steel Knife; add butter to bowl. Microwave vegetables in food processor bowl covered with plastic wrap at High until vegetables are tender, about 5 minutes.

Arrange chicken in clay pot with meatiest portions toward edges of pot. Stir wine, basil, marjoram, and tarragon into vegetable mixture; spoon over chicken. Microwave covered at 70% (Medium High) until chicken is done and juices run clear when thickest pieces are pierced with a fork, about 15 minutes. Add pearl onions and mushrooms to clay pot during last 5 minutes of cooking time. Remove chicken to serving platter; let stand loosely covered with aluminum foil. Mix cornstarch and water; stir into juices in clay pot. Microwave uncovered at High until thickened, 4 to 5 minutes, stirring every 2 minutes. Pour sauce mixture over chicken; sprinkle with reserved parsley.

Tips: You can use a clay pot designed for either conventional or microwave cooking; the latter is simply easier to clean. If you are using the pot for the first time, soak it at least 30 minutes. You can begin soaking any clay pot as far in advance as you wish; the longer it soaks, the better. There is no need to rotate a clay pot during cooking. If you do not have a clay pot, you can prepare this recipe in an oven cooking bag set in a 12″ × 8″ glass baking dish; coat the inside of the bag with 1 tablespoon of flour to prevent it from splitting. Close the bag with a nonmetallic twist tie or string and turn it over halfway through the cooking time. You can also prepare the recipe in a 12″ × 8″ glass baking dish tightly covered with plastic wrap.

To make beef bourguignon, substitute 2 pounds of lean, cubed beef (chuck or sirloin) for the chicken and use red wine instead of white. You may not need to thicken the juices in the pot at the end of the cooking time; if you wish to, stir the cornstarch and water mixture directly into the stew and heat until thickened.

LEMON CHICKEN WITH SNOW PEAS

Oriental sensitivity to balance of seasonings, textures, and colors distinguishes a mild, unusually pretty "stir-fry."

Total Preparation Time: 43 to 49 minutes
Microwave Time: 18 to 22 minutes
Yield: 4 to 6 servings

---

3 large lemons, cut to fit feed tube
1 pound boneless chicken breasts, skinned, cut into ¾-inch pieces
3 tablespoons soy sauce
1 teaspoon granulated sugar
2 teaspoons sesame seeds
1 green onion and top, cut into 1-inch pieces
8 ounces fresh snow peas, ends trimmed
1 tablespoon peanut or vegetable oil
1 teaspoon sesame oil
1 cup water

2 teaspoons chicken-flavor instant bouillon
⅓ cup packed light brown sugar
3 tablespoons cornstarch
½ teaspoon dry mustard
4 to 6 cups hot cooked rice

Slice (Slicing Disc) 1 lemon; reserve. Grate rind from 1 lemon; reserve. Peel 2 whole lemons and cut into quarters. Process (Steel Knife) lemon pulp until all juice is extracted; strain and discard pith and seeds. Mix chicken, 2 tablespoons of the lemon juice, the soy sauce, and granulated sugar in bowl; let stand 15 minutes.

Microwave sesame seeds in glass pie plate, uncovered, at High until toasted, about 3 minutes, stirring after 1½ minutes. Process (Steel Knife) onion until coarsely chopped; remove. Slice (Slicing Disc) snow peas, placing peas in feed tube horizontally. Remove Slicing Disc; microwave peas in food processor bowl, covered with plastic wrap, at High until crisp-tender, about 2 minutes.

Microwave oils in 12″ × 8″ glass baking dish at High until hot. Drain excess liquid from chicken and reserve; microwave chicken in hot oil in glass baking dish, uncovered, at High until chicken loses pink color, 5 to 7 minutes, stirring every 2 minutes. Drain oil; let chicken stand loosely covered while preparing sauce.

Mix water, remaining lemon juice, reserved liquid from chicken, the bouillon, brown sugar, cornstarch, dry mustard, and reserved lemon rind in 4-cup glass measure; microwave uncovered at High until thickened, 5 to 6 minutes, stirring every 2 minutes. Stir sauce and snow peas into chicken; microwave uncovered at High until hot through, about 2 minutes. Spoon onto serving platter. Sprinkle with sesame seeds and onion; garnish with sliced lemon. Serve with rice.

Tips: To slice snow peas horizontally, you may find it easier to pack them into the bottom of the feed tube, which is slightly wider than the top. If any of the snow peas are too long, cut in half to fit.

Slicing makes the texture of the crisp pods more consistent with the delicacy of the chicken.

SAVORY CHICKEN ROLLS

Two major advantages of food processor/
microwave cooking—a stuffing made in seconds
and moister white-meat chicken. Spoon
Mushroom or Fresh Tomato Sauce (see Index)
over the rolls to maximize their savory appeal.

Total Preparation Time: 42 to 47 minutes
Microwave Time: 17 to 20 minutes
Yield: 4 servings

Garlic-Herb Bread Crumbs (see Index)
2 ounces mozzarella cheese, chilled, cut to
　fit feed tube
1 large carrot, pared, cut to fit feed tube
6 medium mushrooms
½ small onion, peeled, cut into halves
4 tablespoons butter or margarine
½ teaspoon salt
⅛ teaspoon white pepper
4 chicken breast halves, skinned, boned
　(about 2 pounds)
Paprika

Make Garlic-Herb Bread Crumbs; dry
crumbs. Shred (Shredding Disc) cheese and
carrot separately; remove. Process (Steel Knife)
mushrooms and onion separately, using on/off
technique, until finely chopped. Microwave
butter in 1-quart glass casserole at High until
melted; reserve half the butter. Stir carrot,
mushrooms, and onion into remaining butter in
casserole. Microwave covered at High until
vegetables are tender, 3 to 4 minutes. Mix in
crumbs, cheese, salt, and pepper. Pound
chicken breasts until even in thickness. Spread
stuffing on chicken breasts; roll up tightly from
narrow end and secure with wooden picks.
Place rolls in 12″ × 8″ glass baking dish; brush
with reserved butter and sprinkle with
paprika. Microwave covered with plastic wrap
at High until chicken is done and juices run
clear when chicken is pierced with a fork,
about 10 minutes, rotating dish ¼ turn after 5
minutes. Let stand covered 5 minutes.

*Tips: When guests surprise you, you can
surprise them with this recipe. All
ingredients can be kept on hand. Make the
dried bread crumbs whenever you have a
supply of going-stale bread; they will keep
for months. Freeze individually wrapped
flattened chicken breast halves up to 2
months; thaw in microwave as needed. In
a pinch, you can substitute canned
mushrooms or omit them. Keep Twice-As-
Fast Sauce Mix (see Index) in the
refrigerator and turn it into any sauce
that suits the supplies in your pantry.*

CHICKEN AND SHRIMP IN FILLO SHELLS

A spectacular entrée for a formal lunch or
elegant brunch. Make the Fillo Pastry Shells
days in advance, if you wish.

Total Preparation Time: 53 to 58 minutes
Microwave Time: 16 to 18 minutes
Yield: 6 servings

Fillo Pastry Shells (see Index)
1½ ounces Parmesan cheese, cut into 1-inch
　pieces
3 ounces Swiss cheese, chilled, cut to fit feed
　tube
6 ounces mushrooms
1 large clove garlic, peeled
3 medium green onions and tops, cut into 1-
　inch pieces
4½ tablespoons Twice-As-Fast Sauce Mix
1½ cups half-and-half
¼ teaspoon salt
⅛ teaspoon white pepper
¾ pound cooked chicken, cut into 1-inch
　pieces
¾ pound cooked, shelled, deveined shrimp
⅓ cup slivered almonds

Make Fillo Pastry Shells. Process (Steel Knife) Parmesan cheese until finely grated; remove. Shred (Shredding Disc) Swiss cheese; remove. Slice (Slicing Disc) mushrooms; remove. With machine running (Steel Knife), drop garlic through feed tube, processing until minced. Add onions to bowl; process using on/off technique until chopped. Microwave onion mixture, mushrooms, and sauce mix in 1-quart glass casserole, covered, at High 4 minutes, stirring after 2 minutes. Stir in half-and-half, salt, and pepper. Microwave uncovered at High until thickened, 5 to 6 minutes, stirring every 1½ minutes with whisk. Stir in cheeses, chicken, and shrimp; microwave uncovered at High until hot through, about 3 minutes. Spoon mixture into fillo shells; sprinkle with almonds.

Tips: One whole, large chicken breast will yield about ¾ pound cooked chicken. Microwave skinned chicken breast in glass baking dish, covered with plastic wrap, at High just until tender and juices run clear, about 7 minutes; remove meat from bones and cut into 1-inch pieces.

One pound of medium shrimp in shells will yield just under ¾ pound cooked, shelled shrimp. Microwave shelled, deveined, uncooked shrimp in 2-cup glass measure, covered with plastic wrap, at High 3 to 4 minutes.

Chicken and shrimp mixture can be topped with seasoned bread crumbs (see Index) and heated in ramekins or shell dishes as above, omitting Fillo Pastry Shells and almonds.

MOCK FRIED CHICKEN BREASTS

Much lighter than true-fried, and much more convenient to prepare. Remove the skin from the chicken if you wish to reduce calories and cholesterol.

Total Preparation Time: 28 to 32 minutes
Microwave Time: 18 to 20 minutes
Yield: 6 servings

Wheat and Walnut Bread Crumbs (see Index)
2 tablespoons butter or margarine
1 egg
6 boneless chicken breast halves (about 2 pounds)

Make Wheat and Walnut Bread Crumbs; dry crumbs. Microwave butter in glass pie plate at High until melted; whisk in egg until smooth. Dip chicken breasts in egg mixture to coat; dip into crumb mixture, pressing crumbs firmly onto chicken. Arrange chicken on microwave meat rack in 12″ × 8″ glass baking dish with meatiest portions toward the edges of dish. Microwave uncovered at High until chicken is tender and juices run clear when thickest portions are pierced with a fork, about 14 minutes.

Tips: Any of the seasoned bread crumb variations can be used in this recipe. Crumbs can be made in advance; see recipe for storage directions.

Two pounds cut-up chicken pieces can be substituted for the boneless breast halves.

CHICKEN LIVERS STROGANOFF

Microwaves protect the tenderness of liver, yielding a texture to match the fine flavor of this brandy-spiked stroganoff. The recipe can easily be doubled for a buffet and set out, with noodles, on a warming tray.

Total Preparation Time: 27 to 31 minutes
Microwave Time: 13 to 14 minutes
Yield: 4 servings

---

4 sprigs parsley
1 medium onion, peeled, cut into 1-inch
    pieces
2 tablespoons butter or margarine
12 ounces chicken livers, cut into halves
4 ounces mushrooms
2 tablespoons brandy
½ cup sour cream
2 tablespoons flour
1 teaspoon chicken-flavor instant bouillon
1 teaspoon Worcestershire sauce
½ teaspoon Dijon-style mustard
Few drops browning and seasoning sauce
Toast points or cooked noodles

Process (Steel Knife) parsley using on/off technique until minced; reserve. Process (Steel Knife) onion using on/off technique until coarsely chopped. Microwave onion and butter in 1½-quart glass casserole, covered, at High 3 minutes. Stir in livers; microwave covered at High until livers lose pink color, 4 to 5 minutes, stirring after 2 minutes. Slice (Slicing Disc) mushrooms; stir into liver mixture. Microwave uncovered at High 2 minutes. Microwave brandy in 1-cup glass measure at High 15 to 20 seconds; ignite and pour over liver mixture. Mix sour cream and flour; stir into liver mixture. Stir in bouillon, Worcestershire sauce, mustard, and browning sauce. Microwave covered at High until hot through, about 3 minutes, stirring after 1½ minutes. Serve over toast points or noodles; sprinkle with reserved parsley.

ROAST CORNISH HENS WITH FRUIT PILAF

Diners who disdain the dryness of conventionally roasted Cornish hens will be delighted by the taste of these. A fruit glaze and a pecan-crunchy, brown rice stuffing flatter the meat perfectly. This is a good holiday alternative to turkey for a small gathering.

Total Preparation Time: 54 to 56 minutes
Microwave Time: 47 to 53 minutes
Yield: 4 servings

2 cups hot water
1½ tablespoons orange juice concentrate
¼ teaspoon salt
⅔ cup uncooked brown rice
1 small cucumber, pared, seeded, cut into 1-
    inch pieces
1 small onion, peeled, cut into quarters
¾ cup pecans
¼ cup raisins
¼ cup dried apricots, cut into halves
2 tablespoons orange marmalade
4 Cornish hens (about 1 pound each)
¼ cup orange marmalade
1½ teaspoons prepared mustard
1 teaspoon distilled white vinegar
1 teaspoon soy sauce
¼ teaspoon browning and seasoning sauce

Microwave hot water, orange concentrate, and salt in 2-quart glass casserole, covered, at High until boiling; stir in rice. Microwave covered at High 5 minutes; stir after 3 minutes. Microwave covered at 50% (Medium) 20 minutes, or until rice is tender and water is absorbed.

Process (Steel Knife) cucumber, onion, pecans, raisins, and apricots using on/off technique until chopped. Stir cucumber mixture into rice; stir in 2 tablespoons marmalade. Stuff cavities of hens with rice mixture. Place hens breast sides down on microwave roasting rack in 12″ × 8″ glass baking dish. Mix ¼ cup marmalade and remaining ingredients; brush hens with half the mixture. Microwave uncovered at High 10 minutes. Turn hens breast sides up; brush with remaining glaze. Microwave uncovered 10 to 15 minutes, or until juices run clear when hens are pierced with fork at inside thigh. Remove hens from oven; cover loosely with aluminum foil. Let stand 6 to 8 minutes before serving.

Tip: To thaw the four frozen Cornish hens, microwave in wrapping at 30% (Medium Low) 20 minutes; then place hens, without unwrapping, in bowl of cold water for 30 minutes. Check manufacturer's manual for special defrosting features of your oven.

ROAST DUCKLING WITH SWEET AND SOUR CABBAGE

Duck skin will not crisp in the microwave oven, but the trade-off is uniformly moist meat. This recipe shows off the succulent dimension of duck with an eastern European-style accompaniment of sausage, cabbage, apples, and caraway.

Total Preparation Time: 64 to 75 minutes
Microwave Time: 54 to 65 minutes
Yield: 4 servings

½ **pound bulk sausage**
1 **pound cabbage (about ½ medium head), cut into wedges to fit feed tube**
2 **medium apples, unpared, cored, cut into 1-inch pieces**
½ **small onion, peeled, cut into 1-inch pieces**
¼ **cup water**
¼ **cup cider vinegar**
2 **tablespoons apricot preserves**
2 **teaspoons caraway seeds**
1 **duckling (4 to 5 pounds)**
¼ **cup orange juice**
1 **tablespoon apricot preserves**
1 **tablespoon browning and seasoning sauce**
1 **small apple, cored, cut into halves (optional)**
Watercress or parsley sprigs

Crumble sausage into 3-quart glass casserole; microwave covered with waxed paper at High until meat loses pink color, about 3 minutes. Drain well. Slice (Slicing Disc) cabbage; add to casserole. Process (Steel Knife) 2 apples and the onion using on/off technique until coarsely chopped; stir into cabbage mixture. Stir water, vinegar, 2 tablespoons preserves, and the caraway seeds into cabbage mixture. Microwave covered at High 8 minutes. Stir

cabbage mixture; let stand covered while duckling is cooking.

Split duckling lengthwise through breastbone. Turn duckling skin side up and press down to crack bones so that duckling will lie flat. Pierce duckling skin liberally with fork. Place duckling on microwave rack in 12″ × 8″ glass baking dish. Mix orange juice, 1 tablespoon preserves, and the browning sauce; reserve.

Microwave duckling uncovered at 70% (Medium High) about 9 minutes per pound; when duckling is done, meat near bone will not be pink and juices will run clear when duckling is pierced with fork at inside thigh. During cooking time, rotate baking dish ¼ turn every 10 minutes, basting duckling with reserved orange juice mixture and shielding wing tips and legs with small pieces of aluminum foil if necessary to prevent overcooking. Remove duckling from oven; cover loosely with aluminum foil and let stand 10 minutes.

Microwave cabbage mixture covered at High until cabbage is tender, 8 to 10 minutes. Slice (Slicing Disc) the small apple. Spoon cabbage mixture onto serving platter; arrange duckling on cabbage. Garnish with sliced apple and watercress. Cut duckling into quarters to serve.

Tip: To crisp skin, transfer duck to broiler pan after microwaving and broil until crisp, about 10 minutes.

TURKEY BREAST WITH HONEY–MUSTARD SAUCE

Make economical, low-cholesterol turkey breast a menu staple by cutting back the cooking time. If you are counting calories, resist adding the sauce and just enjoy the moist, piquant-glazed meat.

Total Preparation Time: 63 to 67 minutes
Microwave Time: 43 to 45 minutes
Yield: 8 to 10 servings

---

4 sprigs watercress or parsley
1 small clove garlic, peeled
½ cup Dijon-style mustard
2 tablespoons butter or margarine
1 tablespoon honey
½ teaspoon dried rosemary leaves
¼ teaspoon dried thyme leaves
1 turkey breast (about 3 pounds)
Paprika
3 tablespoons flour
Milk
Watercress or parsley sprigs

Process (Steel Knife) 4 sprigs watercress until minced. With machine running (Steel Knife), drop garlic through feed tube; process using on/off technique until minced. Add mustard, butter, honey, rosemary, and thyme to bowl; process until smooth.

Place turkey breast upside down on microwave meat rack in 12″ × 8″ glass baking dish; brush with half the mustard mixture. Microwave uncovered at High 5 minutes. Microwave at 50% (Medium) 15 minutes, rotating dish ¼ turn after 7 minutes. Turn breast right side up on rack; brush with mustard sauce. Microwave at 50% (Medium) until meat thermometer inserted in thickest part of meat registers 170° F, 18 to 22 minutes, rotating baking dish ¼ turn and basting with sauce after 10 minutes. Sprinkle turkey with paprika. Let stand loosely covered with aluminum foil 10 minutes.

Pour pan drippings into 2-cup glass measure; stir in remaining mustard mixture and the flour. Stir in enough milk to measure 1¼ cups. Microwave uncovered at High until boiling and thickened, 5 to 7 minutes, stirring with whisk every 2 minutes. Arrange turkey on serving platter; garnish with watercress. Slice and serve with sauce.

Tips: If turkey breast is frozen, thaw according to directions in manufacturer's manual. Or remove from wrapping, place in 12″ × 8″ glass baking dish and microwave covered with waxed paper at High 3 minutes; then microwave at 70% (Medium High) 6 minutes and let stand until thawed, 20 to 30 minutes.

Leftover turkey breast can be used in Turkey Tetrazzini (following recipe) or cut up and turned into a delicious salad with sliced celery and Food Processor Walnut Mayonnaise (see Index). The turkey can also be substituted for the chicken in Chicken and Shrimp in Fillo Shells or Double-Dressed Chicken Salad (see Index).

An inverted plate can be substituted for the microwave meat rack. Do not use a conventional meat thermometer in the microwave oven; use a microwave meat thermometer or remove turkey from the oven to check temperature with an instant-register or a conventional meat thermometer.

TURKEY TETRAZZINI

A favorite use for leftover turkey. This version differs from the classic in that the spaghetti is cooked separately. The revision offers several benefits: the spaghetti stays firm, the dish comes together faster, and the turkey mixture can be prepared ahead of time.

Total Preparation Time: 32 to 36 minutes
Microwave Time: 11 to 14 minutes
Yield: 4 to 6 servings

---

2 ounces brick cheese, chilled, cut to fit feed tube
1 medium green pepper, seeded, cut to fit feed tube
4 ounces mushrooms
1 medium onion, peeled, cut into 1-inch pieces
1 rib celery, cut into 1-inch pieces
2 ounces pimiento
1 tablespoon butter or margarine
12 ounces cooked turkey, cut into 1-inch pieces
6 tablespoons Twice-As-Fast Sauce Mix
2 cups half-and-half
1 tablespoon dry sherry

½ teaspoon dry mustard
⅛ teaspoon white pepper
4 to 6 cups hot cooked spaghetti or noodles

Shred (Shredding Disc) cheese; reserve. Slice (Slicing Disc) green pepper and mushrooms separately. Process (Steel Knife) onion and celery using on/off technique until chopped. Add pimiento to bowl; process using on/off technique until chopped.

Microwave vegetables and butter in 2-quart glass casserole, covered, at High until vegetables are tender, 4 to 5 minutes. Process (Steel Knife) turkey using on/off technique until coarsely chopped; stir into vegetable mixture. Let stand covered while preparing sauce.

Microwave sauce mix in 4-cup glass measure, uncovered, at High 2 to 3 minutes, stirring after 1 minute. Stir in half-and-half, sherry, mustard, and white pepper with whisk. Microwave uncovered at High until mixture boils and thickens, 5 to 6 minutes, whisking every minute. Stir in turkey-vegetable mixture and reserved cheese. Serve over spaghetti or noodles.

Tip: Turkey Tetrazzini, without spaghetti, can be refrigerated covered 2 days; it can be frozen, in a sealed container, up to 1 month.

8 Meat

VEGETABLE-STUFFED STEAK

Slice this rolled flank steak to reveal a pinwheel pattern of beef and colorful vegetables.

Total Preparation Time: 43 to 46 minutes (plus
30 minutes
marinating time)
Microwave Time: 33 to 39 minutes
Yield: 4 to 6 servings

---

1 beef flank steak (1½ to 2 pounds)
½ cup water
½ teaspoon beef-flavor instant bouillon
2 tablespoons teriyaki sauce
1 teaspoon sugar
1 clove garlic, peeled
2 green onions and tops, cut into 1-inch
   pieces
4 ounces broccoli, cut into 1-inch pieces
3 carrots, cut to fit feed tube
4 ounces brick cheese, chilled, cut to fit feed
   tube
½ teaspoon dried dillweed
1 tablespoon cornstarch
2 tablespoons cold water

Pound steak with meat mallet until even in thickness; place in 12″ × 8″ glass baking dish. Mix ½ cup water, the bouillon, teriyaki sauce, and sugar; pour over meat. Let stand covered 30 minutes.

With machine running (Steel Knife), drop garlic through feed tube; process using on/off technique until minced. Add onions and broccoli to bowl; process using on/off technique until minced. Shred (Shredding Disc) carrots and cheese. Combine onion mixture, carrots, cheese, and dillweed.

Remove steak from baking dish, reserving marinade in baking dish. Spoon vegetable mixture on steak. Roll up, beginning with short end; secure with string or wooden picks. Place meat roll in baking dish with marinade; microwave covered at 50% (Medium) 30 to 35 minutes, rotating dish ¼ turn every 5 minutes, and turning steak roll over halfway through cooking time. Transfer meat to serving platter;

let stand loosely covered with aluminum foil 10 minutes.

Strain juices in baking dish into 2-cup glass measure. Mix cornstarch and 2 tablespoons cold water; stir into juices. Microwave uncovered at High until boiling and thickened, 3 to 4 minutes, stirring after 1½ minutes. Serve with sliced flank steak.

Tip: If you wish to save time at the dinner hour, prepare the steak and refrigerate it in the marinade hours ahead of time or overnight. The stuffing can be prepared up to 1 day ahead of time and refrigerated, separately, covered.

SIRLOIN STEAK WITH MUSHROOMS

Steak, mushrooms, and a rich sauce—a popular combination that cleverly masks meat economy.

Total Preparation Time: 32 to 33 minutes
Microwave Time: 17 to 18 minutes
Yield: 4 servings

---

1 ounce Parmesan cheese, cut into 1-inch
   pieces
1½ pounds lean, boneless sirloin steak, cut
   into 4 serving pieces
Salt
Pepper
8 ounces mushrooms
½ cup pitted ripe olives
1 clove garlic, peeled
½ medium onion, peeled, cut into 1-inch
   pieces
3 tablespoons butter or margarine
3 tablespoons flour
½ cup whipping cream
2 tablespoons dry white wine
½ teaspoon Worcestershire sauce
½ teaspoon Dijon-style mustard
2 tablespoons vegetable oil

With machine running (Steel Knife), drop cheese through feed tube, processing until finely grated; reserve.

Pound steak with mallet to scant ½-inch thickness; sprinkle lightly with salt and pepper. Slice (Slicing Disc) mushrooms and olives separately; remove. With machine running (Steel Knife), drop garlic through feed tube, processing until minced. Add onion to bowl; process using on/off technique until chopped. Microwave onion mixture and butter in 4-cup glass measure, uncovered, at High 2 minutes. Stir in flour; microwave at High 1 minute. Stir in cream, wine, Worcestershire sauce, mustard, and olives; microwave uncovered at High until thick, 4 to 5 minutes, stirring with whisk every 2 minutes.

Microwave oil in 12″ × 8″ glass baking dish, uncovered, at High 2 minutes. Add steak; microwave uncovered at High 3 minutes. Turn steak pieces over and top with mushrooms; microwave uncovered at High 2 minutes. Spoon sauce over mushrooms; sprinkle with reserved cheese. Microwave uncovered at 50% (Medium) until steak is desired degree of doneness, about 3 minutes for medium.

CHINESE PEPPER BEEF

The precision provided by the food processor and microwave oven is the key to the ease of this Oriental "stir-fry." No laborious slicing and chopping, no need to stand over a wok! Yet the taste is authentically fresh, and the dish would go well with Steamed Dumplings or a bowl of Won Ton Soup (see Index).

Total Preparation Time: 26 to 29 minutes (plus 30 minutes marinating time and freezing time)
Microwave Time: 15 to 18 minutes
Yield: 6 servings

1 pound beef flank steak, cut to fit feed tube
1 sprig fresh coriander or ½ teaspoon dried coriander leaves
1 slice gingerroot (the size of a dime)
1 clove garlic, peeled
½ cup dry sherry
¼ cup soy sauce
2 teaspoons light brown sugar
2 green onions and tops, cut into 1-inch pieces
2 medium green peppers, seeded, cut to fit feed tube
8 ounces mushrooms
2 tablespoons peanut or vegetable oil
8 ounces snow peas
8 ounces fresh or canned bean sprouts, rinsed, drained
1½ tablespoons cornstarch
1 cup beef broth
6 cups hot cooked rice

Freeze meat until slightly frozen (meat will feel frozen but you can pierce meat with tip of sharp knife); slice (Slicing Disc) and place in 12″ × 8″ glass baking dish. Process (Steel Knife) coriander using on/off technique until minced. With machine running, drop gingerroot and garlic through feed tube, processing until minced. Add sherry, soy sauce, and sugar to bowl; process using on/off technique until blended. Pour mixture over meat; let stand 30 minutes. Drain, reserving marinade.

Process (Steel Knife) onions using on/off technique until chopped; remove. Slice (Slicing Disc) peppers and mushrooms. Microwave oil in 2-quart glass baking dish, uncovered, at High until hot, about 2 minutes. Stir in meat, onions, peppers, mushrooms, snow peas, and bean sprouts. Microwave uncovered at High until vegetables are crisp-tender, 10 to 12 minutes, stirring every 4 minutes. Combine reserved marinade, the cornstarch, and beef broth; stir into meat mixture. Microwave uncovered at High until sauce has thickened, 3 to 4 minutes, stirring after 2 minutes. Serve with rice.

Tips: Beef can be prepared and refrigerated in the marinade hours in advance.

(Tips continued next page)

If you are using canned bean sprouts, crisp them in ice water. If time allows, leave them in the water refrigerated for several hours.

Steam rice conventionally according to package directions while preparing Chinese Pepper Beef for greatest time advantage. To improve fluffiness of rice without rinsing it, which removes nutrients, remove pot from burner 5 minutes before end of recommended cooking time and place several layers of paper toweling between the pot and the lid. Let stand 10 minutes or until ready to serve.

BOURBON POT ROAST

Something wonderful happens to this pot roast in its relatively brief cooking time—the vegetables pick up the distinctive flavor of the bourbon-sauced meat and the juices thicken into a natural gravy.

Total Preparation Time: 86 to 92 minutes
Microwave Time: 76 to 81 minutes
Yield: 6 servings

---

2 cloves garlic, peeled
⅓ cup bourbon
1 boneless beef pot roast (about 3½ pounds)
½ cup water
¼ cup all-purpose flour
½ cup tomato juice
1 teaspoon dry mustard
½ teaspoon beef-flavor instant bouillon
½ teaspoon salt
.½ teaspoon pepper
3 medium potatoes, unpared, cut to fit feed tube
2 carrots, pared, cut to fit feed tube
2 medium onions, peeled, cut to fit feed tube

With machine running (Steel Knife), drop garlic through feed tube; process until minced. Add 1 tablespoon of the bourbon to bowl; process 2 seconds. Rub garlic mixture into pot

roast. Microwave remaining bourbon in 1-cup glass measure, uncovered, at High until hot, 20 to 30 seconds. Ignite and pour over pot roast. Mix water and flour in small bowl; stir in tomato juice, dry mustard, bouillon, salt, and pepper; pour over roast in 12″ × 8″ glass baking dish. Microwave covered with plastic wrap at High 15 minutes; turn roast over. Microwave covered at 50% (Medium) until roast is tender, about 1 hour.

Slice (Slicing Disc) potatoes, carrots, and onions separately; add vegetables to roast during the last 30 minutes of cooking time.

Tips: Use any cut of pot roast, such as boneless chuck, Boston cut, top round, or bottom round. If using a roast thicker than 2 inches, turn it over when you add the vegetables.

Igniting the bourbon burns off the alcohol, eliminating its harsh taste.

CURRY BEEF STEW WITH CHIVE DUMPLINGS

Chopped beef literally "beefs up" the consistency of this curry-seasoned stew, and light dumplings complete the temptation.

Total Preparation Time: 82 to 94 minutes
Microwave Time: 72 to 84 minutes
Yield: 8 servings

---

2 medium onions, peeled, cut into 1-inch pieces
2½ pounds lean beef cubes for stew (1-inch cubes)
3 tablespoons flour
2 cups beef broth
1½ teaspoons curry powder
1 teaspoon salt
¼ teaspoon pepper
½ package (10-ounce size) frozen peas
¼ cup all-purpose flour
⅓ cup cold water
Chive Dumplings (recipe follows)

Process (Steel Knife) onions using on/off technique until chopped; remove. Process (Steel Knife) ¾ pound of the beef using on/off technique until finely chopped. Microwave chopped beef in 4-quart glass casserole, covered, at High until meat loses pink color, 3 to 5 minutes, stirring after 2 minutes; drain. Toss remaining beef cubes with 3 tablespoons flour. Stir beef cubes, onions, broth, curry powder, salt, and pepper into chopped beef. Microwave covered at High 10 minutes; stir. Microwave uncovered at 50% (Medium) until meat is tender, 50 to 60 minutes, stirring every 20 minutes and adding peas during last 10 minutes of cooking time.

Mix ¼ cup flour and the water; stir into stew. Microwave covered at High until boiling, about 4 minutes; boil until thickened, about 1 minute.

Make dumpling mixture. Drop dumpling mixture by spoonfuls onto hot stew. Microwave covered at High until dumplings are cooked, 5 to 7 minutes.

Chive Dumplings

2 cups Baking Mix (see Index)
1 cup milk
1 tablespoon dried chives
¼ teaspoon curry powder

Process (Steel Knife) all ingredients until smooth.

Tips: Unless you have a large-model food processor, chop no more than ½ pound of beef at a time. A larger quantity will result in uneven texture.

Curry Beef Stew, without peas and dumplings, can be frozen, in a covered container, up to 3 months. Add peas when reheating; add dumplings to hot stew.

Substitute different seasonings for the chives to vary the dumplings, if you wish. Dried dillweed or toasted sesame seeds would be good choices. To toast sesame seeds, spread them in a glass baking dish and microwave uncovered at High 2 minutes.

CRUMB-CRUSTED ROAST BEEF

Microwaves protect the juiciness of a naturally tender cut. The roast cooks evenly, without drying out, and the herbed crumbs seal in the juices as they season the meat. Because there is no dry heat in the microwave oven, however, the crumb crust will not get crisp.

Total Preparation Time: 56 to 60 minutes
Microwave Time: 36 to 39 minutes
Yield: 6 to 8 servings

1 **beef tenderloin or eye of round roast**
   (about 4 pounds)
Garlic-Herb Bread Crumbs (See Index)
⅓ **cup butter or margarine**

Place tenderloin on microwave roasting rack in 12″ × 8″ glass baking dish; fold tip end of meat under so that meat is as uniform in thickness as possible. Make Garlic-Herb Bread Crumbs, using whole wheat or French bread. Microwave butter in 1-cup glass measure at High until melted; add to crumb mixture in food processor bowl. Process (Steel Knife) using on/off technique until butter is mixed into crumb mixture; pat mixture on top and sides of tenderloin. Microwave uncovered at High 5 minutes; rotate baking dish ¼ turn. Microwave uncovered at 50% (Medium) until meat thermometer registers 135° F (for medium doneness), about 30 minutes, rotating baking dish ¼ turn every 10 minutes. Let stand loosely covered with aluminum foil until meat thermometer registers 150° F, about 10 minutes. Place on serving platter and carve.

Tips: You can prop up the meat on an overturned heatproof plate if you don't have a microwave roasting rack; remove the plate as soon as you remove the meat from the oven.

Do not use a conventional meat thermometer in the microwave oven. If you don't have a microwave meat thermometer, remove the roast from the oven and check doneness with either an instant-register or a regular meat thermometer.

MUSTARD ROAST BEEF

An easy trick with a sirloin tip roast: rub the meat with a spicy beef suet mixture to guarantee juiciness and flavor appeal in every slice. The suet melts away during cooking, while the seasonings are absorbed by the meat. The leftovers make great sandwiches!

Total Preparation Time: 48 to 53 minutes
Microwave Time: 30 to 35 minutes
Yield: 6 servings

4 ounces beef suet, room temperature, cut into 1-inch pieces
1 tablespoon spicy brown mustard
1 tablespoon light brown sugar
1 teaspoon caraway seeds, crushed
½ teaspoon prepared horseradish
¼ teaspoon ground allspice
1 boneless beef sirloin tip roast (about 3 pounds), all fat trimmed

Process (Steel Knife) suet, mustard, sugar, caraway seeds, horseradish, and allspice until smooth; spread on all surfaces of meat. Place meat on microwave meat rack in 12" × 8" glass baking dish. Microwave uncovered at 70% (Medium High) 15 minutes. Turn meat over; microwave uncovered at 50% (Medium) until meat thermometer registers 135° F (for medium doneness), 15 to 20 minutes. Let stand loosely covered with aluminum foil 10 minutes. Place on serving platter; slice to serve.

Tips: Mustard Roast Beef can be refrigerated, wrapped in aluminum foil, and served cold or at room temperature.
See previous recipe, Crumb-Crusted Roast Beef, for microwave tips.

BASIC MEAT LOAF WITH VARIATIONS

Processor chopping ensures desired leanness for meat loaf and microwave cooking prevents dryness—a fundamental formula that gets even better when you add savory seasonings and a sauce or glaze. Choose from this spectrum of variations—Lemon Meat Loaf with Egg Lemon Sauce, Italian Meat Loaf, and Sweet-Sour Ham Loaf. Or select a sauce, such as Mushroom or Fresh Tomato (see Index), to mate with Basic Meat Loaf. Make an extra meat loaf to slice cold for sandwiches—it's delicious and much less expensive than purchased lunch meat.

Total Preparation Time: 25 to 30 minutes
Microwave Time: 9 to 11 minutes
Yield: 4 to 6 servings

1 sprig parsley
2 slices firm white bread, torn into pieces
½ medium onion, peeled, cut into 1-inch pieces
1 green pepper, seeded, cut into 1-inch pieces
1 egg
½ teaspoon Dijon-style mustard
½ teaspoon salt
¼ teaspoon pepper
1 pound boneless beef round steak, cut into 1-inch pieces
2 tablespoons water
½ teaspoon beef-flavor instant bouillon

Process (Steel Knife) parsley using on/off technique until minced. Add bread to bowl; process using on/off technique until fine crumbs are formed. Add onion and green pepper to bowl; process using on/off technique until chopped. Add egg, mustard, salt, and pepper to bowl; process until blended; remove bread crumb mixture.

Process (Steel Knife) beef using on/off technique until finely chopped. Microwave water and bouillon in 1-cup glass measure at High until boiling; stir to dissolve bouillon. Add bouillon mixture to bowl; process using on/off technique until blended.

Combine meat and bread crumb mixture; pat into 6-cup plastic or glass ring mold. Microwave uncovered at High until meat loses pink color, 8 to 10 minutes, rotating mold ¼ turn after five minutes. Let stand loosely covered with aluminum foil 5 minutes. Invert onto serving platter.

Tips: Unless you have a large-model food processor, chop no more than ½ pound beef at a time.

Although you can process beef without any fat, meat loaf, burgers, and meatballs will be juicier, yet not greasy, if you leave some fat on the meat; 10% fat is the preferred ratio of fat to lean.

Lean, boneless pork and veal can be substituted for part of the beef; one-third each of beef, pork, and veal is the traditional meat loaf mix.

A 2-quart glass casserole, with a glass placed open end up in the center, can be substituted for the ring mold.

Meat loaves can be frozen, raw or cooked, tightly wrapped, up to 1 month. To thaw, microwave according to manufacturer's manual. Toppings for Italian Meat Loaf and Sweet-Sour Ham Loaf can be added prior to freezing or after thawing.

VARIATIONS

LEMON MEAT LOAF: Make Basic Meat Loaf as above, processing 1 tablespoon lemon juice, 1 tablespoon grated lemon rind, and ¼ teaspoon dried savory leaves with the egg and mustard. Complete as in Basic Meat Loaf Recipe above.

Make Egg Lemon Sauce (recipe follows); serve with meat loaf.

Egg Lemon Sauce

Yield: about 1¼ cups

2 tablespoons butter or margarine
2 tablespoons flour
½ cup chicken broth
½ cup milk
1 egg yolk
¼ cup whipping cream
3 to 4 tablespoons lemon juice

1 teaspoon grated lemon rind
⅛ teaspoon salt
1/16 teaspoon pepper

Microwave butter in 4-cup glass measure at High until melted; stir in flour. Microwave uncovered at High 30 seconds. Stir in broth and milk; microwave uncovered at High until sauce boils and thickens, about 4 minutes, stirring with whisk every 2 minutes.

Mix egg yolk and cream in small bowl; stir part of sauce mixture into egg mixture. Stir egg mixture into sauce mixture. Microwave uncovered at High until mixture boils and thickens, 1½ to 2 minutes, stirring with whisk after 1 minute. Stir in remaining ingredients.

ITALIAN MEAT LOAF: With machine running (Steel Knife), drop ½ ounce Parmesan cheese through feed tube; process until finely grated. Shred (Shredding Disc) 3 ounces chilled mozzarella cheese, cut to fit feed tube.

Make Basic Meat Loaf, processing (Steel Knife) 1 peeled garlic clove with the parsley, and 4 pitted ripe olives with the onion and green pepper. Stir three-fourths of the cheeses and ¼ cup tomato sauce into meat loaf mixture; stir in ¼ teaspoon dried basil leaves and ¼ teaspoon dried oregano leaves. Complete as in Basic Meat Loaf recipe above.

Invert cooked meat loaf onto serving platter; top with 2 tablespoons tomato sauce and remaining cheeses; let stand loosely covered with aluminum foil 5 minutes.

SWEET-SOUR HAM LOAF: Make Basic Meat Loaf, processing 2 sweet pickles (cut into 1-inch pieces), ½ cup blanched almonds, and ½ cup mixed dried fruit with the onion and green pepper. Substitute 4 ounces of cooked ham (cut into 1-inch pieces) for 4 ounces of the beef.

Combine ⅓ cup apricot preserves, 1 tablespoon cider vinegar, 2 tablespoons catsup, and 2 teaspoons soy sauce; stir all but 1 tablespoon of this mixture into the bouillon mixture. Complete meat loaf as in Basic Meat Loaf recipe above.

Invert cooked meat loaf onto serving platter; top with 1 tablespoon of preserve mixture; let stand loosely covered with aluminum foil 5 minutes.

TRIPLE THREAT CHILI

Hot pepper power three ways! Add a fourth, if you wish, with hot Italian sausage. The texture of processor-chopped beef shows up especially well in chili. Be careful not to overprocess the meat—it should be slightly chunky.

Total Preparation Time: 45 to 48 minutes
Microwave Time: 23 to 24 minutes
Yield: 6 servings (about 1⅓ cups each)

---

8 ounces hot or mild Italian sausage, cut into ½-inch pieces
1 cup water
1 clove garlic, peeled
1 medium onion, peeled, cut into 1-inch pieces
1 medium green pepper, seeded, cut into 1-inch pieces
1 tablespoon vegetable oil
12 ounces boneless beef round steak, excess fat trimmed, cut into 1-inch pieces
2 cans (16 ounces each) tomatoes, undrained
2 cans (15 ounces each) pinto beans, drained
3 tablespoons tomato paste
2 tablespoons Worcestershire sauce
1 tablespoon sugar
1 to 2 teaspoons crushed dried red pepper
½ to 1 teaspoon chili powder
1 or 2 dashes red pepper sauce

Microwave sausage in water in 1-quart glass casserole, uncovered, at High until sausage loses pink color, about 5 minutes; drain well. With machine running (Steel Knife), drop garlic through feed tube, processing until minced. Add onion and green pepper to bowl; process using on/off technique until coarsely chopped. Microwave onion mixture and oil in a 3-quart glass casserole, uncovered, at High 4 minutes.

Process (Steel Knife) round steak using on/off technique until coarsely chopped; stir into onion mixture. Microwave uncovered at High until beef loses pink color, about 4 minutes,

stirring after 2 minutes. Process (Steel Knife) tomatoes using on/off technique until coarsely chopped. Stir tomatoes, sausage, and remaining ingredients into casserole; microwave uncovered at High until boiling, about 10 minutes, stirring after 5 minutes.

Tips: Unless you have a large-model food processor, chop no more than ½ pound beef at a time.

Triple Threat Chili can be frozen up to 1 month. Freeze individual portions for quick lunches, suppers, or snacks, or freeze in a single container for a do-ahead party dish.

ENCHILADA CASSEROLE

A creamy tortilla casserole with fresh Mexican flavor. You might want to make two batches and freeze them for a party, since the rich taste and serving convenience will please both guests and host.

Total Preparation Time: 55 to 57 minutes
Microwave Time: 17 to 19 minutes
Yield: 4 servings

Hot Salsa (optional; see Index)
4 large sprigs fresh coriander
1 clove garlic, peeled
1 medium onion, peeled, cut into 1-inch pieces
2 jalapeño peppers, seeded, cut into quarters
2 tablespoons vegetable oil
1 can (10 ounces) green chili enchilada sauce
1 cup sour cream
1 pound lean, boneless beef round steak, cut into 1-inch pieces
¼ teaspoon ground cumin
½ teaspoon salt
8 corn tortillas
8 ounces Mexican white cheese (queso blanco) or feta cheese, crumbled

Make Hot Salsa.

Process (Steel Knife) coriander using on/off technique until minced. With machine running, drop garlic through feed tube, processing until minced. Add onion and peppers to bowl; process using on/off technique until chopped. Microwave vegetable mixture and oil in 1-quart glass casserole, covered, at High 4 minutes, stirring after 2 minutes. Add enchilada sauce and sour cream; microwave covered at High 2 minutes, stirring after 1 minute.

Process (Steel Knife) beef until chopped. Microwave beef and cumin in 1½-quart glass casserole, uncovered, at High until meat loses pink color, about 6 minutes; stir in salt.

Dip tortilla into sauce mixture; spoon 2 heaping tablespoons meat mixture and 2 tablespoons crumbled cheese in center of tortilla and roll up. Place seam side down in 12″ × 8″ glass baking dish; repeat with remaining tortillas, sauce mixture, meat mixture, and cheese. Spoon remaining sauce over tortillas; sprinkle with cheese. Microwave uncovered at High 5 minutes, rotating dish ¼ turn after 2½ minutes. Let stand loosely covered with aluminum foil on counter top 10 minutes. Serve with Hot Salsa.

Tips: Be careful not to touch eyes when handling jalapeño peppers, as the juice can cause irritation.

Shredded Muenster or Monterey Jack cheese can be substituted for the queso blanco; shred (Shredding Disc) cheese after vegetables have been chopped. If you are using feta cheese and it is salty, rinse it well in cold water and squeeze dry in several layers of cheesecloth or a dish towel.

Top Enchilada Casserole with chopped tomato and avocado instead of Hot Salsa, if you wish. Use 1 medium tomato, cored and cut into 1-inch pieces, and 1 medium avocado, peeled, pitted, and cut into 1-inch pieces. Process (Steel Knife) tomato and avocado separately, using on/off technique, until chopped.

Casserole can be frozen up to 1 month, either uncooked or cooked. Top with Hot Salsa or chopped vegetables after

reheating. To freeze uncooked casserole, line baking dish with heavy-duty aluminum foil before assembling ingredients. Wrap foil around food and freeze in dish until firm; then remove dish and wrap food in an additional sheet of foil. Remove foil and replace food in casserole before reheating.

BRAISED LIVER AND ONIONS

Exceedingly tender baby beef liver with a fresh, crisp accent of sliced leek and the traditional topping of crumbled bacon.

Total Preparation Time: 28 to 32 minutes
Microwave Time: 16 to 19 minutes
Yield: 4 servings

1 **medium leek, cleaned, or 6 green onions and tops, cut to fit feed tube**
1 **rib celery, cut to fit feed tube**
2 **tablespoons dry white wine**
4 **slices bacon**
1 **pound baby beef liver**
¼ **cup all-purpose flour**
¼ **teaspoon dried chervil leaves**
⅛ **to ¼ teaspoon cayenne pepper**
1 **small tomato, cut into 1-inch pieces**

Slice (Slicing Disc) leek and celery; microwave leek, celery, and wine in 1-quart glass casserole, covered, at High until vegetables are tender, 4 to 5 minutes. Microwave bacon in glass baking dish, uncovered, at High until crisp, 5 to 6 minutes. Drain bacon and crumble; reserve drippings.

Cut liver, if necessary, so that pieces are similar in size. Coat liver with combined flour, chervil, and cayenne pepper. Microwave liver in bacon drippings in 12″ × 8″ glass baking dish, covered with waxed paper, at High 3 minutes, turning liver after 1½ minutes. Process (Steel Knife) tomato using on/off technique until chopped. Sprinkle leek mixture and tomato over liver. Microwave, covered with waxed paper, at High 4 to 5 minutes, or until liver loses pink color; let stand 5 minutes. Arrange on serving plate; sprinkle with bacon.

THREE–MEAT GOULASH

The mingled juices of three kinds of meat yield unsurpassed flavor. Remember this recipe when you have a crowd to feed—it comes together quickly and makes a large quantity.

Total Preparation Time: 88 to 93 minutes
Microwave Time: 83 to 85 minutes
Yield: 8 servings

---

8 ounces mushrooms
3 medium onions, peeled, cut to fit feed tube
4 green onions and tops, cut to fit feed tube
2 tablespoons butter or margarine
4 medium tomatoes, seeded, cut into 1-inch pieces
1 pound beef cubes for stew
1 pound pork cubes for stew
1 pound veal cubes for stew
½ can (6-ounce size) tomato paste
½ teaspoon caraway seeds
¼ teaspoon dried dillweed
1 cup water
1 tablespoon beef-flavor instant bouillon
1 tablespoon paprika
2 teaspoons salt
½ teaspoon pepper
1 cup sour cream
¼ cup all-purpose flour
4 to 6 cups hot cooked noodles (optional)

Slice (Slicing Disc) mushrooms, onions, and green onions. Microwave vegetable mixture and butter in 4-quart glass casserole, covered, at High until vegetables are tender, 8 to 10 minutes, stirring every 4 minutes. Process (Steel Knife) tomatoes using on/off technique until coarsely chopped; stir into mushroom mixture. Stir in meats, tomato paste, caraway seeds, dillweed, water, bouillon, paprika, salt, and pepper. Microwave covered with plastic wrap at High 10 minutes; microwave covered with plastic wrap at 50% (Medium) until meat is tender, about 1 hour, stirring after 30 minutes. Mix sour cream and flour; stir into stew. Microwave covered at 50% (Medium) until thickened, about 5 minutes, stirring after 3 minutes. Serve over noodles.

Tips: Cook noodles conventionally, while the goulash is cooking, for maximum time advantage. Serve the goulash with thick slices of rye, pumpernickel, or Three-Grain Bread (see Index), instead of noodles, if you wish.

One-half cup dry white or red wine or beer can be substituted for ½ cup of the water specified in the recipe.

Three-Meat Goulash can be prepared up to the addition of sour cream and flour and frozen up to 2 months. You may wish to remove and freeze half the goulash before adding the sour cream and proceed as above, using half the sour cream and flour to complete the remaining portion.

To store leftover tomato paste, pour a thin layer of vegetable oil over the paste in the can and refrigerate; pour off the oil when you're ready to use the paste. Leftover paste can also be frozen. Place teaspoons of paste on a sheet of waxed paper, freeze until firm, and transfer to a plastic bag; remove portions as needed.

VEAL ROLLS WITH PROSCIUTTO

An elegant entrée that highlights veal economically. There's a great advantage, when you're entertaining, in not having to watch and turn the veal continuously, as you would if you sautéed the rolls conventionally.

Total Preparation Time: 30 to 35 minutes
Microwave Time: 12 to 15 minutes
Yield: 4 servings

---

6 sprigs parsley
1 ounce Parmesan cheese, cut into 1-inch pieces
1 clove garlic, peeled
½ medium onion, peeled, cut into 1-inch pieces
4 ounces mozzarella cheese, chilled, cut into 1-inch pieces

4 ounces prosciutto, cut into 1-inch pieces
¼ teaspoon dried savory leaves
8 veal scallops, pounded paper-thin (about 1 pound)
½ cup dry white wine
1 tablespoon cornstarch
¼ cup cold water

Process (Steel Knife) parsley using on/off technique until minced. With machine running, drop Parmesan cheese and garlic through feed tube; process until finely grated. Add onion, mozzarella, prosciutto, and savory to bowl; process using on/off technique until mixture is chopped and thoroughly mixed.

Divide cheese mixture on veal scallops; roll up and secure with wooden picks. Microwave veal rolls and wine in 12″ × 8″ glass baking dish covered with plastic wrap at High until veal is cooked and juices run clear when veal is pierced with a fork, 10 to 12 minutes, rotating dish ¼ turn every 4 minutes. Arrange veal rolls on serving platter; cover loosely with aluminum foil. Pour pan juices into 2-cup measure. Mix cornstarch and cold water; stir into pan juices. Microwave sauce uncovered at High until thickened, 2 to 3 minutes, stirring with whisk every minute. Spoon sauce over veal rolls.

Tips: Use good-quality veal scallops, preferably cut from the loin, for meat that can be pounded to most attractive thinness. Other cuts of boneless veal will cook to tenderness in this recipe, but it is much harder to flatten them.

Prosciutto can be found in the deli sections of large supermarkets or in specialty delicatessens. Smoked ham can be substituted.

PORK CHOPS GRUYÈRE

The nutty flavor of Gruyère, blended with a robust mustard, distinguishes these quick, carefree pork chops.

Total Preparation Time: 29 to 35 minutes
Microwave Time: 14 to 20 minutes
Yield: 4 servings

4 to 6 loin pork chops (½ inch thick each)
Browning and seasoning sauce
Salt
Pepper
4 sprigs parsley
4 ounces Gruyère or Swiss cheese, chilled, cut to fit feed tube
2 tablespoons whipping cream or half-and-half
1½ tablespoons Dijon-style mustard

Brush chops lightly on both sides with browning sauce. Arrange chops in 12″ × 8″ glass baking dish, with meatiest portions toward edges of dish. Microwave covered with waxed paper at 70% (Medium High) until chops lose their pink color, 12 to 18 minutes, draining chops and rotating dish ¼ turn halfway through cooking time. Sprinkle chops lightly with salt and pepper. Let stand loosely covered with aluminum foil 10 minutes.

Process (Steel Knife) parsley using on/off technique until minced; remove. Shred (Shredding Disc) cheese; mix cheese, cream, and mustard. Sprinkle cheese mixture over chops. Microwave uncovered at 70% (Medium High) until cheese is melted, about 2 minutes. Sprinkle with parsley.

ROAST LOIN OF PORK WITH APPLES

Microwave sweet potato-stuffed pork in clay to save more than two-thirds of the time it would take to achieve an equally moist roast in a conventional oven. Then serve the roast with spiced apples "baked" with the pork. It's a perfect Sunday dinner for cooks who'd like to take the day off!

Total Preparation Time: 72 to 75 minutes
Microwave Time: 42 to 45 minutes
Yield: 8 servings

1 medium sweet potato, pared, cut to fit feed tube
¼ cup butter or margarine
¼ cup packed light brown sugar
½ cup pecans
⅓ cup dark raisins
2 tablespoons light rum
⅛ teaspoon ground nutmeg
Pinch ground cardamom
4 medium tart apples, pared, cored
1 boned, rolled, tied pork loin roast (about 3 pounds)

Soak clay pot in water 15 minutes. Slice (Slicing Disc) potato; remove. Process (Steel Knife) butter and sugar until smooth; add pecans, raisins, rum, nutmeg, and cardamom. Process (Steel Knife) using on/off technique until coarsely chopped. Stuff apples with 3 to 4 tablespoons of the butter mixture. Add potato to bowl with remaining butter mixture; process (Steel Knife) using on/off technique until finely chopped.

Cut 4 to 6 slices in pork roast, making cuts 2 inches deep and 2 inches apart; spoon potato mixture into cuts. Place roast in clay pot; microwave covered at 50% (Medium) 30 minutes. Microwave covered at High 5 minutes. Add apples to pot; microwave covered at High until apples are crisp-tender and roast registers 160° F on meat thermometer, 7 to 10 minutes. Let stand loosely covered with aluminum foil until roast registers 170° F on meat thermometer, about 15 minutes. Arrange meat on serving platter; cut apples into halves and arrange around roast.

Tip: You can use a clay pot designed for either conventional or microwave cooking. If you are using the pot for the first time, soak it at least 30 minutes. There is no need to rotate a clay pot during cooking. If you do not have a clay pot, you can prepare this recipe in an oven cooking bag set in a 12″ × 8″ glass baking dish; coat the inside of the bag with 1 tablespoon of flour to prevent it from splitting. Close the bag with a nonmetallic twist tie or string and turn it over halfway through the first 30 minutes of cooking. Let roast stand in the bag instead of covered with aluminum foil. The recipe can also be prepared in a 12″ × 8″ glass baking dish tightly covered with plastic wrap.

SWEET MUSTARD GLAZED RIBS

Meaty, country-style ribs in a thick, unusually good, sweet-tangy sauce.

Total Preparation Time: 45 to 52 minutes
Microwave Time: 35 to 42 minutes
Yield: 4 servings

2 pounds country-style pork ribs, cut into serving-size pieces
½ teaspoon salt
¼ teaspoon pepper
¼ cup water
1 large green onion and top, cut into 1-inch pieces
2 large dill pickles, cut into 1-inch pieces
1 clove garlic, peeled
2 to 3 tablespoons sugar
1 tablespoon flour
1 tablespoon dry mustard
1 egg yolk
1 cup whipping cream or half-and-half
1 to 2 teaspoons teriyaki sauce
2 tablespoons cider vinegar

Sprinkle both sides of ribs with salt and pepper. Arrange in 12″ × 8″ glass baking dish with meatiest portions of ribs toward edges of dish; add water. Microwave covered with waxed paper at 70% (Medium High) for 5 minutes; drain ribs and turn over. Microwave covered with waxed paper at 50% (Medium) until ribs are fork tender and juices run clear, 20 to 25 minutes; turn ribs over after 10 minutes. Drain well. Process (Steel Knife) onion and pickles using on/off technique until chopped; sprinkle over ribs. Microwave covered with waxed paper at 70% (Medium High) 10 minutes; drain ribs and rearrange.

With machine running (Steel Knife), process garlic until minced. Add remaining ingredients except vinegar to bowl; process until smooth. Microwave in 4-cup glass measure uncovered at High until thick, 3 to 4 minutes, stirring with whisk every minute. Stir in vinegar. Spoon sauce over ribs; microwave uncovered at High until hot through, 2 to 3 minutes.

Tip: Two pounds of loin pork chops can be substituted for the ribs.

SPINACH-STUFFED HAM

An extremely attractive and generous ham that's equally appropriate for a sit-down dinner or a festive brunch buffet.

Total Preparation Time: 65 to 70 minutes
Microwave Time: 50 to 52 minutes
Yield: 14 to 16 servings

---

2 cloves garlic, peeled
½ medium onion, peeled, cut into 1-inch pieces
6 ounces mushrooms
2 tablespoons butter or margarine
⅔ cup walnut pieces
2 packages (10 ounces each) frozen chopped spinach, thawed, well drained
3 tablespoons Twice-As-Fast Sauce Mix (see Index)
¼ teaspoon ground mace
3 ounces Swiss cheese, chilled, cut to fit feed tube
1 5-pound packaged or canned ham

With machine running (Steel Knife), drop garlic through feed tube, processing until minced. Add onion to bowl; process using on/off technique until finely chopped. Process (Steel Knife) mushrooms until finely chopped. Microwave butter in 1½-quart glass casserole at High until melted. Stir in onion mixture and mushrooms; microwave covered at High until onion is tender, about 3 minutes.

Process (Steel Knife) walnuts until finely chopped; stir into onion mixture with spinach, sauce mix, and mace. Microwave covered at High 3 minutes. Shred (Shredding Disc) cheese. Reserve ¼ cup cheese; stir remaining cheese into spinach mixture.

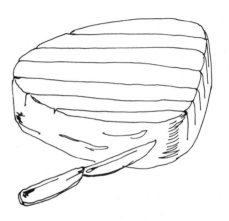

Cut ham lengthwise into slices 1 inch apart, cutting to, but not through, bottom of ham. Spoon spinach mixture into cuts; place ham in 12″ × 8″ glass baking dish. Microwave covered with waxed paper at 50% (Medium) until hot through, about 8 minutes per pound; rotate baking dish ¼ turn every 10 minutes. Sprinkle spinach mixture with reserved ¼ cup cheese; microwave uncovered at High until cheese is melted, about 2 minutes.

Tip: The ham is cut lengthwise to create pockets for the spinach-walnut mixture so that each serving will feature "stripes" of the meat and stuffing.

ZUCCHINI–HAM LOAF

.Fill the center of this glazed, zucchini-flecked ring with steamed carrots, Brussels sprouts, cauliflower, or broccoli—a fresh look for a refreshingly moist loaf.

Total Preparation Time: 50 to 55 minutes
Microwave Time: 24 to 27 minutes
Yield: 8 servings

Dill Sauce (see Index)
Fresh Bread Crumbs (see Index)
1 medium zucchini, cut to fit feed tube
1 small onion, peeled, cut into 1-inch pieces
1½ pounds smoked ham, cut into 1-inch pieces
1 pound uncooked pork, excess fat trimmed, cut into 1-inch pieces
2 eggs
3 tablespoons half-and-half or milk
1 teaspoon prepared mustard
¼ teaspoon ground mace
⅛ teaspoon ground cloves
1½ tablespoons butter or margarine
2 tablespoons light brown sugar

Make Dill Sauce. Make Bread Crumbs; do not dry crumbs.

Shred (Shredding Disc) zucchini; drain well between layers of paper toweling. Process (Steel Knife) onion using on/off technique until finely chopped; remove. Process (Steel Knife) ham using on/off technique until finely chopped; remove. Process (Steel Knife) pork using on/off technique until finely chopped. Mix zucchini, onion, ham, pork, bread crumbs, eggs, half-and-half, mustard, mace, and cloves.

Pat mixture into 6-cup microwave ring mold (or into 2-quart glass casserole, with custard cup placed open end up in center). Microwave uncovered at High 15 minutes, rotating mold ¼ turn every 5 minutes. Let stand loosely covered with aluminum foil 5 minutes.

Microwave butter and sugar in 1-cup glass measure at High until butter is melted and sugar is dissolved. Invert ham loaf on serving plate; spoon butter glaze over. Microwave Dill Sauce at High until hot through; serve with ham loaf.

Tips: Unless you have a large-model food processor, chop no more than ½ pound of meat at a time.

Zucchini-Ham Loaf can be frozen without the glaze, tightly wrapped, up to 1 month. Add glaze after reheating.

SAUSAGE HASH–BROWN SKILLET

The superior flavor of homemade sausage raises a country-kitchen skillet dish to company-brunch status. Prepare the sausage mixture separately for fried breakfast patties or a poultry stuffing.

Total Preparation Time: 48 to 51 minutes
Microwave Time: 26 to 29 minutes
Yield: 6 servings

Sour Cream–Green Onion Sauce (see Index)
¼ cup milk
¼ cup sour cream
4 ounces Cheddar cheese, chilled, cut to fit feed tube
½ medium onion, peeled, cut into 1-inch pieces
1 rib celery, cut into 1-inch pieces
¼ cup water
1 teaspoon dried marjoram leaves
1 teaspoon dried sage leaves
½ teaspoon dried thyme leaves
¼ teaspoon dried savory leaves
1 bay leaf
Dash nutmeg
1 teaspoon salt
1 teaspoon pepper
¾ pound lean boneless pork, cut into 1-inch pieces
¼ pound pork fat, cut into 1-inch pieces
¾ package (24-ounce size) frozen hash-brown potatoes

Make Sour Cream-Green Onion Sauce; stir in milk and sour cream. Shred (Shredding Disc) cheese; remove. Process (Steel Knife) onion and celery using on/off technique until finely chopped.

Microwave water, marjoram, sage, thyme, savory, bay leaf, nutmeg, salt, and pepper in 1-cup glass measure, uncovered, at High 1 minute; remove bay leaf and discard. Process (Steel Knife) pork using on/off technique until finely chopped; process (Steel Knife) pork fat using on/off technique until finely chopped. Mix meat, fat, and herb mixture in 12″ × 8″ glass baking dish. Microwave covered with waxed paper at High until meat loses pink color, 4 to 5 minutes, stirring after 2 minutes. Drain excess fat. Let stand covered with waxed paper 2 minutes. Spread sausage evenly in baking dish.

Microwave potatoes in 1-quart glass casserole, uncovered, at 10% (Low) until potatoes are thawed, about 6 minutes, stirring after 3 minutes. Stir Sour Cream-Green Onion Sauce, ½ cup of the cheese, the onion, and celery into potatoes; spoon potato mixture over sausage in baking dish. Microwave uncovered at 70% (Medium High) until hot through, 13 to 15 minutes, rotating baking dish ¼ turn after 6 minutes. Sprinkle with remaining cheese; microwave uncovered at High 2 minutes. Let stand covered with aluminum foil 5 minutes.

Tips: Unless you have a large-model food processor, chop no more than ½ pound of meat at a time. The ratio of ¼ pound fat to ¾ pound pork results in juicy sausages.

To make sausage for other uses, follow second paragraph as above, but do not microwave meat. Sausage mixture can be prepared, shaped into a roll, and sliced for convenient freezer storage; separate slices with waxed paper, wrap in freezer wrap, and freeze up to 2 months.

FRUIT-STUFFED LEG OF LAMB

Savor the pure harmony of lamb and spiced fruit in a fragrant, all-occasions entrée. The food processor quickly turns part of the fruit into a natural sauce for the festive rolled lamb.

Total Preparation Time: 65 to 70 minutes
Microwave Time: 44 to 52 minutes
Yield: 8 servings

1 cup dried apples
1 cup dried apricots
2 tablespoons flour
1 can (12 ounces) apricot nectar
1 cup apple juice
⅛ teaspoon ground allspice
⅛ teaspoon ground cloves
1 boned, rolled, leg of lamb (about 3 pounds)
½ teaspoon ground cinnamon
3 tablespoons brandy
Mint or watercress sprigs

Process (Steel Knife) apples, apricots, and flour using on/off technique until fruit is finely chopped. Microwave fruit mixture, apricot nectar, apple juice, allspice, and cloves in 1½-quart glass casserole, uncovered, at High 10 minutes, or until fruit is tender, stirring every 3 minutes. Lay lamb flat on counter top; spoon half the fruit mixture on lamb. Roll lamb up and tie with string in several places; place in 12″ × 8″ glass baking dish. Rub cinnamon onto lamb; spoon remaining fruit mixture around lamb. Microwave uncovered at 50% (Medium) 11 to 13 minutes per pound until meat thermometer registers 160° F, rotating baking dish ¼ turn every 15 minutes. Let roast stand loosely covered with aluminum foil for 10 minutes.

Process (Steel Knife) fruit, pan drippings, and brandy until smooth. Microwave in 4-cup glass measure, uncovered, at High until hot through, about 45 seconds. Place roast on serving platter and carve; garnish with mint. Serve with fruit sauce.

Tip: The microwave time specified in the recipe will produce a tender, well-done roast. If you prefer medium-rare lamb, microwave 9 to 11 minutes per pound, until meat thermometer registers 150° F. Do not use a conventional meat thermometer in the microwave oven; if you do not have a microwave meat thermometer, remove roast from the oven and check doneness with an instant-register or a regular thermometer.

MOROCCAN LAMB STEW

An extraordinary lamb stew, with haunting overtones of fragrant spices, almonds, and raisins. Feature it on a Middle Eastern-style dinner menu with an appetizer of Eggplant Dip with Pita Triangles and Baklava for dessert (see Index).

Total Preparation Time: 50 to 55 minutes
Microwave Time: 38 to 43 minutes
Yield: 4 servings

---

1 clove garlic, peeled
1 medium onion, peeled, cut into 1-inch pieces
2 tablespoons vegetable oil
¼ teaspoon ground cinnamon
⅛ teaspoon ground ginger
⅛ teaspoon ground turmeric
¹⁄₁₆ teaspoon ground cloves
4 medium tomatoes, seeded, cut into 1-inch pieces
1½ pounds boneless lamb cubes for stew, excess fat trimmed
2 tablespoons flour
1 tablespoon beef-flavor instant bouillon
¼ cup cold water
¼ to ½ teaspoon salt
¼ teaspoon pepper
Turmeric Rice (see Index)
¼ cup slivered almonds
2 tablespoons golden raisins
Parsley sprigs

With machine running (Steel Knife), drop garlic through feed tube, processing until minced. Add onion to bowl; process using on/off technique until chopped. Microwave onion mixture and oil in 2½-quart glass casserole, covered, at High 3 to 4 minutes. Stir in cinnamon, ginger, turmeric, and cloves; microwave uncovered at High 2 minutes.

Process (Steel Knife) tomatoes using on/off technique until coarsely chopped; stir tomatoes and lamb into casserole. Microwave covered at High 10 minutes; microwave uncovered at 50% (Medium) 10 minutes, stirring every 5 minutes. Mix flour, bouillon, and water; stir into lamb

mixture. Microwave covered at 50% (Medium) until lamb is tender, about 10 to 15 minutes. Season to taste with salt and pepper. Let stand 5 minutes.

Make Turmeric Rice conventionally while microwaving lamb mixture.

Microwave almonds in glass pie plate, uncovered, at High until toasted, about 3 minutes, stirring after 1½ minutes. Spoon lamb mixture onto rimmed platter; garnish with almonds, raisins, and parsley. Serve with Turmeric Rice.

Tip: Moroccan Lamb Stew can be cooked 1 day in advance without garnishes or Turmeric Rice; refrigerate covered. Add garnishes and make rice before serving. The stew can be frozen, tightly covered, up to 1 month.

GREEK MEATBALL KEBABS

A novel way to present a Greek menu classic. Wrap herbed lamb meatballs in microwave-softened grapevine leaves and cook the packets on skewers for convenient serving.

Total Preparation Time: 51 to 59 minutes
Microwave Time: 25 to 28 minutes
Yield: 4 servings

---

16 grapevine leaves, rinsed, drained
3 cups water
¾ cup dry Bread Crumbs (see Index)
1 clove garlic, peeled
1 small onion, peeled, cut into 1-inch pieces
1¼ pounds boneless lamb, cut into 1-inch pieces
¼ teaspoon dried oregano leaves
⅛ teaspoon dried mint leaves
½ teaspoon salt
1 egg
2 tablespoons plain yogurt
1 small tomato, cut into quarters
4 medium mushrooms
¼ cup butter or margarine
Yogurt Sauce (recipe follows)

Microwave grapevine leaves and water in 2-quart glass casserole, uncovered, at High until boiling, about 8 minutes; let boil 2 minutes. Rinse with cold water and drain well.

Make Bread Crumbs; dry crumbs and reserve. With machine running (Steel Knife), drop garlic through feed tube, processing until minced. Add onion to bowl; process using on/off technique until finely chopped. Process (Steel Knife) lamb using on/off technique until finely chopped. Mix meat, onion mixture, bread crumbs, oregano, mint, salt, egg, and yogurt; form into 16 meatballs. Wrap meatballs in grapevine leaves; place 2 meatballs each on 8 bamboo skewers. Place a tomato quarter or mushroom on the end of each skewer.

Lay skewers across 12″ × 8″ glass baking dish. Microwave butter in 1-cup glass measure uncovered at High until melted; brush over meatballs. Microwave meatballs covered with waxed paper at High until meatballs are cooked, about 10 minutes, rearranging skewers and basting with remaining butter after 5 minutes. Let stand loosely covered 5 minutes.

Make Yogurt Sauce; serve with meatballs.

Yogurt Sauce

Yield: about 1 cup

½ **small onion, peeled, cut into 1-inch pieces**
1 **cup plain yogurt**
1 **teaspoon dried mint leaves**

Process (Steel Knife) onion using on/off technique until chopped; mix with yogurt and mint. Refrigerate until serving time.

Tips: *Grapevine leaves can be found in large supermarkets and Greek or Middle Eastern groceries. They usually are packed in brine and must be rinsed with cold water before using.*

Unless you have a large-model food processor, chop no more than ½ pound of meat at a time.

The meatball packets can be cooked without skewers; arrange in a circle in a glass pie plate and proceed as above, rotating dish ¼ turn halfway through cooking time.

Greek Meatball Kebabs can be served as an appetizer; allow 1 kebab per serving.

9 Rice, Grains, and Pasta

RICE AND SEASONED VARIATIONS

Combine the convenience of microwave rice with the infinite versatility of processor-chopped seasonings. All variations can be made with conventionally cooked rice, too, and doubled or tripled when you're preparing larger quantities of rice. Rice reheats well in the microwave, so you may wish to renew plain leftovers with any of the seasoning blends.

Just a few of the serving possibilities: Turmeric Rice or Minted Rice with curries; Coriander Rice with any Mexican entrée; Cardamom Rice with meat loaf or pot roast; Peanut Rice with barbequed spareribs or roast pork; Pimiento Rice with goulash or stroganoff.

Total Preparation Time: 26 to 29 minutes
Microwave Time: 19 to 22 minutes
Yield: 3 to 4 cups

2¼ cups hot water, chicken broth, or beef broth
1 teaspoon salt (optional; omit if using broth)
1 cup uncooked long-grain or converted rice

Microwave water and salt in 2-quart glass casserole, uncovered, at High until boiling; stir in rice. Microwave covered at High until rice is tender and water is absorbed, 16 to 18 minutes, stirring after 8 minutes. Let stand covered 5 minutes.

VARIATIONS

ONION RICE: Process (Steel Knife) 1 small onion, peeled and cut into 1-inch pieces, using on/off technique until chopped. Microwave with 1 tablespoon butter or margarine in small glass bowl, covered, at High until onion is tender, about 4 minutes. Make rice as above, stirring onion into cooked rice.

TURMERIC RICE: Make rice as above, stirring ⅛ teaspoon ground turmeric into boiling water with rice. Stir ¼ to ½ teaspoon ground ginger into cooked rice.

CORIANDER RICE: Process (Steel Knife) 2 sprigs coriander using on/off technique until minced. Make rice as above, stirring coriander and 2 teaspoons dried chives into cooked rice.

TOMATO RICE: Make rice as above, stirring 1 teaspoon dried basil leaves and ½ teaspoon dried rosemary leaves into cooked rice; stir in 2 tablespoons tomato paste and ¼ cup sour cream.

CARDAMOM RICE: Make rice as above, stirring ¼ teaspoon ground cardamom into cooked rice.

MINTED RICE: Process (Steel Knife) 3 sprigs mint and 2 sprigs parsley using on/off technique until minced. Make rice as above, stirring mint and parsley into cooked rice.

PEANUT RICE: Process (Steel Knife) ½ cup peanuts using on/off technique until chopped. Process (Steel Knife) ¼ large red pepper (cut into 1-inch pieces) and 1 green onion and top (cut into 1-inch pieces) using on/off technique until chopped. Microwave pepper, onion, and 1 tablespoon butter in small glass bowl, covered, at High until tender, about 3 minutes. Make rice as above, stirring onion mixture, peanuts, and ¼ teaspoon curry powder into cooked rice.

PARMESAN RICE: Process (Steel Knife) 1 to 2 ounces Parmesan cheese (cut into 1-inch pieces) using on/off technique until finely grated. Make rice as above, stirring cheese into cooked rice.

PIMIENTO RICE: Process (Steel Knife) 2 whole pimientos (cut into 1-inch pieces) using on/off technique until coarsely chopped. Make rice as above, stirring pimiento and ½ teaspoon paprika into cooked rice.

SPINACH RICE

You may wish to double the recipe for this creamy green rice dish since the leftovers will disappear quickly—especially at lunch the next day.

Total Preparation Time: 35 to 40 minutes
Microwave Time: 15 to 19 minutes
Yield: 6 servings

½ ounce Parmesan cheese, cut into 1-inch pieces
10 ounces fresh spinach, stems removed
1 tablespoon water
½ medium onion, peeled, cut into 1-inch pieces
2 ounces mushrooms
2 slices bacon
2 ounces brick cheese, chilled, cut to fit feed tube
2 cups cooked rice
⅓ cup half-and-half
2 eggs, beaten
¹⁄₁₆ teaspoon ground nutmeg
½ teaspoon salt
⅛ teaspoon white pepper

With machine running (Steel Knife), drop Parmesan cheese through feed tube, processing until finely grated; reserve. Slice (Slicing Disc) spinach; microwave spinach and water in 3-quart glass casserole, covered, at High until cooked, 4 to 5 minutes. Drain thoroughly in a strainer, pressing to remove excess moisture.

Process (Steel Knife) onion using on/off technique until coarsely chopped; add mushrooms to bowl; process using on/off technique until coarsely chopped. Microwave bacon in 1½-quart glass casserole, uncovered, at High until crisp, about 3 minutes. Crumble bacon; reserve 1 tablespoon drippings in casserole. Microwave onion mixture in drippings, covered, at High until onion is tender, 2 to 3 minutes.

Shred (Shredding Disc) brick cheese. Stir brick cheese, spinach, and remaining ingredients except Parmesan cheese into onion mixture. Microwave covered at 70% (Medium High) until all liquid is absorbed, 6 to 8 minutes, stirring after 4 minutes. Stir in Parmesan cheese; let stand covered 5 minutes.

Tips: Cook rice conventionally or in the microwave oven, as directed in Rice and Seasoned Variations (previous recipe), using ⅔ cup rice and 1⅓ cups water. Reduce salt proportionately, or omit, if desired.

One 10-ounce package frozen chopped spinach can be substituted for the sliced fresh spinach; remove paper wrapper, cut slits in box, and microwave at High 4 to 5 minutes. Drain as above.

TEX–MEX RICE

A winning side dish for outdoor barbecues, but also a quick, nutritious lunch. Use mild chilies, or omit them, to please timid tastes.

Total Preparation Time: 29 to 32 minutes
Microwave Time: 9 to 12 minutes
Yield: 6 servings

2 sprigs fresh coriander or ½ teaspoon dried coriander leaves
2 sprigs fresh parsley
4 ounces Monterey Jack cheese, chilled, cut to fit feed tube
1 ounce Cheddar cheese, chilled, cut to fit feed tube
2 cloves garlic, peeled
1 medium onion, peeled, cut into 1-inch pieces
2 to 3 hot or mild green chili peppers, seeded, cut into 1-inch pieces
8 ounces boneless beef chuck, excess fat trimmed, cut into 1-inch pieces
3 cups cooked rice
1½ cups sour cream
¼ teaspoon ground cumin
¼ teaspoon salt

Process (Steel Knife) coriander and parsley using on/off technique until minced; remove. Shred (Shredding Disc) cheeses separately; reserve. With machine running (Steel Knife), drop garlic through feed tube, processing until minced. Add onion and peppers to bowl; process using on/off technique until finely chopped. Process (Steel Knife) beef using on/off technique until finely chopped. Microwave beef and onion mixture in 2½-quart glass casserole, covered, at High until meat loses pink color, 3 to 4 minutes, stirring after 2 minutes. Stir coriander, parsley, Monterey Jack cheese, and all remaining ingredients except Cheddar cheese into casserole. Microwave covered at High until hot through, 6 to 8 minutes, stirring after 3 minutes. Sprinkle Cheddar cheese over top; let stand covered 5 minutes.

Tip: Cook rice conventionally or as directed in *Rice and Seasoned Variations (see Index).*

ORIENTAL FRIED RICE

An exciting alternative to plain rice with Chinese Pepper Beef (see Index). However, the Chinese view this type of melange as the snack-time answer to leftover rice, and you may wish to also.

Total Preparation Time: 20 to 24 minutes
Microwave Time: 11 to 12 minutes
Yield: 4 servings

---

2 sprigs fresh coriander or parsley
8 ounces fresh green beans, trimmed
3 tablespoons water
3 to 4 cups cooked rice
1 tablespoon peanut or vegetable oil
4 ounces smoked ham, cut into 1-inch pieces
2 ounces mushrooms
1 green onion and top, cut into 1-inch pieces
2 eggs, beaten
2 tablespoons soy sauce
1 teaspoon sugar
Soy sauce

Process (Steel Knife) coriander using on/off technique until minced; remove. Slice (Slicing Disc) beans, placing beans in feed tube vertically. Microwave beans and water in 1-quart glass casserole dish, covered, at High until crisp-tender, about 4 minutes; drain. Microwave rice and oil in 2-quart glass casserole, uncovered, at High until hot through, about 3 minutes, stirring after 1½ minutes.

Process (Steel Knife) ham using on/off technique until coarsely chopped. Process (Steel Knife) mushrooms and onion using on/off technique until coarsely chopped. Mix eggs, 2 tablespoons soy sauce, and the sugar. Stir beans, ham, mushroom mixture, and egg mixture into hot rice. Microwave uncovered at High until eggs are set, 4 to 5 minutes, stirring every 2 minutes. Sprinkle with coriander; serve with additional soy sauce.

Tips: For a quick variation, substitute one 10-ounce package frozen peas for the green beans and do not slice. Remove paper wrapper, cut several slits in box, and microwave at High 5 minutes; drain.

Cook rice conventionally or as directed in *Rice and Seasoned Variations (see Index).*

Cooked chicken or beef, cut into 1-inch pieces, can be substituted for the ham. Four ounces shrimp can also be substituted; small shrimp need not be chopped.

PASTITSIO

The Mediterranean legacy of spices highlights a layered casserole crowned with a custard-like sauce. The classic formula calls for macaroni; this rice variation is lighter and more versatile. Serve small squares with chicken, fish, or lamb. Or increase the portion size for a one-dish entrée.

Total Preparation Time: 58 to 59 minutes
Microwave Time: 28 to 29 minutes
Yield: 8 servings

---

1 ounce Parmesan cheese, cut into 1-inch
   pieces
¼ cup blanched almonds
1 medium onion, peeled, cut into 1-inch
   pieces
2 ounces mushrooms
½ pound boneless beef chunk, cut into 1-inch
   pieces
½ pound boneless lean lamb, cut into 1-inch
   pieces
¼ cup golden raisins
¼ cup tomato sauce
¼ teaspoon dried marjoram leaves
⅛ teaspoon ground cinnamon
1/16 teaspoon ground allspice
1/16 teaspoon ground cloves
1 teaspoon salt
1/16 teaspoon pepper
4 cups cooked rice
2 eggs, beaten
½ teaspoon salt
⅔ cup Twice-As-Fast Sauce Mix
2½ cups half-and-half
½ teaspoon salt
2 eggs, beaten

With machine running (Steel Knife), drop
Parmesan cheese through feed tube, processing
until finely grated; remove. Process (Steel
Knife) almonds using on/off technique until
finely chopped; remove. Process (Steel Knife)
onion and mushrooms using on/off technique
until finely chopped; remove. Process (Steel
Knife) beef and lamb using on/off technique
until finely chopped. Microwave beef, lamb,
and onion mixture in 1½-quart glass casserole,
covered, at High until meat loses pink color, 3
to 4 minutes, stirring after 2 minutes. Drain.
Stir in almonds, raisins, tomato sauce,
marjoram, cinnamon, allspice, cloves, 1
teaspoon salt, and the pepper.
  Combine rice, 2 eggs, and ½ teaspoon salt.
Combine sauce mix, half-and-half, and ½
teaspoon salt in 4-cup glass measure.
Microwave uncovered at High until thickened,
about 5 minutes, stirring with whisk every 1½
minutes. Stir about ¼ cup sauce mixture into 2
eggs; stir egg mixture into sauce mixture.
  Spoon half the rice mixture in bottom of
greased 12″ × 8″ glass baking dish; sprinkle
with half the Parmesan cheese. Spoon meat

mixture over rice mixture; spoon remaining
rice mixture over meat mixture. Pour sauce
over rice mixture; microwave uncovered at 70%
(Medium High) until sauce is just set in the
center, about 20 minutes, rotating dish ¼ turn
every 5 minutes. Sprinkle with remaining
Parmesan cheese; let stand loosely covered with
aluminum foil 5 minutes. Cut into squares to
serve.

*Tips: Unless you have a large-model food
      processor, chop no more than ½ pound
      meat at a time.
        Meat mixture can be made 1 day in
      advance; refrigerate covered.
        Cook rice conventionally or as directed
      in Rice and Seasoned Variations (see
      Index).*

SHERRIED BROWN RICE WITH MUSHROOMS AND PORK

A most cosmopolitan accompaniment for
broiled or roasted meats, fish, or poultry. Dried
mushrooms, almonds, sherry, and orange rind
underline—and refine—the delicious nutty
flavor of brown rice. In larger portions, it's an
entrée high in B vitamins, iron, and meat
economy.

Total Preparation Time: 60 to 63 minutes
Microwave Time: 48 to 55 minutes
Yield: 10 to 12 servings

---

1 cup hot water
12 Chinese dried mushrooms
3 cups hot water
1 teaspoon salt
1 cup uncooked brown rice
½ cup blanched almonds
2 ribs celery, cut to fit feed tube
½ medium onion, peeled, cut into 1-inch
   pieces
1 pound lean boneless pork, cut into ½-inch
   pieces
¼ cup dry sherry
½ cup sour cream
1 teaspoon grated orange rind

Pour 1 cup hot water over mushrooms; let stand until mushrooms are soft, 10 to 20 minutes.

Microwave 3 cups water and the salt in 3-quart glass casserole, uncovered, at High until boiling, about 4 minutes. Stir in rice; microwave uncovered at High until rice is tender and liquid is absorbed, 30 to 35 minutes, stirring after 15 minutes. Let stand covered 5 minutes.

Process (Steel Knife) almonds until coarsely chopped; remove. Drain mushrooms; cut out tough stems. Slice (Slicing Disc) celery and mushrooms. Process (Steel Knife) onion using on/off technique until chopped. Microwave pork and ¼ cup sherry in 1-quart glass casserole, covered, at High until meat loses pink color, 7 to 9 minutes. Drain, reserving 2 tablespoons cooking liquid.

Microwave celery, mushrooms, and onion in reserved cooking liquid in 1-quart glass casserole, covered, at High until onion is tender, about 4 minutes. Stir pork mixture, vegetable mixture, almonds, sour cream, and rind into rice; microwave covered at High until hot through, about 3 minutes.

Tip: To microwave plain brown rice for other uses, follow the second paragraph as above. The yield will be about 4 cups.

APPLE–ALMOND KASHA

Wonderful with chicken or lamb, this mixture features the protein and mineral wealth of buckwheat and the natural sweetness of apples and raisins.

Total Preparation Time: 29 to 33 minutes
Microwave Time: 20 to 23 minutes
Yield: 6 to 8 servings

---

1 cup medium-grain kasha (buckwheat groats)
1 egg
2 cups chicken broth
2 medium apples, pared, cored, cut into 1-inch pieces
½ cup golden raisins
¼ teaspoon ground cinnamon
⅛ teaspoon ground nutmeg
⅓ cup plain yogurt
2 teaspoons vanilla
⅓ cup blanched almonds
2 teaspoons butter or margarine

Microwave kasha in 1½-quart glass casserole, uncovered, at High 2 minutes. Stir in egg; microwave uncovered at High 1½ minutes, or until egg is set (mixture will appear very dry).

Microwave broth in 2-cup glass measure at High until boiling, 5 to 6 minutes. Stir broth into kasha. Microwave covered at High 4 minutes, stirring after 2 minutes.

Process (Steel Knife) apples, raisins, cinnamon, and nutmeg using on/off technique until apples are chopped; stir into kasha mixture. Microwave covered at High until kasha is tender, about 5 minutes. Stir in yogurt and vanilla; let stand 5 minutes.

Process (Steel Knife) almonds using on/off technique until chopped. Microwave butter in glass pie plate at High until melted. Stir in almonds; microwave uncovered at High until toasted, 2 to 3 minutes. Sprinkle over kasha before serving.

Tips: Substitute water for the chicken broth and serve Apple-Almond Kasha with milk or cream for a nutritious breakfast. Cholesterol-counters can omit the egg (or use 2 egg whites) and almonds and enjoy the kasha with yogurt for a very satisfying lunch.

To microwave plain kasha, follow the first and second paragraphs above but increase cooking time to about 8 minutes, stirring every 3 minutes; let stand 5 minutes. The yield will be about 3 cups. If you wish to add chopped onion to the plain kasha, process (Steel Knife) ½ medium onion, cut into quarters, until finely chopped. Microwave onion in 1-cup glass measure with 2 tablespoons butter or margarine, covered, at High 5 minutes; stir into cooked kasha.

Kasha can be found in large supermarkets and in health food stores. It is usually sold in fine, medium, or whole grain. The whole grains remain slightly more separate during cooking for a fluffier texture, which some people prefer. The fine grain is appropriate for cereal or soup.

POLENTA

The easiest possible preparation of an Italian classic. It is superb with grilled Italian sausage, Italian Meat Loaf, or Chicken Provençal (see Index). Omit the Fresh Tomato Sauce, if you wish, and serve with melted butter.

Total Preparation Time: 20 to 22 minutes
Microwave Time: 10 to 12 minutes
Yield: 6 servings

Fresh Tomato Sauce (optional; see Index) or melted butter
4 sprigs parsley
2 ounces Parmesan cheese, cut into 1-inch pieces
1 medium onion, peeled, cut into 1-inch pieces
¼ cup butter or margarine
3½ cups water
1 cup coarse-ground yellow cornmeal
½ teaspoon salt

Make Fresh Tomato Sauce.

Process (Steel Knife) parsley using on/off technique until minced. With machine running, add cheese through feed tube, processing until finely grated; reserve. Process (Steel Knife) onion using on/off technique until finely chopped. Microwave onion and 2 tablespoons of the butter in 2-cup glass measure, covered with plastic wrap, at High until onion is tender, about 3 minutes. Microwave water in 8½″ × 4½″ × 2½″ glass loaf pan at High until simmering. Add cornmeal and salt gradually, stirring continuously. Microwave uncovered at High until mixture boils and thickens, 3 to 5 minutes, stirring after 1½ minutes; let boil 1 minute. Stir in reserved cheese mixture, the onion mixture, and remaining 2 tablespoons

butter. Let stand covered 5 minutes. Spoon onto plates. Serve hot with Fresh Tomato Sauce.

Tips: Polenta will thicken to slicing consistency as it cools. To slice it, loosen edges of Polenta with tip of knife; invert onto plate. Cut into ½- to ¾-inch slices; cut slices into 1½-inch pieces. Microwave slices loosely covered with waxed paper at 50% (Medium) until hot, about 2 minutes. Serve with Fresh Tomato Sauce or melted butter.

If desired, Polenta can be fried. Heat browning dish in microwave at High 5 minutes. Slice Polenta into ¾- to 1-inch slices as above; place on hot browning dish. Microwave uncovered at High 30 seconds; turn slices over. Microwave uncovered at High until Polenta is hot through, 1 to 1½ minutes. Serve with Fresh Tomato Sauce or melted butter.

GARLIC GRITS

You should be warned about these nutty, great-tasting grits—it's all too easy to devour the whole bowlful if nobody else is around to help!

Total Preparation Time: 30 to 35 minutes
Microwave Time: 20 to 23 minutes
Yield: 4 to 6 servings

1 cup grits
3 cups water
1 teaspoon salt
⅓ cup walnuts
⅓ cup pecans
4 ounces Cheddar cheese, chilled, cut to fit feed tube
2 cloves garlic, peeled
¼ cup mayonnaise or salad dressing
¼ teaspoon ground allspice
⅛ teaspoon dried thyme leaves
¼ teaspoon salt

Microwave grits, water, and 1 teaspoon salt in 1½-quart glass casserole, covered, at High 11 to 13 minutes, or until water is absorbed, stirring after 7 minutes. Let stand 5 minutes.

Process (Steel Knife) nuts using on/off technique until chopped. Microwave nuts in glass pie plate, uncovered, at High until toasted, 3 to 4 minutes, stirring after 2 minutes. Shred (Shredding Disc) cheese. With machine running (Steel Knife), drop garlic through feed tube, processing until minced.

Reserve 2 tablespoons of the nuts and ¼ cup of the cheese mixture; stir remaining ingredients into grits. Microwave covered at High until hot through, about 6 minutes, stirring after 3 minutes. Sprinkle edge of grits mixture with reserved nuts; sprinkle reserved cheese mixture in center. Let stand loosely covered with aluminum foil 5 minutes.

Tip: To microwave plain grits, follow the first paragraph above. The yield will be about 3 cups.

¼ teaspoon pepper
3 ounces salted cashews

Microwave barley in 2-quart glass casserole, uncovered, at High 3 minutes, stirring after 1½ minutes. Process (Steel Knife) parsley using on/off technique until minced. Add onion to bowl; process using on/off technique until chopped, and remove. Slice (Slicing Disc) carrot, mushrooms, and celery separately. Stir beef stock, onion mixture, carrot, celery, marjoram, caraway seeds, and pepper into barley. Microwave uncovered at High until barley is tender, 35 to 40 minutes, stirring every 10 minutes.

Stir mushrooms and cashews into barley mixture during last 10 minutes of cooking time.

Tip: To microwave plain barley, follow the first paragraph above, omitting vegetables, herbs, and pepper. Substitute chicken stock for the beef stock, if you wish. The yield will be 3 to 4 cups.

BARLEY CASSEROLE

The marvelous flavor and mingled textures of this casserole will justify the cooking time required by the barley. It is one of the best things that ever happened to a pot roast dinner!

Total Preparation Time: 45 to 50 minutes
Microwave Time: 38 to 43 minutes
Yield: 6 to 8 servings

1 cup uncooked pearl barley
10 sprigs parsley
1 medium onion, peeled, cut into 1-inch pieces
1 medium carrot, pared, cut to fit feed tube
4 ounces mushrooms
1 rib celery, cut to fit feed tube
4 cups beef stock
½ teaspoon dried marjoram leaves
¼ teaspoon caraway seeds

EGGPLANT SPAGHETTI

A marvelous first course or a side dish with baked chicken or grilled meats. But if you love eggplant, you'll want to make a whole meal of this lyrical dish.

Total Preparation Time: 25 to 28 minutes
Microwave Time: 16 to 18 minutes
Yield: 6 to 8 servings

2 sprigs parsley
1 clove garlic, peeled
1 medium eggplant (about 1 pound), pared, cut to fit feed tube
4 ounces mushrooms
4 green onions and tops, cut to fit feed tube
2 tablespoons olive or vegetable oil
1 can (28 ounces) Italian-style plum tomatoes, undrained, cut into quarters
2 cans (6 ounces each) tomato paste

2 tablespoons dry white wine
2 teaspoons dried oregano leaves
½ teaspoon dried basil leaves
1 teaspoon sugar
1 teaspoon salt
⅛ teaspoon pepper
1 pound spaghetti, cooked

Process (Steel Knife) parsley using on/off technique until minced. With machine running, drop garlic through feed tube, processing until minced; remove. Slice (Slicing Disc) eggplant, mushrooms, and onions. Microwave garlic mixture, eggplant, mushrooms, onions, and oil in 3-quart glass casserole, covered, at High until vegetables are tender, about 6 minutes, stirring after 3 minutes.

Process (Steel Knife) tomatoes and liquid using on/off technique until chopped. Stir tomatoes and remaining ingredients except spaghetti into eggplant mixture; microwave uncovered at High 10 minutes, stirring after 5 minutes. Serve sauce over hot spaghetti.

Tips: If you can obtain fresh basil, substitute 2 large leaves for the ½ teaspoon dried and mince them with the parsley.

Good olive oil will enhance any vegetable sauce; choose an imported light oil from Italy or Spain. A heavy olive oil with an intense flavor will overwhelm the other seasonings; so mix ½ tablespoon of a heavier oil with 1½ tablespoons of vegetable oil.

Cook spaghetti conventionally since there is no microwave time savings with more than 8 ounces of pasta.

SPAGHETTI CARBONARA

Another identity for spaghetti—flecked with bacon, ham, and eggs. It's somewhat lighter than the meat-sauced standby, yet needs only a large tossed salad to complete a supper menu.

Total Preparation Time: 28 to 34 minutes
Microwave Time: 20 to 26 minutes
Yield: 4 to 6 servings

4 cups water
8 ounces uncooked spaghetti
1 tablespoon olive or vegetable oil
1 teaspoon salt
4 slices bacon
2 ounces Parmesan cheese, cut into 1-inch pieces
6 ounces Canadian-style bacon or ham, cut into 1-inch pieces
2 tablespoons butter or margarine
1 tablespoon olive or vegetable oil
3 eggs
⅛ teaspoon pepper

Microwave water in 4-cup glass measure at High until boiling. Arrange spaghetti in 12″ × 8″ glass baking dish; sprinkle with 1 tablespoon oil and the salt. Pour boiling water over spaghetti; microwave covered with plastic wrap at High until spaghetti is al dente, 8 to 10 minutes, stirring twice. Drain.

Microwave bacon in glass baking dish, covered with paper toweling, at High until bacon is crisp, 3 to 4 minutes. Drain and crumble.

With machine running (Steel Knife), drop cheese through feed tube, processing until finely grated. Process (Steel Knife) Canadian-style bacon using on/off technique until chopped.

Microwave butter and 1 tablespoon oil in 2-quart glass casserole at High until butter is melted; whisk in eggs until smooth. Stir in spaghetti, grated cheese, Canadian-style bacon, bacon, and pepper. Microwave uncovered at High until eggs are set, 3 to 4 minutes, stirring every minute.

Tip: Spaghetti can be cooked conventionally, if desired.

PASTA PRIMAVERA

The name of this Italian rite translates to springtime pasta, a concept beautifully detailed with mushrooms, carrots, asparagus, and zucchini—or any fresh vegetable you wish to substitute. Serve it as a first course, according to tradition, or as a warm-weather entrée.

Total Preparation Time: 36 to 44 minutes
Microwave Time: 28 to 33 minutes
Yield: 4 to 6 servings

---

4 cups water
8 ounces uncooked linguine
1 tablespoon olive or vegetable oil
1 teaspoon salt
2 ounces Parmesan cheese, cut into 1-inch pieces
1 clove garlic, peeled
1 green onion and top, cut into 1-inch pieces
1 tablespoon butter or margarine
4 ounces mushrooms
2 medium carrots, pared, cut to fit feed tube
4 ounces fresh asparagus, tips cut off and reserved, stalks cut to fit feed tube
2 medium zucchini, cut to fit feed tube
¼ cup water
¼ cup butter or margarine
1 cup whipping cream or half-and-half
¼ teaspoon white pepper
⅛ to ¼ teaspoon freshly grated nutmeg

Microwave 4 cups water in 4-cup glass measure at High until boiling. Arrange linguine in 12″ × 8″ glass baking dish; sprinkle with oil and salt. Pour boiling water over linguine. Microwave covered with plastic wrap at High until linguine is al dente, 5 to 7 minutes, stirring twice. Drain.

With machine running (Steel Knife), drop cheese through feed tube, processing until finely grated; reserve. With machine running (Steel Knife), drop garlic through feed tube, processing until minced. Add onion to bowl; process using on/off technique until finely chopped. Microwave onion mixture and 1 tablespoon butter in 1-quart casserole, uncovered, at High until onion is tender, 2 to 3 minutes. Slice (Slicing Disc) mushrooms; add to onion mixture and microwave uncovered at High 3 minutes. Drain.

Slice (Slicing Disc) carrots, asparagus stalks, and zucchini separately. Microwave carrots and ¼ cup water in 2-quart glass casserole, covered, at High 2 minutes. Add asparagus tips and stalks to casserole; microwave covered at High 2 minutes. Add zucchini to casserole; microwave covered at High until vegetables are crisp-tender, about 2 minutes.

Microwave ¼ cup butter and the cream in 12″ × 8″ glass baking dish, uncovered, at High until cream is slightly thickened, 4 to 5 minutes, stirring after 2 minutes. Stir in reserved cheese; stir in linguine and vegetables, tossing to coat with sauce. Sprinkle with pepper and nutmeg. Microwave uncovered at High until hot through, about 3 minutes.

Tips: To microwave plain noodles, follow the first paragraph above. Linguine can be cooked conventionally, if desired, according to package directions.

Substitute broccoli, yellow summer squash, green or red peppers, or shelled peas for an equal weight or volume of any of the vegetables. Microwave sliced peppers as directed above for carrots, sliced broccoli as directed for asparagus, sliced yellow squash or peas as directed for zucchini.

GREEN NOODLES WITH YOGURT–DILL SAUCE

This slightly tangy flavor scheme of green noodles and pale sauce adds magic to a meal of broiled fish or chicken.

Total Preparation Time: 17 to 18 minutes
Microwave Time: 7 to 8 minutes
Yield: 4 to 6 servings

---

2 large sprigs parsley
1 clove garlic, peeled
½ small onion, peeled, cut into 1-inch pieces
1 green onion and top, cut into 1-inch pieces
1 cup plain yogurt
¼ cup small curd cottage cheese
½ package (3-ounce size) cream cheese, softened

1½ tablespoons Twice-As-Fast Sauce Mix
  (see Index)
2 tablespoons butter or margarine, softened
1½ teaspoons dried dillweed or 4 sprigs
  fresh dill
1 teaspoon dried marjoram
¼ teaspoon salt
1/16 teaspoon white pepper
12 ounces green noodles, cooked

Process (Steel Knife) parsley using on/off technique until minced; with machine running, add garlic through feed tube, processing until minced. Add onions to bowl; process (Steel Knife) using on/off technique until chopped. Add onion mixture, yogurt, cottage cheese, cream cheese, sauce mix, butter, dill, marjoram, salt, and pepper to bowl; process (Steel Knife) until mixture is smooth. Transfer mixture to 2-quart glass casserole; microwave uncovered at High until slightly thickened, 5 to 6 minutes, stirring every 2 minutes. Stir in noodles; microwave uncovered at High until hot through, about 2 minutes.

Tips: Cook noodles conventionally, since there is no microwave time savings with more than 8 ounces of pasta.

If using fresh dill, process it with the parsley.

Cooked sauce can be refrigerated covered up to 2 days.

LINGUINE WITH SPINACH–CLAM SAUCE

A fast answer to longings for pasta with Italian-style clam sauce, and a delightful change from the commonplace "red" or "white." Serve as a first course or a light entrée.

Total Preparation Time: 25 to 27 minutes
Microwave Time: 17 to 18 minutes
Yield: 4 servings

1 package (10 ounces) frozen chopped
  spinach
1 ounce Parmesan cheese, cut into 1-inch
  pieces
1 sprig parsley
1 clove garlic, peeled
1 shallot or ¼ small onion, peeled
3 tablespoons butter or margarine
3 tablespoons flour
2 cans (6½ ounces each) minced clams,
  undrained
1 cup whipping cream or half-and-half
8 ounces linguine, cooked
⅛ teaspoon ground nutmeg
1/16 teaspoon pepper

Remove paper wrapper and make 1 or 2 slits in spinach package; microwave at High until cooked, 4 to 5 minutes. Drain thoroughly in a strainer, pressing to remove excess moisture.

With machine running (Steel Knife), drop cheese through feed tube; process until finely grated, and reserve. Process (Steel Knife) parsley using on/off technique until minced. With machine running, drop garlic and shallot through feed tube, processing until minced. Microwave garlic mixture and butter in 2-quart glass measure, uncovered, at High until shallot is tender, about 3 minutes. Stir in flour; microwave uncovered at High 2 minutes. Stir in clams, clam liquor, and cream; microwave uncovered at High until thickened, about 6 minutes, stirring with whisk every 2 minutes. Stir in spinach; microwave uncovered at High 2 minutes, or until hot through.

Arrange linguine on serving platter; pour sauce over and toss. Sprinkle with nutmeg, pepper, and reserved cheese.

Tips: Microwave linguine according to first paragraph of Pasta Primavera (see Index) or cook conventionally.

Ten ounces of fresh spinach can be substituted for the frozen. Microwave with the water that clings from washing in a glass casserole, covered, at High until tender, about 3 minutes. Drain well; process (Steel Knife) using on/off technique until finely chopped.

CHICKEN LASAGNA

This three-part recipe yields a hearty entrée of unusually rich flavor and creamy texture. Turn to it for the relaxed serving pace of a one-dish entrée, whether for casual entertaining or family dinners.

Total Preparation Time: 90 to 97 minutes
Microwave Time: 72 to 78 minutes
Yield: 8 servings

5½ cups water
1 tablespoon vegetable oil
½ teaspoon salt
12 lasagna noodles
2 ounces Parmesan cheese, cut into 1-inch pieces
12 ounces mozzarella cheese, chilled, cut to fit feed tube
1 medium carrot, pared, cut into 1-inch pieces
1 rib celery, cut into 1-inch pieces
1 medium onion, peeled, cut into 1-inch pieces
1 medium green pepper, seeded, cut into 1-inch pieces
1 tablespoon olive or vegetable oil
6 medium tomatoes, seeded, cut into 1-inch pieces
2 cans (15 ounces each) tomato sauce
1½ teaspoons sugar
1 teaspoon dried basil leaves
½ teaspoon dried oregano leaves
¼ teaspoon dried marjoram leaves
2 large sprigs parsley
1 clove garlic, peeled
12 ounces cooked, skinned, boned chicken (light and dark meat), cut into 1-inch pieces
16 ounces ricotta cheese
3 eggs, beaten
¼ teaspoon salt
⅛ teaspoon pepper

Microwave water, 1 tablespoon oil, and ½ teaspoon salt in 12″ × 8″ glass baking dish at High until boiling; add noodles. Microwave covered with plastic wrap at High until noodles are al dente, about 10 minutes. Drain; rinse with cold water.

With machine running (Steel Knife), drop Parmesan cheese through feed tube, processing until finely grated; remove. Shred (Shredding Disc) mozzarella cheese; remove. Process (Steel Knife) carrot, celery, onion, and green pepper using on/off technique until finely chopped. Microwave vegetable mixture and 1 tablespoon oil in 2-quart glass casserole, covered, at High until tender, about 4 minutes.

Process (Steel Knife) tomatoes using on/off technique until coarsely chopped. Stir tomatoes, tomato sauce, sugar, basil, oregano, and marjoram into vegetable mixture in casserole. Microwave uncovered at High 25 minutes, or until thickened, stirring every 5 minutes.

Process (Steel Knife) parsley using on/off technique until minced. With machine running, drop garlic through feed tube, processing until minced. Add chicken to bowl; process using on/off technique until coarsely chopped. Mix chicken mixture, 2 cups of the mozzarella, 2 tablespoons of the Parmesan, the ricotta cheese, eggs, ¼ teaspoon salt, and the pepper.

Layer 4 lasagna noodles in bottom of 12″ × 8″ glass baking dish. Spread half the chicken mixture over noodles; spoon a third of the sauce mixture over chicken mixture. Repeat layers, ending with remaining sauce. Microwave uncovered at 50% (Medium) 20 minutes, rotating dish ¼ turn every 5 minutes. Microwave uncovered at High until bubbly, about 5 minutes. Sprinkle remaining mozzarella and Parmesan cheese over top. Let stand loosely covered 10 minutes. Cut into squares to serve.

Tips: Noodles can be cooked conventionally, according to package directions.

To microwave chicken, arrange skinned chicken pieces in a 12″ × 8″ glass baking dish with meatiest portions toward edges of dish. Microwave covered with plastic wrap at High, about 7 minutes per pound. Let stand until cool enough to remove meat from bones; cut meat into 1-inch pieces. Two pounds of mixed light and dark meat pieces will yield about 12 ounces of cooked chicken.

Chicken and sauce mixtures can be made 1 day in advance; refrigerate separately, covered. Chicken Lasagna can be assembled 1 hour before cooking.

minutes, or until hot through, rotating dish ¼ turn every 5 minutes. Sprinkle with remaining mozzarella cheese; let stand loosely covered 5 minutes.

CHEESE MANICOTTI WITH MEAT SAUCE

The suspense of stuffed pasta is heightened by the aroma of a spicy meat sauce—and well satisfied by the contrast between sauce and three-cheese stuffing.

Total Preparation Time: 47 to 55 minutes
Microwave Time: 24 to 29 minutes
Yield: 6 servings

Meat Sauce (recipe follows)
4 ounces mozzarella cheese, chilled, cut to fit feed tube
4 sprigs parsley
1 ounce Parmesan cheese, cut into 1-inch pieces
1 clove garlic, peeled
1 small onion, peeled, cut into 1-inch pieces
16 ounces ricotta cheese
2 eggs
½ teaspoon dried basil leaves
12 cooked manicotti

Make Meat Sauce.
Shred (Shredding Disc) mozzarella cheese; remove. Process (Steel Knife) parsley using on/off technique until minced. With machine running, drop Parmesan cheese through feed tube, processing until finely grated. With machine running, drop garlic through feed tube, processing until minced. Add onion to bowl; process using on/off technique until finely chopped. Add ricotta cheese, half the mozzarella cheese, the eggs, and basil to bowl; process using on/off technique just until blended (do not overprocess or consistency of filling will be too thin).
Spoon half the Meat Sauce in bottom of 12″ × 8″ glass baking dish. Fill manicotti with cheese mixture; arrange in baking dish. Spoon remaining Meat Sauce over manicotti. Microwave uncovered at High 13 to 15

Meat Sauce

Yield: 6 cups

12 ounces Italian sausage, casing removed, crumbled
4 ounces pepperoni sausage, cut into 1-inch pieces
¼ large green pepper, seeded, cut into 1-inch pieces
6 medium tomatoes, seeded, cut into 1-inch pieces
2 cans (6 ounces each) tomato paste
½ cup water
¼ cup dry white wine
2 tablespoons light brown sugar
½ teaspoon dried oregano leaves
¼ teaspoon dried marjoram leaves
¼ teaspoon dried thyme leaves
½ teaspoon salt
⅛ teaspoon pepper

Microwave Italian sausage in 3-quart glass casserole, uncovered, at High until meat loses pink color, 5 to 6 minutes, stirring after 3 minutes; drain well. Process (Steel Knife) pepperoni using on/off technique until finely chopped; remove. Process (Steel Knife) green pepper using on/off technique until chopped. Add tomatoes to bowl; process using on/off technique until chopped. Stir pepperoni, tomato mixture, and remaining ingredients into Italian sausage; microwave loosely covered with waxed paper at High until sauce is slightly thickened, about 8 minutes, stirring after 4 minutes.

Tips: Microwave manicotti according to first paragraph of Chicken Lasagna (previous recipe) or cook conventionally.

Cheese mixture can be made 1 day in advance; refrigerate covered. Meat Sauce can be made and refrigerated covered 2 days in advance, or frozen in a covered container up to 1 month.

Ratatouille
Braised Kale
Cauliflower with Avocado and Almonds
Stir-Fried Broccoli and Walnuts
French-Style Vegetable Puree
Corn Soufflé
Onion-Apple Bake
Shredded Carrot Casserole
Green Beans and Tomatoes
Zucchini-Potato Pancake
Potatoes Gratin
Sweet Potato Pudding
Baked Sweet Potatoes with Seasoned Butter
Spaghetti Squash with Parmesan-Garlic Butter
Stuffed Acorn Squash
Tomato Timbales

10 Vegetables

RATATOUILLE

A versatile French classic. Serve it hot or at
room temperature with beef, lamb, chicken, or
sliced sausages. Or chill it and arrange
portions on lettuce leaves as a first course.

Total Preparation Time: 35 to 40 minutes
Microwave Time: 20 to 25 minutes
Yield: 6 servings

---

1 small eggplant, pared, cut to fit feed tube
1 medium green pepper, seeded, cut to fit
   feed tube
12 pitted ripe olives
2 cloves garlic, peeled
2 small onions, peeled, cut into quarters
1 can (16 ounces) Italian-style plum
   tomatoes, undrained, cut into quarters
2 tablespoons olive or vegetable oil
¼ cup red wine vinegar
2 tablespoons light brown sugar
2 tablespoons tomato paste
1 tablespoon drained capers
¼ teaspoon dried basil leaves
⅛ teaspoon dried tarragon leaves
⅛ teaspoon dried oregano leaves
¼ teaspoon salt
⅛ teaspoon pepper
⅓ cup pine nuts or slivered almonds

Slice (Slicing Disc) eggplant, green pepper,
and olives; remove. With machine running
(Steel Knife), drop garlic through feed tube,
processing until minced. Add onions to bowl;
process using on/off technique until coarsely
chopped; remove. Process (Steel Knife)
tomatoes and liquid using on/off technique until
coarsely chopped. Microwave onion mixture,
eggplant, green pepper, olives, tomatoes, and
oil in 2-quart glass casserole, covered, at High
until eggplant is tender, 12 to 15 minutes,
stirring every 5 minutes. Stir in remaining
ingredients except nuts; microwave covered at
50% (Medium) 8 to 10 minutes. Stir in nuts.

*Tip: When full-flavored tomatoes are available,
   substitute 2 large, fresh tomatoes, cored
   and cut into 1-inch pieces, for the canned
   tomatoes. Substitute fresh herbs, using*

*twice the amounts of dried or more,
according to taste; chop them with the
onions.*

BRAISED KALE

The appearance of kale in the market is one
of the first, and best, signs of spring. The
ruffled leaves have both a wonderful flavor and
extremely high vitamin A content.

Total Preparation Time: 28 to 29 minutes
Microwave Time: 17 to 18 minutes
Yield: 4 servings

---

4 slices bacon
1 medium leek or 6 green onions and tops,
   cleaned, cut to fit feed tube
1 pound kale, stems removed
½ cup water
1 teaspoon chicken-flavor instant bouillon
⅓ cup sour cream or sour half-and-half
1 teaspoon Dijon-style mustard
⅛ teaspoon pepper

Microwave bacon in 2-quart glass casserole,
uncovered, at High until crisp, about 4
minutes. Drain bacon and crumble; reserve
drippings.
Slice (Slicing Disc) leek; microwave in bacon
drippings in casserole, covered, at High until
tender, 3 to 4 minutes, stirring after 2 minutes.
Slice (Slicing Disc) kale. Stir kale, water, and
bouillon into casserole. Microwave covered at
High until kale is tender, about 10 minutes,
stirring after 5 minutes. Drain well. Stir in
sour cream, mustard, and pepper; sprinkle
with bacon.

*Tips: To slice kale, stack the leaves neatly, roll
   up, and insert the roll vertically in the
   food processor feed tube, through the
   bottom of the tube if necessary. Slice with
   light pressure.*

*   Use this recipe to enjoy the taste and
   nutrition benefits of all the deep-green,*

leafy vegetables, such as collards and turnip greens, that usually require long simmering on top of the stove. You can also substitute spinach; because it is much more tender than kale, spinach will require only about 5 minutes of microwave cooking.

CAULIFLOWER WITH AVOCADO AND ALMONDS

If you like guacamole, this will become your favorite way to serve cauliflower. The whole cauliflower, draped with lime-piqued avocado sauce, is both handsome and delicious.

Total Preparation Time: 20 to 22 minutes
Microwave Time: 9 to 11 minutes
Yield: 6 servings

2 tablespoons blanched almonds
½ head iceberg lettuce, cut into wedges to fit feed tube
1 green onion and top, cut into 1-inch pieces
1 medium avocado, peeled, pitted, cut into 1-inch pieces
1 tablespoon lime juice
¼ teaspoon ground nutmeg
1 medium head cauliflower, core removed
½ cup chicken broth
1 tablespoon pimiento pieces

Process (Steel Knife) almonds until coarsely chopped. Microwave almonds in glass pie plate, uncovered, at High until toasted, about 2 minutes, stirring after 1 minute.

Slice (Slicing Disc) lettuce; arrange in layer on serving plate and refrigerate. Process (Steel Knife) onion using on/off technique until finely chopped; add avocado, lime juice, and nutmeg to bowl, and process using on/off technique until almost smooth. Refrigerate.

Microwave cauliflower and broth in glass pie plate, covered with plastic wrap, at High until crisp-tender, 7 to 9 minutes, rotating casserole ¼ turn after 4 minutes.

Serve cauliflower warm or refrigerate and serve cold. Place cauliflower on lettuce on serving plate; spoon avocado mixture over cauliflower. Sprinkle with almonds; garnish with pimiento.

STIR-FRIED BROCCOLI AND WALNUTS

Food processor slicing turns broccoli stalks into slim, attractive disks, and quick cooking protects crisp-tender texture. It's a good way to preserve the high vitamin C content of broccoli, which can be destroyed by prolonged heat.

Total Preparation Time: 19 to 22 minutes
Microwave Time: 9 to 12 minutes
Yield: 4 servings

½ cup walnuts
1 small onion, peeled, cut into quarters
12 ounces fresh broccoli, cut to fit feed tube
1 tablespoon olive or vegetable oil
¼ cup chicken broth
2 teaspoons soy sauce
1 teaspoon sugar

Process (Steel Knife) walnuts using on/off technique until coarsely chopped. Microwave in glass pie plate uncovered at High until toasted, 2 to 3 minutes, stirring every minute.

Process (Steel Knife) onion using on/off technique until chopped; remove. Slice (Slicing Disc) broccoli. Microwave oil in 1-quart glass casserole, uncovered, until hot, 1 minute. Stir in onion; microwave uncovered at High until tender, 2 to 3 minutes. Stir in broccoli, chicken broth, soy sauce, and sugar. Microwave covered at High until broccoli is crisp-tender, 4 to 5 minutes. Sprinkle with walnuts.

Tip: Substitute asparagus for the broccoli, if you wish. With either broccoli or asparagus, you can cut off and reserve small flowerets or tips prior to slicing and microwave them with the sliced vegetable as above.

FRENCH–STYLE VEGETABLE PUREE

·Update a refined French accompaniment for roast meats. The shredded potato thickener for pureed peas is classic, but microwave cooking allows you to achieve optimum consistency without the hours of stove-top simmering that used to be required.

Total Preparation·Time: 44 to 52 minutes
Microwave Time: 28 to 34 minutes
Yield: 4 servings

---

2 small Idaho potatoes (about 12 ounces)
2 packages (10 ounces each) frozen peas
¼ to ⅓ cup whipping cream
¼ cup butter or margarine, softened
Salt
Pepper
Freshly ground nutmeg

Pierce potatoes in several places with fork. Microwave on paper toweling at High until tender, 6 to 7 minutes; wrap in aluminum foil and let stand 5 minutes. Peel potatoes. Shred (Shredding Disc) potatoes; spoon into 1½-quart casserole.

Remove wrappers and make 1 or 2 slashes in each box of peas; microwave in boxes at High until tender, 10 to 12 minutes. Process (Steel Knife) until smooth; stir into potato. Microwave uncovered at High until very thick, 10 to 12 minutes, stirring every 2 minutes. Stir in cream, 1 tablespoon at a time; stir in butter, 1 tablespoon at a time, until incorporated. Season to taste with salt, pepper, and nutmeg. Microwave covered at High until hot through, about 2 to 4 minutes.

Tips: French-Style Vegetable Puree can be made with various fresh or frozen vegetables, including carrots, broccoli, asparagus, and winter squash. Substitute 1½ pounds fresh vegetable for the frozen peas; slice (Slicing Disc) vegetable or cut into 1-inch pieces. Microwave fresh vegetables with 2 tablespoons water in 1½-quart glass casserole, covered, at High until vegetables are tender, 10 to 12 minutes. Proceed with recipe as above. Substitute 2 packages (10 ounces each) frozen vegetable for the peas; cook as above.

Remove paper wrapping from boxes of frozen vegetables to prevent the printing ink from staining the bottom of the oven.

CORN SOUFFLÉ

Because all ingredients can be kept on hand, this is a good recipe to remember for winter suppers and unexpected guests.

Total Preparation Time: 40 to 46 minutes
Microwave Time: 28 to 34 minutes
Yield: 6 to 8 servings

¼ cup Twice-As-Fast Sauce Mix (see Index)
1 teaspoon chicken-flavor instant bouillon
½ teaspoon dried savory leaves
¼ teaspoon dried marjoram leaves
¹⁄₁₆ teaspoon white pepper
1¼ cups milk
4 ounces Cheddar cheese, chilled, cut to fit feed tube
1 can (12 ounces) whole-kernel corn, drained
6 egg yolks
6 egg whites
2 tablespoons sugar
1 tablespoon flour
2 tablespoons water
1 teaspoon lemon juice

Microwave sauce mix in 1½-quart glass casserole at High, uncovered, 2 minutes, stirring after 1 minute. Stir in bouillon, savory, marjoram, and pepper; stir in milk. Microwave uncovered at High until sauce boils and thickens, 3 to 4 minutes, stirring with whisk every minute.

Shred (Shredding Disc) cheese. Stir cheese into sauce mixture; microwave covered at High just to boiling, about 3 minutes, stirring after 2 minutes. Process (Steel Knife) half the corn using on/off technique until minced. Add egg yolks to bowl; process using on/off technique until blended. Stir corn mixture and remaining corn into sauce mixture.

Insert Steel Knife in clean processor bowl. Add egg whites, sugar, and flour; with machine running, pour combined water and lemon juice through feed tube. Process until egg whites are stiff, about 2 minutes. Fold egg whites into corn mixture. Pour mixture into ungreased 2-quart glass soufflé dish. Microwave uncovered at 50% (Medium) until center is almost set, 20 to 25 minutes, rotating soufflé dish ¼ turn every 5 minutes. Serve immediately.

Tip: In a rare exception to the no-wash Twice As Fast rule, you will need to wash and dry the food processor workbowl before processing the egg whites in this recipe.

ONION–APPLE BAKE

Serendipity for a menu of pork or poultry, and a revitalizing relish for leftover turkey or ham.

Total Preparation Time: 20 to 23 minutes
Microwave Time: 10 to 13 minutes
Yield: 6 to 8 servings

---

3 tablespoons butter or margarine
⅓ cup packed light brown sugar
¼ teaspoon dry mustard
¼ teaspoon chicken-flavor instant bouillon
⅛ teaspoon ground mace
1 pound yellow onions, peeled, cut to fit feed tube
3 medium apples, pared, cored, cut into halves

Microwave butter in 2-quart glass casserole at High until melted; stir in sugar, mustard, bouillon, and mace.

Slice (Slicing Disc) onions and apples; add to casserole, stirring to coat with butter mixture. Microwave covered at High until tender, 8 to 10 minutes, stirring every 4 minutes.

SHREDDED CARROT CASSEROLE

A festive, pudding-like dish—especially welcome at holiday tables and when winter produce markets make carrots the best fresh vegetable choice.

Total Preparation Time: 45 to 50 minutes
Microwave Time: 36 to 41 minutes
Yield: 4 to 6 servings

---

1 cup blanched almonds
1 pound carrots, pared, cut to fit feed tube
2 cups milk
1 cup whipping cream or half-and-half
⅔ cup golden raisins
¼ cup packed light brown sugar
½ stick cinnamon
2 cloves
2 to 4 tablespoons plain yogurt

Process (Steel Knife) almonds using on/off technique until coarsely chopped; remove. Shred (Shredding Disc) carrots. Combine carrots, half the almonds, and the remaining ingredients except yogurt in 2-quart glass casserole. Microwave covered at High 6 minutes. Microwave uncovered until carrots have absorbed almost all the liquid, 30 to 35 minutes, stirring every 10 minutes. Remove cinnamon stick. Stir in yogurt; top with remaining almonds.

GREEN BEANS AND TOMATOES

An irresistible adaptation of a Greek specialty—green beans braised just to tenderness with fresh tomatoes, garlic, and herbs.

Total Preparation Time: 40 to 42 minutes
Microwave Time: 30 to 32 minutes
Yield: 4 servings

Fresh Tomato Sauce (see Index)
1 clove garlic, peeled
¾ pound green beans, trimmed
½ teaspoon dried basil leaves
⅛ teaspoon dried oregano leaves

Make Fresh Tomato Sauce, adding 1 additional clove garlic and using 1½-quart glass casserole. Stir beans, basil, and oregano into sauce; microwave covered at High until beans are tender, about 10 minutes, stirring after 5 minutes.

Tips: Green beans vary greatly in texture according to age and size. Very small green beans may require less cooking time; check for doneness when you stir them. If beans are thick and not very fresh, you may want to French-cut them prior to cooking; if so, place beans horizontally in the feed tube and slice (Slicing Disc).

Zucchini can be substituted for the green beans. Cut ¾ pound zucchini to fit feed tube and slice; microwave at High as above until tender, about 5 minutes.

ZUCCHINI–POTATO PANCAKE

This delightful treat fits all kinds of menus, for it can accompany anything from scrambled eggs to delicately sauced chicken.

Total Preparation Time: 28 to 31 minutes
Microwave Time: 6½ to 7 minutes
Yield: 4 servings

½ slice day-old bread, torn into pieces
1 ounce Parmesan cheese, cut into 1-inch pieces
1 medium zucchini, cut to fit feed tube
1 medium potato, pared, cut to fit feed tube
1 clove garlic, peeled
½ medium onion, peeled, cut into 1-inch pieces
1 egg
1 tablespoon mayonnaise or salad dressing
¼ teaspoon dried marjoram leaves

⅛ teaspoon dried dillweed
¼ teaspoon salt
1/16 teaspoon white pepper
Paprika

Process (Steel Knife) bread to form fine crumbs; reserve. With machine running (Steel Knife), drop cheese through feed tube; process until finely ground and reserve. Shred (Shredding Disc) zucchini; reserve. Shred potato; soak potato in ice water to cover for 15 minutes. Drain; pat dry between layers of paper toweling. Microwave potato in lightly greased 9″ glass pie plate, covered with plastic wrap, at High 2 minutes.

With machine running (Steel Knife), drop garlic through feed tube, processing until minced. Add onion to bowl; process using on/off technique until finely chopped. Stir onion mixture, zucchini, bread crumbs, egg, mayonnaise, marjoram, dillweed, salt, and pepper into potato in pie plate. Pat mixture evenly on bottom and one-third up side of pie plate. Microwave covered with plastic wrap at High 2½ minutes. Sprinkle with reserved cheese; microwave uncovered at High 2 minutes, or until cheese is melted. Sprinkle with paprika. Slide onto serving plate; cut into wedges to serve.

Tip: The shredded potato must be soaked to remove excess starch.

POTATOES GRATIN

When you're looking for a fast, flavorful potato casserole, this recipe is the answer!

Total Preparation Time: 22 to 24 minutes
Microwave Time: 16 to 20 minutes
Yield: 6 servings

1¼ pounds potatoes (about 4 medium), pared, cut to fit feed tube
2 tablespoons water
2 ounces Cheddar cheese, chilled, cut to fit feed tube

1 small onion, peeled, cut into quarters
1 small rib celery, cut into 1-inch pieces
3 tablespoons Twice-As-Fast Sauce Mix
1 cup half-and-half or milk
½ cup sour cream
1 tablespoon dried chives
Salt
Pepper
Paprika

Slice (Slicing Disc) potatoes; microwave with water in 1½-quart glass casserole, covered, at High until tender, 4 to 5 minutes, rotating casserole ¼ turn after 2 minutes. Drain any excess liquid.

Shred (Shredding Disc) cheese; remove. Process (Steel Knife) onion and celery, using on/off technique, until finely chopped. Microwave sauce mix in 4-cup glass measure at High, uncovered, 2 minutes, stirring after 1 minute. Stir in onion, celery, and half-and-half; microwave at High, uncovered, until sauce boils and thickens, about 3 minutes, stirring with whisk every minute. Stir in cheese until melted; stir in sour cream and chives. Season to taste with salt and pepper.

Stir sauce mixture into potatoes. Microwave uncovered at 70% (Medium High) until hot through, 7 to 9 minutes. Sprinkle with paprika.

SWEET POTATO PUDDING

Shredded sweet potatoes lighten this version of an all-American tradition. Use firm pressure on the food processor pusher to shred raw potatoes most efficiently.

Total Preparation Time: 22 to 24 minutes
Microwave Time: 12 to 14 minutes
Yield: 6 servings

½ cup pecans
1 pound sweet potatoes, pared, cut to fit
   feed tube
¼ cup packed light brown sugar

2 tablespoons flour
2 tablespoons granulated sugar
¼ cup milk
1 tablespoon orange-flavored liqueur
Grated rind of 1 orange
⅛ teaspoon ground mace
Dash ground allspice
2 tablespoons butter or margarine
2 tablespoons light brown sugar

Process (Steel Knife) pecans using on/off technique until finely chopped; remove. Shred (Shredding Disc) sweet potatoes. Combine potatoes, ¼ cup brown sugar, the flour, granulated sugar, milk, liqueur, orange rind, mace, and allspice in a greased 1-quart glass casserole. Dot with butter; sprinkle with 2 tablespoons brown sugar and the pecans. Microwave covered at High until potatoes are set, about 12 minutes, rotating dish ¼ turn every 4 minutes.

BAKED SWEET POTATOES WITH SEASONED BUTTER

When Columbus arrived in America, he discovered sweet potatoes, among other things. But he could not have realized what a treasury of vitamin A he had found! Accord this economical root vegetable regal treatment with fruit-seasoned butters.

Total Preparation Time: 9 to 11 minutes
Microwave Time: 7 to 9 minutes
Yield: 4 servings

4 medium sweet potatoes
Strawberry or Chutney Butter (see Index)

Pierce potatoes with fork. Microwave on paper toweling at High until tender, 7 to 9 minutes. Make desired butter. Pierce tops of potatoes and press to open; spoon butter in potatoes.

SPAGHETTI SQUASH WITH PARMESAN–GARLIC BUTTER

A marvelous trick played on pasta—
"spaghetti" harvested from the garden and
tossed with a light, Italian-style sauce. The
squash microwaves beautifully, yielding fluffy
strands of pulp when cut open.

Total Preparation Time: 19 to 23 minutes
Microwave Time: 15 to 18 minutes
Yield: 6 to 8 servings

---

1 large spaghetti squash (about 3½ pounds)
Parmesan-Garlic Butter (see Index)

Pierce squash in several places with fork.
Microwave on paper toweling at High until
skin yields to gentle pressure, 15 to 18 minutes,
turning squash over after 6 minutes.

Make Parmesan-Garlic Butter. Cut squash
lengthwise into halves; scoop out seeds and
discard. Fluff strands of squash with fork.
Spoon butter over; toss until melted. Serve
from squash halves.

STUFFED ACORN SQUASH

A naturally sweet and tart filling of apple
and prunes for golden winter squash.
Purchased sausage turns it into a delectable
entrée, but Homemade Sausage (see Index)
turns it into a feast!

Total Preparation Time: 27 to 28 minutes
Microwave Time: 18 to 19 minutes
Yield: 8 servings

---

2 medium acorn squash
½ cup pitted prunes
⅓ cup water
⅔ cup walnuts
¼ cup packed light brown sugar
¼ teaspoon ground cinnamon

⅛ teaspoon ground nutmeg
1 medium green apple, pared, cored, cut into 1-inch pieces
3 tablespoons butter or margarine

Pierce squash several times with fork; place
in microwave oven. Microwave uncovered at
High 5 minutes. Cut squash into quarters;
scoop out seeds and discard. Place squash, cut
sides up, in glass baking dish. Microwave
covered with plastic wrap at High just until
tender, about 5 minutes. Let stand loosely
covered with aluminum foil.

Microwave prunes and water in 1-quart glass
casserole, uncovered, at High 3 minutes; drain
well. Process (Steel Knife) walnuts, sugar,
cinnamon, and nutmeg using on/off technique
until coarsely chopped; add prunes and apple
to bowl. Process using on/off technique until
apple is coarsely chopped. Spoon mixture onto
squash quarters. Microwave butter in glass
custard cup at High until melted; drizzle over
squash. Microwave loosely covered at High
until hot through, 3 to 4 minutes.

*Tip: To add sausage to Stuffed Acorn Squash,
cut squash into halves instead of quarters
and microwave as above. Microwave 8
ounces bulk sausage in 1-quart glass
casserole, covered, at High until pink color
disappears, about 3 minutes. Drain well;
mix sausage into chopped prune mixture.
Fill sausage halves with prune mixture;
microwave as above. Makes 4 servings.*

TOMATO TIMBALES

In French cuisine, a timbale is a savory
custard baked in a small, drum-shaped mold.
This rosy version meets the classic standard of
delicacy but does not require the usual, slow
water-bath baking, since microwaves cook with
remarkable evenness and without dry heat.
The result is an impressive first course or an
exquisite vegetable accent for roast meats,
steaks, chops, or poultry.

Total Preparation Time: 39 to 43 minutes
Microwave Time: 29 to 33 minutes
Yield: 6 servings

Fresh Tomato Sauce (see Index)
**1 ounce Parmesan cheese, cut into 1-inch
  pieces**
**3 tablespoons Twice-As-Fast Sauce Mix (see
  Index)**
½ cup milk
2 eggs, beaten
Watercress or parsley sprigs

Make Fresh Tomato Sauce.

Process (Steel Knife) cheese until finely grated. Microwave sauce mix in 4-cup glass measure, uncovered, at High 2 minutes, stirring with whisk every minute. Stir in milk; microwave uncovered at High until mixture boils and thickens, 2 to 3 minutes, stirring every minute (mixture will be extremely thick).

Stir Fresh Tomato Sauce into sauce mix; stir in eggs and grated cheese. Spoon mixture into 6 ungreased 6-ounce glass custard cups. Arrange cups in circle in oven. Microwave uncovered at High until set, 5 to 7 minutes, rotating cups ¼ turn after 3 minutes. Let stand 5 minutes.

Loosen edges of cups with knife; unmold onto serving plate. Garnish each with sprig of watercress.

Tips: For a dramatic entrée presentation, unmold individual timbales onto large dinner plates after you have arranged the meat portions; then spoon a serving of steamed green vegetables onto the plate for maximum color contrast.

To serve timbales as a first course, unmold them onto salad-size plates, garnish with watercress, and spoon Butter Sauce (see Index) around, not over, each serving.

Wilted Greens Salad
Hot and Cold Roquefort Salad
Asparagus and Cucumber Arcs Vinaigrette
Layered Vegetable Salad with Garlic Dressing
Artichokes with Vegetables Vinaigrette
Zucchini Salad with Pineapple Dressing
Bean Salad with Anise Vinaigrette
Double-Dressed Chicken Salad
Creamiest Potato Salad
Salade Niçoise
Molded Vegetable Salad
Spiced Fruit Salad
Fruit Salad with Pineapple-Cream Dressing

11 Salads

WILTED GREENS SALAD

Assorted greens, olives, and water chestnuts refresh an easy variation of spinach salad with hot bacon dressing.

Total Preparation Time: 17 to 20 minutes
Microwave Time: 7 to 10 minutes
Yield: 4 to 6 servings

4 ounces romaine
3 ounces fresh spinach, stems discarded
3 ounces iceberg lettuce, cut into wedges to fit feed tube
1 small onion, peeled, cut to fit feed tube
4 ounces mushrooms
½ cup pitted ripe olives
1 can (6 ounces) water chestnuts, drained
¼ pound bacon
3 tablespoons sugar
¼ cup catsup
¼ cup cider vinegar
2 tablespoons water
1 teaspoon Worcestershire sauce
½ teaspoon dry mustard
1 teaspoon salt
⅛ teaspoon pepper

Slice (Slicing Disc) greens, onion, mushrooms, olives, and water chestnuts.

Microwave bacon in 2½-quart glass casserole, uncovered, at High until crisp, about 5 minutes, rotating casserole ¼ turn after 2½ minutes. Remove bacon and crumble. Stir sugar and remaining ingredients into bacon drippings; microwave uncovered at High until boiling, about 2 minutes; add sliced greens and vegetables to casserole and toss. Sprinkle with bacon. Serve immediately.

Tips: To slice romaine and spinach in the food processor, arrange leaves in a neat stack, roll up and insert the roll vertically in the feed tube, inserting through the bottom if necessary; slice with light pressure on the pusher. Outer leaves of iceberg lettuce can be sliced the same way, or you can cut the lettuce into wedges to fit the feed tube and slice as you would cabbage. For

maximum convenience, leave the sliced greens and other vegetables in the food processor bowl until the dressing has been made; then add the greens to the casserole and toss.

HOT AND COLD ROQUEFORT SALAD

The contrast between the melting, tangy dressing and cool, crisp lettuce makes this salad memorable.

Total Preparation Time: 7 to 10 minutes
Microwave Time: 2 to 3 minutes
Yield: 6 servings

2 ounces Parmesan cheese, cut into 1-inch pieces
½ green onion and top, cut into 1-inch pieces
1 cup Food Processor Mayonnaise (see Index)
¼ teaspoon prepared horseradish
¼ teaspoon dried basil leaves
3 ounces Roquefort or bleu cheese
6 wedges iceberg lettuce (½ inch thick), well chilled
Paprika

With machine running (Steel Knife), drop Parmesan cheese through feed tube, processing until finely grated. Add onion to bowl; process using on/off technique until finely chopped.

Make Food Processor Mayonnaise; add Parmesan cheese mixture, horseradish, and basil to bowl; process until smooth. Add Roquefort cheese; process using on/off technique just until blended.

Microwave mayonnaise mixture in 2-cup glass measure, covered, at 50% (Medium) just until hot, about 2 minutes, stirring after 1 minute (do not overcook, as mixture will separate). Spread mixture over lettuce wedges; sprinkle with paprika. Serve immediately.

Tip: Mayonnaise mixture may be prepared 1 day in advance; refrigerate covered and heat just before serving.

Tip: To seed cucumber, cut it lengthwise into halves. Cut around center with a paring knife and remove seeds in a strip, or scoop out seeds with a spoon.

ASPARAGUS AND CUCUMBER ARCS VINAIGRETTE

A superb marinated salad for a picnic or patio brunch. The dressing makes it a good match for all Oriental-style menus, too.

Total Preparation Time: 16 to 18 minutes (plus chilling time)
Microwave Time: 7 to 9 minutes
Yield: 4 to 6 servings

---

1 tablespoon sesame seeds
8 ounces fresh asparagus
1 medium cucumber, pared, seeded, cut to fit feed tube
½ medium onion, peeled, cut to fit feed tube
¼ cup water
¼ cup cider vinegar
2 tablespoons teriyaki sauce
1 tablespoon vegetable oil
2 tablespoons sugar
¼ teaspoon dry mustard
¹⁄₁₆ teaspoon ground ginger

Spread sesame seeds on bottom of glass pie plate; microwave uncovered at High until golden, 2 to 3 minutes, stirring every minute. Cut tips off asparagus and reserve; cut stalks to fit feed tube. Slice (Slicing Disc) asparagus stalks, cucumber, and onion separately. Microwave asparagus stalks, reserved tips, and water in 1-quart glass casserole, covered, at High until asparagus is crisp-tender, 4 to 5 minutes. Rinse with cold water and drain.

Add cucumber and onion to casserole. Microwave vinegar and remaining ingredients in 1-cup glass measure, uncovered, at High 1 minute. Stir with whisk; pour over vegetables and toss. Refrigerate covered at least 1 hour for flavors to blend. Sprinkle with sesame seeds before serving.

LAYERED VEGETABLE SALAD WITH GARLIC DRESSING

This extremely attractive salad benefits from overnight refrigeration. Add a layer or two of sliced or chopped ham, turkey, or roast beef and you'll have a completely do-ahead entrée.

Total Preparation Time: 25 to 28 minutes (plus overnight refrigeration)
Microwave Time: 11 to 14 minutes
Yield: 8 servings

Garlic Dressing (recipe follows)
1 small head cauliflower, cut into flowerets
¼ cup water
6 ounces fresh snow peas
4 sprigs parsley
4 ounces mushrooms
6 ounces fresh spinach, stems discarded
1 small red onion, cut into halves
2 large carrots, pared, cut to fit feed tube
6 ounces fresh bean sprouts, rinsed, well drained

Make Garlic Dressing.

Microwave cauliflower and water in 1½-quart glass casserole, covered, at High until cauliflower is crisp-tender, 6 to 8 minutes. Add snow peas to casserole for last 3 minutes of cooking time. Rinse vegetables with cold water; drain well.

Process (Steel Knife) parsley using on/off technique until minced; remove. Slice (Slicing Disc) mushrooms, spinach, and onion separately. Shred (Shredding Disc) carrots. Layer vegetables in a salad bowl. Spread Garlic Dressing over top; sprinkle with parsley. Refrigerate loosely covered overnight. Toss before serving.

Garlic Dressing

¼ cup all-purpose flour
2 tablespoons sugar
¾ teaspoon dry mustard
½ teaspoon salt
Pinch cayenne pepper
¾ cup water
2 egg yolks
¼ cup white wine vinegar
1 small clove garlic
1-inch piece onion
2 tablespoons vegetable oil
½ cup sour cream
1 teaspoon prepared horseradish

Combine flour, sugar, mustard, salt, and cayenne pepper in 4-cup glass measure; stir in water. Mix egg yolks and vinegar; stir into flour mixture. Microwave uncovered at 50% (Medium) until thickened, 5 to 6 minutes, stirring with whisk every 2 minutes.

With machine running (Steel Knife), drop garlic and onion through feed tube, processing until minced. Add cooked dressing to bowl; with machine running, add oil through feed tube, 1 tablespoon at a time. Add sour cream and horseradish to bowl; process using on/off technique until blended. Refrigerate covered until ready to use. Makes about 1¾ cups.

Tips: Vegetables can be layered any way you wish. But do place at least some of the snow peas or carrots on top to provide color contrast for the pale dressing.

With the addition of 1 pound of sliced or cubed cooked meat or poultry, the salad will yield 4 to 6 entrée servings.

ARTICHOKES WITH VEGETABLES VINAIGRETTE

A versatile combination, fancy enough for a dinner party first course, yet perfectly convenient for a picnic.

Total Preparation Time: 35 to 40 minutes (plus chilling time)
Microwave Time: 12 to 14 minutes
Yield: 4 servings

¼ cup red wine vinegar
¼ cup water
2 tablespoons lemon juice
2 tablespoons sugar
1 tablespoon dried chives
¼ teaspoon crumbled dried bay leaves
¼ teaspoon salt
⅛ teaspoon pepper
4 ounces mushrooms
1 small red or green pepper, seeded, cut to fit feed tube
1 small zucchini, cut to fit feed tube
1 rib celery, cut to fit feed tube
6 pitted ripe olives
2 medium artichokes, cut lengthwise into halves
4 teaspoons lemon juice
½ cup water

Microwave vinegar, ¼ cup water, 2 tablespoons lemon juice, the sugar, chives, bay leaves, salt, and ground pepper in 2-cup glass measure at High for 2 minutes, or until boiling. Let stand until room temperature.

Slice (Slicing Disc) mushrooms, red pepper, zucchini, celery, and olives; arrange in bowl and pour vinegar mixture over. Refrigerate covered at least 1 hour for flavors to blend.

Sprinkle cut edges of artichokes with 4 teaspoons lemon juice; arrange, cut sides up, in glass baking dish. Add ½ cup water; microwave covered with plastic wrap at High until tender, 10 to 12 minutes, rotating dish ¼ turn every 4 minutes. Cool artichokes until warm; remove chokes with spoon. Cool to room temperature; refrigerate until serving time. Spoon vegetable mixture into artichoke halves.

Tips: Artichokes with Vegetables Vinaigrette can be served hot as a first course or side dish. Remove chokes from artichokes before cooking; microwave as above. Microwave vegetables in vinegar mixture uncovered at 70% (Medium High) until hot through, about 3 minutes; spoon into hot artichoke halves.

To prepare fresh artichokes for cooking, cut off stems, remove tough bottom leaves and trim leaf tips with kitchen shears or a paring knife.

Tips: Muenster or brick cheese can be substituted for the Swiss.

Dressing may be prepared hours in advance and allowed to stand covered at room temperature. But do not toss with vegetables until ready to serve.

ZUCCHINI SALAD WITH PINEAPPLE DRESSING

Use whatever salad greens look best in the market to make this a year-round salad. It goes well with meat loaf, lamb, or broiled chicken.

Total Preparation Time: 18 to 19 minutes
Microwave Time: 3 to 4 minutes
Yield: 8 servings

½ cup pineapple preserves
¼ cup tarragon vinegar
¼ cup vegetable oil
¼ teaspoon dried mint leaves
4 ounces Swiss cheese, chilled, cut to fit feed tube
2 medium zucchini, cut to fit feed tube
1 small red onion, peeled, cut to fit feed tube
2 tablespoons water
6 cups assorted salad greens, cut into bite-size pieces

Microwave preserves, vinegar, oil, and mint leaves in 2-cup glass measure uncovered at 50% (Medium) until preserves are melted and mixture just comes to a boil, about 1 minute. Stir; let stand until room temperature.

Shred (Shredding Disc) cheese; reserve. Slice (Slicing Disc) zucchini and onion separately. Microwave zucchini and water in 1-quart glass casserole, covered, at High 2 minutes. Drain; cool to room temperature.

Combine greens, reserved cheese, zucchini, and onion in salad bowl; pour dressing over and toss.

BEAN SALAD WITH ANISE VINAIGRETTE

Economical and nutritious three-bean salad refashioned with sweet red onion and a hint of anise.

Total Preparation Time: 19 to 23 minutes (plus chilling time)
Microwave Time: 10 to 13 minutes
Yield: 10 to 12 servings

1 package (10 ounces) frozen baby lima beans
12 ounces fresh green beans, ends trimmed
2 tablespoons water
1 large red onion, cut to fit feed tube
1 can (15½ ounces) kidney beans, drained
⅔ cup distilled white vinegar
⅔ cup vegetable oil
¼ teaspoon anise seed, crushed
1 teaspoon sugar
½ teaspoon Dijon-style mustard
1 teaspoon salt
1/16 teaspoon pepper

Remove wrapper and make 1 or 2 slashes in box of lima beans; microwave in box at High until beans are tender, 4 to 5 minutes. Slice (Slicing Disc) green beans, arranging beans horizontally in feed tube. Microwave green beans and water in 2-quart glass casserole, covered, at High until beans are crisp-tender, 4 to 6 minutes; drain. Slice (Slicing Disc) onion; stir lima beans, onion, and kidney beans into green beans. Microwave remaining ingredients in 2-cup glass measure, uncovered, at High until hot, about 2 minutes; pour over bean mixture and toss. Cool to room temperature; refrigerate until chilled, about 4 hours.

DOUBLE-DRESSED CHICKEN SALAD

The food processor and microwave oven make it easy to assemble the most important elements of a great chicken salad—moist chicken and a delicate mayonnaise.

Total Preparation Time: 22 to 25 minutes (plus chilling time)
Microwave Time: 9 to 11 minutes
Yield: 4 to 6 servings

---

1 pound boneless chicken breast halves, skinned
½ cup water
½ teaspoon chicken-flavor instant bouillon
½ cup pecans
1 can (6 ounces) water chestnuts, drained
2 sprigs parsley
2 tablespoons cider vinegar
¼ teaspoon salt
⅛ teaspoon pepper
⅓ cup vegetable oil
¼ cup Cucumber Mayonnaise (see Index)
¼ cup sour cream
1 teaspoon dried dillweed
½ teaspoon spicy brown mustard
2 hard-cooked eggs, peeled, cut into quarters

Microwave chicken, water, and bouillon in 1½-quart glass casserole, covered, at High until chicken is done and juices run clear when chicken is pierced with a fork, about 7 minutes; turn chicken over after 4 minutes and rotate casserole ¼ turn. Let chicken cool until warm; cut into 1-inch pieces.

Microwave pecans in glass pie plate, uncovered, at High 2 to 3 minutes until toasted, stirring every minute. Slice (Slicing Disc) water chestnuts; remove. Process (Steel Knife) pecans until finely chopped; process chicken until coarsely chopped. Combine water chestnuts, pecans, and chicken in medium bowl. Process (Steel Knife) parsley using on/off technique until minced; add vinegar, salt, and pepper to bowl. With machine running (Steel Knife), add oil through feed tube. Pour dressing over chicken mixture and toss. Refrigerate covered 1 hour for flavors to blend.

Make Cucumber Mayonnaise; stir in sour cream, dillweed, and mustard; spoon over chicken mixture and toss. Spoon into serving bowl; garnish with hard-cooked egg.

Tips: Because this is a fine-textured chicken salad, it makes an excellent appetizer or sandwich spread.

Chicken and mayonnaise mixtures can be prepared 1 day in advance; refrigerate separately, covered, and combine just before serving.

Serve Double-Dressed Chicken Salad with Garlic-Herb Toast (see Index), if you wish. For change-of-pace sandwiches, spread the salad in pita bread halves.

CREAMIEST POTATO SALAD

Shredded cheese makes potato salad creamier than ever, and microwave cooking ensures perfect potato texture.

Total Preparation Time: 19 to 20 minutes (plus chilling time)
Microwave Time: 9 to 10 minutes
Yield: 6 servings

---

1 pound potatoes, pared, cut to fit feed tube
¼ cup water
4 ounces brick cheese, chilled, cut to fit feed tube
2 ounces Cheddar cheese, chilled, cut to fit feed tube
1 green pepper, seeded, cut into 1-inch pieces
1 small onion, peeled, cut into 1-inch pieces
⅓ cup mayonnaise or salad dressing
⅓ cup sour cream
1½ teaspoons spicy brown mustard
½ teaspoon salt
⅛ teaspoon white pepper
4 slices bacon

Slice (Slicing Disc) potatoes; microwave potatoes and water in 1½-quart glass casserole, covered, at High until just tender, 5 to 6 minutes. Drain; let stand covered 5 minutes. Cool to room temperature.

Shred (Shredding Disc) cheeses; remove. Process (Steel Knife) green pepper and onion using on/off technique until chopped. Combine potatoes, cheeses, green pepper, and onion in large bowl. Mix mayonnaise, sour cream, mustard, salt, and pepper; pour over potato mixture and stir. Refrigerate several hours or overnight (texture of salad is creamiest if refrigerated overnight).

Microwave bacon in glass baking dish, covered with paper toweling, at High until crisp, about 4 minutes. Drain bacon and crumble; sprinkle over salad.

Tip: Swiss, Muenster, Colby, or Monterey Jack cheeses can be substituted for the brick and Cheddar.

SALAD NIÇOISE

Chicken replaces the more traditional anchovies or tuna in this sublime entrée salad. The microwaved dressing is absorbed quickly and thoroughly by the cooked, sliced vegetables, eliminating the need to marinate for fullest flavor.

Total Preparation Time: 40 to 45 minutes
Microwave Time: 18 to 21 minutes
Yield: 4 servings

1 pound boneless chicken breast halves, skinned
⅛ **teaspoon ground nutmeg**
8 **ounces fresh green beans, trimmed**
¼ **cup water**
2 **medium potatoes, pared, cut to fit feed tube**
2 **tablespoons water**

12 **pitted ripe olives**
½ **small head iceberg lettuce, cut into wedges to fit feed tube**
1 **small red onion, peeled, cut to fit feed tube**
2 **tomatoes, seeded, cut into 1-inch pieces**
½ **cup olive or vegetable oil**
¼ **cup white wine vinegar**
¾ **teaspoon dried tarragon leaves**
¼ **teaspoon salt**
⅛ **teaspoon pepper**
2 **hard-cooked eggs, peeled, cut into quarters**

Arrange chicken in glass baking dish. Sprinkle chicken with nutmeg. Microwave covered with plastic wrap at High until chicken is done and juices run clear when chicken is pierced with a fork, about 7 minutes; turn chicken over after 4 minutes and rotate dish ¼ turn. Drain and cool to room temperature. Cut into strips; refrigerate covered.

Slice (Slicing Disc) green beans, arranging beans horizontally in feed tube. Microwave beans and water in glass baking dish, covered, at High until beans are crisp-tender, about 5 minutes, stirring after 3 minutes. Drain and cool to room temperature; refrigerate covered. Slice (Slicing Disc) potatoes. Microwave potatoes and 2 tablespoons water in glass baking dish, covered, at High until tender, about 5 minutes, rotating dish ¼ turn after 3 minutes; drain. Cool to room temperature; refrigerate.

Slice (Slicing Disc) olives, lettuce, and onion separately. Process (Steel Knife) tomatoes using on/off technique until coarsely chopped.

Arrange lettuce on serving platter; arrange chicken and vegetables attractively on lettuce. Microwave oil, vinegar, tarragon, salt, and pepper in 1-cup glass measure, uncovered, at High just until boiling; stir with whisk and drizzle over salad. Garnish with egg.

Tip: Do not attempt to hard-cook eggs in the microwave oven (unless you have cookware specially designed for that purpose); for conventional cooking directions, see Index.

MOLDED VEGETABLE SALAD

A pretty vegetable mold comes together remarkably quickly with microwaves and the food processor.

Total Preparation Time: 27 to 28 minutes (plus
chilling time)
Microwave Time: 5 to 6 minutes
Yield: 8 servings

1 cup hot water
1 package (3 ounces) lemon or lime gelatin
¼ cup dry white wine
½ cup cold water
¼ teaspoon dried basil leaves
⅛ teaspoon dried tarragon leaves
¼ medium head cauliflower, cut into
   flowerets
4 medium mushroom caps, fluted if desired
1 ounce fresh spinach, stems discarded
2 ounces mushrooms
¼ medium cucumber, cut to fit feed tube
¼ large red or green pepper, seeded, cut
   into 1-inch pieces
½ small onion, peeled, cut into 1-inch pieces
1 tablespoon water
Lettuce leaves

Microwave 1 cup hot water in 4-cup glass measure at High until boiling; stir in gelatin until dissolved. Stir in wine, ½ cup cold water, the basil, and tarragon. Pour ½ cup of the gelatin mixture in bottom of lightly greased 6-cup ring mold; refrigerate.

Reserve 5 flowerets and the mushroom caps; slice (Slicing Disc) remaining cauliflower, the spinach, mushrooms, and cucumber separately. Process (Steel Knife) red pepper and onion using on/off technique until coarsely chopped. Microwave reserved flowerets, sliced cauliflower, and 1 tablespoon water in 1-quart glass casserole, covered, at High for 3 minutes. Rinse with cold water and drain. Arrange flowerets and fluted mushroom caps on gelatin in mold; layer remaining vegetables in mold. Pour remaining gelatin mixture over vegetables; refrigerate until set, 6 to 8 hours.

Loosen edge of mold with tip of sharp knife; dip mold briefly in warm water. Unmold on lettuce leaves on serving plate.

Tip: To flute mushroom caps, hold each mushroom by the stem and use a sharp paring knife to pare away a thin strip of the cap. Hold the knife blade diagonally and cut from the crown of the cap to the edge. Rotate the mushroom and continue cutting away strips until you have a pinwheel pattern. Remove stem and reserve for other use.

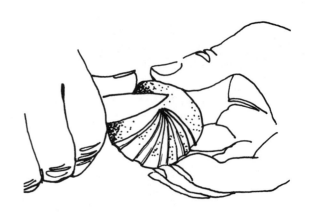

SPICED FRUIT SALAD

Golden in color and fragrant with spices, this is a good holiday season buffet mold. Save time by plumping dried fruit and dissolving gelatin in one step. Because of the way the salad is layered, the gelatin does not need to set before the fruit is added.

Total Preparation Time: 22 to 23 minutes (plus
chilling time)
Microwave Time: 5 to 6 minutes
Yield: 8 servings

1 cup mixed dried fruit
2 cups water
2 packages (3 ounces each) apricot gelatin
1 cup walnut pieces
1 medium apple, cored, cut into 1-inch
   pieces

1 rib celery, cut to fit feed tube
¼ cup golden raisins
⅛ teaspoon ground cloves
⅛ teaspoon ground allspice
⅛ teaspoon ground cinnamon
1 cup tonic or mineral water

Process (Steel Knife) dried fruit using on/off technique until chopped; stir into 2 cups water in 4-cup glass measure. Microwave uncovered at High until boiling; boil 1 minute. Stir in gelatin until dissolved and let stand until room temperature.

Process (Steel Knife) walnuts and apple separately, using on/off technique, until coarsely chopped; remove. Slice (Slicing Disc) celery. Stir walnuts, apple, celery, raisins, cloves, allspice, cinnamon, and tonic into gelatin mixture; pour into lightly greased 6-cup mold. Refrigerate until set, 6 to 8 hours.

Loosen edge of mold with tip of sharp knife. Dip mold briefly in warm water; unmold on serving plate.

FRUIT SALAD WITH PINEAPPLE–CREAM DRESSING

A brunch or warm-weather lunch highlight. For a party buffet, arrange the fruit on a serving platter and allow guests to help themselves to the dressing separately. Substitute any fruit in season; melon, oranges, apples, pears, blueberries, and grapes (unsliced) would all be delicious.

Total Preparation Time: 18 to 20 minutes (plus chilling time)
Microwave Time: 3 to 5 minutes
Yield: 6 to 8 servings

Pineapple-Cream Dressing (recipe follows)
1 pineapple, pared, cored, cut to fit feed tube
2 medium bananas, peeled, cut to fit feed tube
1 pint strawberries, hulled
Lettuce leaves
Mint sprigs (optional)

Make Pineapple-Cream Dressing. Slice (Slicing Disc) fruits; arrange fruits attractively on salad plates lined with lettuce leaves. Spoon dressing over; garnish with mint sprigs.

Pineapple-Cream Dressing

Yield: about 1½ cups

2 tablespoons butter or margarine
2 tablespoons cornstarch
¾ cup whipping cream or half-and-half
½ cup pineapple juice
2 tablespoons lemon juice
¼ cup sugar
¼ teaspoon dry mustard
¼ teaspoon paprika
¼ teaspoon salt

Microwave butter in 4-cup glass measure at High until melted. Stir in cornstarch; stir in remaining ingredients. Microwave uncovered at High until thickened, 2 to 3 minutes, stirring with a whisk every minute. Cool to room temperature. Refrigerate until chilled.

Tip: Pineapple-Cream Dressing may be made 1 day in advance; refrigerate covered. Slice fruit as close to serving time as possible; if salad will be set out on a buffet, substitute a fruit that will not darken, such as oranges or honeydew melon, for the bananas.

12 When Calories Count

MARINATED SHRIMP AND ORANGE SALAD
(about 265 calories per serving)

There's absolutely nothing "dietetic" about this calorie-wise, colorful salad—it just happens to be as light and refreshing as it looks!

Total Preparation Time: 16 to 18 minutes (plus chilling time)
Microwave Time: 9 to 10 minutes
Yield: 6 servings

---

2 large sprigs parsley
1 clove garlic, peeled
1 medium onion, peeled, cut to fit feed tube
⅓ cup vegetable oil
½ cup cider vinegar
3 tablespoons lemon juice
3 tablespoons catsup
1½ tablespoons brown sugar
1 tablespoon lime juice
1 teaspoon teriyaki sauce
½ teaspoon dry mustard
¼ teaspoon paprika
⅛ teaspoon cayenne pepper
1¼ pounds shelled, deveined, uncooked shrimp
2 medium oranges, peeled, cut vertically into halves
½ medium head lettuce, cut into wedges to fit feed tube

Process (Steel Knife) parsley using on/off technique until minced. With machine running, drop garlic through feed tube, processing until minced; remove. Slice (Slicing Disc) onion. Microwave garlic mixture, onion, and oil in 1½-quart glass casserole, covered, at High until onion is tender, about 5 minutes, stirring after 2½ minutes. Stir in remaining ingredients except shrimp, oranges, and lettuce. Microwave covered at High until boiling, about 3 minutes. Stir in shrimp; microwave covered at High until shrimp turn pink, 1 to 2 minutes. Slice (Slicing Disc) oranges; stir into shrimp mixture. Refrigerate until chilled, about 2 hours.

Slice (Slicing Disc) lettuce; arrange on serving plates. Drain shrimp mixture and spoon over lettuce.

Tips: If you're watching cholesterol as well as calories, you may want to substitute 3 boneless chicken breast halves, skinned (about 1¼ pounds), for the shrimp. Cut chicken into 1-inch pieces (or slice partially frozen chicken breasts with Slicing Disc after slicing onion) and proceed as above; after stirring chicken into sauce, microwave covered at High until chicken is cooked, about 7 minutes.

To get more juice from lemon and lime, microwave fruit at High 15 seconds.

ORIENTAL ROAST BEEF SALAD
(about 175 calories per serving)

An economy of calories, time, and beef that measures up to all appetites. The potato and dressing are cooked in the food processor bowl for minimal cleanup.

Total Preparation Time: 23 to 26 minutes (plus chilling time)
Microwave Time: 6 to 8 minutes
Yield: 4 servings

---

8 ounces thinly sliced, cooked, lean roast beef
1 medium potato, pared, cut to fit feed tube
2 tablespoons water
1 medium green pepper, seeded, cut to fit feed tube
1 medium onion, peeled, cut to fit feed tube
4 ounces mushrooms
2 sprigs fresh coriander or ½ teaspoon dried coriander leaves
1 clove garlic, peeled
½ cup water
⅓ cup red wine vinegar
2 teaspoons beef-flavor instant bouillon
2 teaspoons soy sauce
¼ teaspoon dried marjoram leaves
¼ teaspoon dried oregano leaves
⅛ teaspoon ground ginger
⅛ teaspoon pepper

Arrange beef in 12″ × 8″ glass baking dish. Slice (Slicing Disc) potato. Microwave potato and 2 tablespoons water in glass casserole or measuring cup, covered, at High until tender, about 4 minutes; add to beef. Slice (Slicing Disc) green pepper, onion, and mushrooms; add to beef.

Process (Steel Knife) coriander using on/off technique until minced. With machine running, drop garlic through feed tube, processing until minced. Add remaining ingredients to bowl, processing until blended. Remove Steel Knife; microwave mixture in food processor bowl, uncovered, at High just to boiling, about 2 minutes. Pour over meat mixture and toss. Let stand until room temperature; refrigerate until chilled.

Tip: Oriental Roast Beef Salad can be prepared 1 day in advance; refrigerate covered. It is an excellent choice for picnics, as all ingredients travel well. If you wish to double the recipe, microwave the potato slices about 6 minutes and proceed as above.

HOT AND COLD TACO SALAD
(about 150 calories per serving)

Contrasting layers of cool greens, hot beef, tomatoes, and cheese provide the satisfaction of Mexican food without the calamitous calories.

Total Preparation Time: 15 to 20 minutes
Microwave Time: 3 to 5 minutes
Yield: 4 servings

---

2 large sprigs fresh coriander or ½ teaspoon dried coriander leaves
12 ounces assorted salad greens
1 ounce Monterey Jack or brick cheese, chilled, cut to fit feed tube
12 cherry tomatoes
2 green onions and tops, cut into 1-inch pieces
12 ounces lean, boneless beef round steak, cut into 1-inch pieces
¼ cup chili sauce

2 teaspoons chili powder
¼ teaspoon ground cumin
¼ teaspoon salt
¹⁄₁₆ teaspoon cayenne pepper

Process (Steel Knife) coriander using on/off technique until minced; reserve. Slice (Slicing Disc) greens; place in salad bowl and refrigerate. Shred (Shredding Disc) cheese; remove. Slice (Slicing Disc) tomatoes; remove. Process (Steel Knife) onions and meat using on/off technique until chopped. Microwave meat and onion mixture in 1-quart glass casserole, covered, at High until meat loses pink color, 3 to 5 minutes, stirring after 2 minutes. Drain well.

Stir chili sauce, chili powder, cumin, salt, and cayenne pepper into meat mixture. Spoon hot meat mixture over greens; garnish with reserved coriander, the cheese, and tomatoes.

Tips: If you are using iceberg lettuce, cut it into wedges to fit the feed tube. Stack other greens, such as romaine or spinach, and roll up; insert rolls of leaves vertically into feed tube, inserting from bottom, if necessary, to slice. Slice cherry tomatoes as you would olives; place them in the feed tube and slice with firm pressure.

Unless you have a large-model food processor, chop no more than ½ pound of beef at a time. In the above recipe, you can chop half of the beef and transfer it to the casserole; then chop the remaining beef with the onions.

VEGETABLE–STUFFED EGGPLANT PARMESAN
(about 275 calories per serving)

Because of its lightness, this is an unusually appealing way to serve eggplant. Those who aren't counting calories would enjoy smaller portions as a side dish with Mediterranean-flavored entrées, such as Veal Rolls with Prosciutto or Lemon Meat Loaf (see Index).

Total Preparation Time: 28 to 33 minutes
Microwave Time: 11 to 14 minutes
Yield: 4 servings

1 eggplant (about 1 pound)
2 ounces Parmesan cheese, cut into 1-inch pieces
4 ounces Muenster cheese, chilled, cut to fit feed tube
2 sprigs watercress or parsley
1 clove garlic, peeled
½ cup walnuts
½ medium onion, peeled, cut into 1-inch pieces
1 carrot, pared, cut into 1-inch pieces
1 rib celery, cut into 1-inch pieces
1 tablespoon water
1 tomato, seeded, cut into 1-inch pieces
½ teaspoon dried basil leaves
¼ teaspoon salt
1/16 teaspoon white pepper

Pierce eggplant in several places with fork. Microwave on paper toweling at High until tender, 5 to 6 minutes. Process (Steel Knife) Parmesan cheese until finely grated; remove. Shred (Shredding Disc) Muenster cheese; remove. Process (Steel Knife) watercress using on/off technique until minced. With machine running (Steel Knife), add garlic through feed tube; process until minced. Add walnuts, onion, carrot, and celery to bowl; process using on/off technique until finely chopped. Remove Steel Knife; microwave vegetable mixture and water in food processor bowl, covered with plastic wrap, at High until vegetables are crisp-tender, about 3 minutes. Drain thoroughly.

Cut eggplant lengthwise into halves; scoop out interior of eggplant and cut into 1-inch pieces. Add eggplant pieces, tomato, Parmesan cheese, basil, salt, and pepper to food processor bowl; process using on/off technique until eggplant is chopped. Stir eggplant mixture and half of the Muenster cheese into vegetable mixture; spoon into eggplant shells. Place in glass baking dish. Microwave uncovered at High until hot through, 2 to 3 minutes. Sprinkle with remaining Muenster cheese; microwave uncovered at High until cheese

melts, about 1 minute. Cut each shell into halves to serve.

Tip: If you are on a low-sodium diet, you may wish to omit the salt and reduce the amount of Parmesan cheese; the eggplant mixture will still be quite flavorful.

GARDEN BAKED FISH FILLETS
(about 130 calories per serving)

Chopped and shredded vegetables give a low-calorie dish the look and taste of abundance.

Total Preparation Time: 15 to 18 minutes
Microwave Time: 4 to 5 minutes
Yield: 4 servings

4 sprigs parsley
1 clove garlic, peeled
3 tablespoons lemon juice
¾ teaspoon soy sauce
½ teaspoon dried dillweed
½ teaspoon dried basil leaves
¼ teaspoon Dijon-style mustard
1 small cucumber, pared, seeded, cut into 1-inch pieces
1 pound turbot or other white fish fillets
1 carrot, pared, cut to fit feed tube
2 radishes, ends trimmed

Process (Steel Knife) parsley using on/off technique until minced. With machine running, drop garlic through feed tube, processing until minced. Add lemon juice, soy sauce, dillweed, basil, and mustard to bowl; process until blended. Add cucumber to bowl; process using on/off technique until chopped.

Layer fish in 12″ × 8″ glass baking dish, folding thin ends of fillets under. Spoon cucumber mixture evenly over fish.

Shred (Shredding Disc) carrot and radishes; sprinkle evenly over fish. Microwave covered with plastic wrap at High until fish is tender and flakes with a fork, 4 to 5 minutes, rotating dish ¼ turn after 2 minutes. Arrange on serving platter.

YOGURT CHICKEN
(about 175 calories per serving)

This dish tastes much, much richer than it is, due to the lavish, sweet scent of the spices and the creaminess of the sauce. Marinate the chicken at least an hour, or overnight, for the seasonings to blend. The salt can easily be omitted for low-sodium diets.

Total Preparation Time: 28 to 30 minutes (plus marinating time)
Microwave Time: 13 to 18 minutes
Yield: 4 servings

---

2 sprigs fresh coriander or ½ teaspoon dried coriander leaves
1 small clove garlic, peeled
½ cup plain low-fat yogurt
1 teaspoon paprika
½ teaspoon ground cinnamon
¼ teaspoon ground nutmeg
⅛ teaspoon ground cardamom
1 teaspoon salt
1/16 teaspoon cayenne pepper
4 small chicken breast halves, skinned (about 1½ pounds)
Chicken broth
1 tablespoon flour
2 tablespoons water
1 small lemon, cut to fit feed tube
Coriander or parsley sprigs

Process (Steel Knife) 2 sprigs coriander using on/off technique until minced. With machine running, drop garlic through feed tube, processing until minced. Add yogurt, paprika, cinnamon, nutmeg, cardamom, salt, and cayenne pepper to bowl; process (Steel Knife) using on/off technique until mixed. Arrange chicken in glass baking dish, with meatiest portions toward edges of dish. Pour yogurt marinade over chicken. Refrigerate covered with waxed paper 1 to 2 hours.

Microwave chicken in baking dish with yogurt marinade, covered with waxed paper, until chicken is tender and juices run clear when chicken is pierced with a fork in thickest parts, 10 to 13 minutes; rearrange chicken pieces and coat with marinade after 6 minutes.

Arrange chicken on serving plate; cover loosely with aluminum foil. Pour pan juices and marinade into 2-cup glass measure; add chicken broth to make ½ cup. Stir in combined flour and water to make sauce. Microwave uncovered at 50% (Medium) just until boiling, 3 to 4 minutes, stirring every 2 minutes. Pour sauce over chicken. Slice (Slicing Disc) lemon. Garnish chicken with lemon and coriander or parsley sprigs.

MOO SHU PORK
IN CABBAGE LEAVES
(about 290 calories per serving)

A classic Chinese pork mixture rolled up in cabbage or lettuce leaves can make you forget you're counting calories. Serve the delicate rolls as an appetizer or first-course for all-purpose entertaining, too—and especially if Won Ton Soup or Lemon Chicken with Snow Peas (see Index) will follow on the menu.

Total Preparation Time: 30 to 32 minutes
Microwave Time: 13 to 15 minutes
Yield: 4 servings

---

1 cup water
⅓ cup Chinese dried mushrooms
2 large leaves Chinese cabbage, cut to fit feed tube
1 piece gingerroot (the size of a dime)
1 can (6 ounces) water chestnuts, drained
8 ounces lean boneless pork, cut into 1-inch pieces
2 tablespoons soy sauce
2 teaspoons dry sherry
½ teaspoon sugar
1 tablespoon cornstarch
1 green onion and top, cut into 1-inch pieces
4 eggs
¼ teaspoon salt
⅛ teaspoon white pepper
Chinese cabbage leaves

Microwave 1 cup water in 2-cup glass measure at High until boiling; stir in mushrooms. Let stand until mushrooms are soft, 15 to 20 minutes. Drain, reserving ¼ cup liquid; cut out tough centers and discard.

Slice (Slicing Disc) 2 cabbage leaves; remove. With machine running (Steel Knife), drop gingerroot through feed tube, processing until minced. Add water chestnuts to bowl; process (Steel Knife) using on/off technique until finely chopped. Add pork, mushrooms, soy sauce, sherry, and sugar to bowl; process (Steel Knife) using on/off technique just until pork is chopped.

Microwave meat mixture and sliced cabbage in 2-quart glass casserole, uncovered, at High until pork loses pink color, 7 to 8 minutes, stirring every 4 minutes. Stir in combined cornstarch and ¼ cup reserved liquid; microwave uncovered at High until thickened, about 2 minutes.

Process (Steel Knife) onion until coarsely chopped; add eggs, salt, and pepper to bowl. Process (Steel Knife) using on/off technique until blended. Remove Steel Knife; microwave egg mixture in food processor bowl uncovered at High until set, 2 to 3 minutes, stirring every minute. Stir egg mixture into pork mixture.

To serve, spoon pork mixture onto cabbage leaves and roll up.

Tips: Chinese cabbage, a delicately tangy green, can be found in the produce section of a large supermarket or Oriental grocery. The ruffled leaves are stiff enough to be stacked and inserted into the food processor feed tube without being rolled up; slice with light pressure. Romaine lettuce can be substituted for the Chinese cabbage, both in the meat mixture and as a wrapper.

ONION–SMOTHERED STEAK
(about 315 calories per serving)

Everything you ever wanted on a diet but were afraid to touch—beef, beer, and a thick onion gravy. You can fool everyone with this dish, including yourself!

Total Preparation Time: 40 to 42 minutes
Microwave Time: 22 to 24 minutes
Yield: 6 servings

1½ **pounds lean, boneless beef round steak, cut into ½-inch strips**
1 **cup beer**
4 **medium onions, peeled, cut to fit feed tube**
3 **tablespoons butter or margarine**
2 **teaspoons brown sugar**
3 **tablespoons flour**
½ **teaspoon dry mustard**
½ **cup beef broth**
¼ **teaspoon dried marjoram leaves**
¼ **teaspoon dried oregano leaves**
¼ **teaspoon dried thyme leaves**
¼ **teaspoon dried savory leaves**
Browning and seasoning sauce

Combine beef and beer in 2-quart glass casserole; let stand 15 minutes. Drain, reserving ½ cup beer.

Slice (Slicing Disc) onions. Microwave onions, butter, and sugar in 2-quart glass casserole, covered, at High until onions are golden, about 10 minutes, stirring every 3 minutes. Stir in flour and mustard; microwave uncovered at High 2 minutes. Stir in reserved ½ cup beer, the broth, marjoram, oregano, thyme, savory, and a few drops browning sauce; microwave uncovered at High 2 minutes. Stir in beef; microwave covered at High until meat loses pink color and is tender, 8 to 10 minutes, stirring every 3 minutes. Let stand covered 10 minutes before serving.

Tip: Because round steak is not a tender cut, it is important to cut it into very thin strips. If you wish to slice the meat in the food processor, cut it into pieces to fit the feed tube; be sure that the grain of the meat is lengthwise, so that you will slice across it. Place the pieces on aluminum foil-lined plate of a baking sheet and freeze until semi-firm (you should still be able to pierce it with a knife). Insert pieces in the feed tube and slice (Slicing Disc) with firm pressure.

13 Sandwiches and Snacks

SLOPPY JOES

These fresh-tasting Sloppy Joes offer a very good reason to buy extra when beef is on sale and keep it ready in the freezer. The sliced pepper garnish may be omitted, although its crisp counterpoint enlivens the saucy meat.

Total Preparation Time: 25 to 28 minutes
Microwave Time: 10 to 13 minutes
Yield: 6 servings

---

1 pound boneless sirloin or beef round steak
1 medium onion, peeled, cut into 1-inch pieces
1 rib celery, cut into 1-inch pieces
1 large green pepper, seeded, cut into 1-inch pieces
¾ cup chili sauce
2 tablespoons light brown sugar
1 tablespoon cider vinegar
1 teaspoon Worcestershire sauce
½ teaspoon Garlic Salt (see Index)
¼ teaspoon dry mustard
1/16 teaspoon pepper
1 large green pepper, seeded, cut to fit feed tube
6 onion rolls or hamburger buns

Trim excess fat from meat, leaving about 2 ounces (two 1-inch pieces); cut meat into 1-inch pieces. Process (Steel Knife) meat using on/off technique until finely chopped. Process (Steel Knife) onion, celery, and green pepper pieces using on/off technique until chopped. Microwave meat and vegetables in 1½-quart glass casserole, covered, at High until meat loses pink color and vegetables are tender, about 5 minutes, stirring after 2½ minutes. Stir in remaining ingredients except large green pepper and rolls; microwave covered at High until hot through, about 5 minutes, stirring after 2 minutes.

Slice (Slicing Disc) large green pepper. Spoon meat mixture onto bottoms of rolls; top with green pepper slices and roll tops.

Tips: Unless you have a large-model food processor, do not chop more than ½ pound of beef at a time.

The cooked meat mixture can be frozen in a covered container up to 1 month.

To warm rolls, arrange them in a circle on paper toweling; microwave at 70% (Medium High) until just warm to the touch, 30 to 40 seconds.

WESTERN ROUNDUPS

A Denver-style scrambled omelet paired with sourdough bread and sliced avocado.

Total Preparation Time: 17 to 21 minutes
Microwave Time: 7 to 11 minutes
Yield: 4 servings

---

1 ounce Monterey Jack or brick cheese, chilled, cut to fit feed tube
4 ounces smoked ham, cut into 1-inch pieces
½ medium red or green pepper, seeded, cut into 1-inch pieces
1 green onion and top, cut into 1-inch pieces
1 tablespoon butter or margarine
3 eggs
1 tablespoon whipping cream or half-and-half
⅛ teaspoon salt
⅛ to ¼ teaspoon cayenne pepper
1 small avocado, peeled, pitted, cut to fit feed tube
4 slices sourdough bread, toasted

Shred (Shredding Disc) cheese; reserve. Process (Steel Knife) ham, pepper, and onion using on/off technique until coarsely chopped. Microwave ham mixture and butter in 1-quart glass casserole, uncovered, at High until vegetables are tender, 2 to 3 minutes. Mix eggs, cream, salt, and cayenne pepper; stir into ham mixture. Microwave uncovered at High until eggs are set but still moist, 5 to 8 minutes, stirring every 2 minutes. Sprinkle with reserved cheese; let stand covered until cheese melts, about 2 minutes.

Slice (Slicing Disc) avocado. Spoon egg mixture onto bread slices; garnish with avocado.

Tips: Toast bread conventionally; it will dry out in the microwave oven long before it browns.

    Four ounces of cooked bacon, crumbled, can be substituted for the chopped ham. Canadian bacon can also be substituted; proceed as above.

ITALIAN BEEF WITH PEPPERS

An herb-accented sauce makes the most of leftover or deli roast beef. Prepare it without the tomato sauce for a beef-in-gravy-style sandwich.

Total Preparation Time: 25 to 30 minutes
Microwave Time: 18 to 21 minutes
Yield: 4 servings

---

2 cloves garlic, peeled
2 small onions, peeled, cut into 1-inch pieces
1 tablespoon butter or margarine
1¼ cups water
1 cup tomato sauce (optional)
¼ cup red wine vinegar
1 tablespoon beef-flavor instant bouillon
1 tablespoon brown sugar
1 tablespoon crushed dried red pepper
1 teaspoon dried basil leaves
½ teaspoon dried oregano leaves
¼ teaspoon browning and seasoning sauce (optional; use if not using tomato sauce)
2 medium green peppers, seeded, cut to fit feed tube
½ pound thinly sliced, cooked roast beef
4 Italian rolls, split

With machine running (Steel Knife), drop garlic through feed tube, processing until minced. Add onions to bowl; process using on/off technique until chopped. Microwave onion mixture and butter in 2-quart glass casserole, uncovered, at High until onions are tender, about 4 minutes. Stir in remaining ingredients except green peppers, beef, and rolls; microwave covered at High until boiling, 4 to 5 minutes.

Slice (Slicing Disc) green peppers; stir into sauce. Microwave covered at High until peppers are tender, 5 to 7 minutes. Stir in beef; microwave covered at High until hot through, about 4 minutes.

Place rolls in oven on paper toweling; microwave at 70% (Medium High) 30 seconds. Spoon meat mixture into rolls.

Tip: One-half pound cooked Italian sausage can be substituted for the roast beef. Do not omit the tomato sauce. To grill sausage, preheat browning dish at High 5 minutes. Cut sausage into 1½-inch pieces; arrange on preheated dish. Microwave uncovered at High until sausage loses pink color, about 5 minutes, turning sausage over twice. Drain sausage and cut pieces into halves; proceed as above.

HOT TURKEY SURPRISE

The surprise of chopped apple and chutney lies beneath a puff of savory meringue. Process egg whites first to avoid washing the food processor bowl.

Total Preparation Time: 16 to 21 minutes
Microwave Time: 4 to 6 minutes
Yield: 4 servings

---

2 egg whites
¼ teaspoon dry mustard
¼ cup blanched almonds
1 medium apple, cored, cut into 1-inch pieces
3 tablespoons chutney
8 ounces thinly sliced, cooked turkey
4 slices Italian bread

Process (Steel Knife) egg whites and mustard until stiff peaks form; reserve. Process (Steel Knife) almonds using on/off technique until chopped; remove. Process (Steel Knife) apple using on/off technique until chopped; add chutney to bowl. Process just until blended.

Microwave almonds in glass pie plate, uncovered, at High until toasted, 2 to 3 minutes, stirring after 1 minute.

Arrange turkey on bread; spoon apple mixture over turkey. Spoon meringue over apple mixture; sprinkle with almonds. Microwave on paper toweling, uncovered, at High until meringue is firm to touch, 2 to 3 minutes. Serve hot.

Tip: Microwave sandwich only until meringue is firm; the meringue will not brown.

HAM SALAD ROLLS

A delicious, crunchy ham salad dressed up with lightly sweetened dill sauce.

Total Preparation Time: 15 to 19 minutes
Microwave Time: 4 to 6 minutes
Yield: 4 servings

½ cup walnuts
8 ounces smoked ham, cut into 1-inch pieces
½ medium onion, peeled, cut into 1-inch pieces
2 small sweet pickles, cut into 1-inch pieces
1 rib celery, cut into 1-inch pieces
¼ to ⅓ cup sour cream
½ teaspoon Dijon-style mustard
2 French or hard rolls
Dill Sauce (optional; see Index)
2 teaspoons honey (optional)

Process (Steel Knife) walnuts using on/off technique until chopped; reserve 1½ tablespoons. Add ham, onion, pickles, celery, sour cream, and mustard to walnuts in bowl; process (Steel Knife) using on/off technique until finely chopped.

Cut rolls lengthwise into halves; scoop out centers (reserve cutout parts for bread crumbs or other use). Fill rolls with ham mixture.

Make Dill Sauce, stirring in honey. Microwave rolls on paper toweling at 70% (Medium High) until hot through, 4 to 6

minutes; spoon sauce over. Sprinkle with reserved walnuts.

Tip: For a cold sandwich or appetizer spread, follow the first paragraph of the recipe; do not reserve walnuts. Substitute mayonnaise for the sour cream, if you wish.

PITA POCKETS

Although pita rounds were introduced to America via Middle Eastern markets, they closely resemble a type of Chinese bread. So it's no coincidence that they provide sturdy holders for an Oriental stir-fry filling.

Total Preparation Time: 22 to 24 minutes
Microwave Time: 16 to 17 minutes
Yield: 6 servings

---

8 ounces lean boneless pork, cut into ¼-inch strips
1 tablespoon vegetable oil
2 ribs celery, cut to fit feed tube
3 green onions and tops, cut to fit feed tube
1 can (6 ounces) water chestnuts, drained
8 ounces fresh or canned bean sprouts, rinsed, well drained
2 tablespoons teriyaki sauce
1 tablespoon cornstarch
¼ cup cold water
2 teaspoon sesame seeds
3 pita breads, cut into halves

Microwave pork and oil in 1-quart glass casserole, uncovered, at High until pork loses pink color, about 6 minutes, stirring after 3 minutes. Slice (Slicing Disc) celery, onions, and water chestnuts; stir into pork. Stir bean sprouts and teriyaki sauce into pork mixture. Microwave uncovered at High 5 minutes, stirring after 3 minutes. Mix cornstarch and cold water; stir into pork mixture. Microwave uncovered at High 5 minutes, until thickened, about 3 minutes, stirring after 1½ minutes.

Microwave sesame seeds in glass pie plate uncovered at High until toasted, about 2 minutes, stirring after 1 minute. Open pockets in breads; fill with pork mixture. Sprinkle with sesame seeds.

Tip: *To crisp canned bean sprouts, place them in ice water for 10 minutes, or as long as time allows.*

CHOPPED REUBENS ON RYE

The new, improved Reuben—four layers of robust flavor! This recipe makes most economical use of costly ingredients with food processor chopping, blending, and shredding.

Total Preparation Time: 18 to 20 minutes
Microwave Time: 8 to 10 minutes
Yield: 6 servings

---

4 ounces Swiss cheese, chilled, cut to fit feed tube
8 ounces cooked corned beef, cut into 1-inch pieces
¼ cup canned sliced beets, well drained
¼ medium onion, peeled, cut into 1-inch pieces
2 medium sweet pickles, cut into 1-inch pieces
⅓ cup mayonnaise or salad dressing
2 tablespoons catsup
⅛ teaspoon prepared horseradish
6 slices rye bread
1 can (14 ounces) sauerkraut, well drained

Shred (Shredding Disc) cheese; remove. Process (Steel Knife) corned beef and beets using on/off technique until coarsely chopped; remove. Process (Steel Knife) onion, pickles, mayonnaise, catsup, and horseradish until onion is finely chopped.

Spread bread slices with onion mixture; top with sauerkraut, corned beef mixture, and shredded cheese. Place sandwiches on 2 plates lined with paper toweling; microwave at 70%

(Medium High) until hot through, 8 to 10 minutes rotating plates ¼ turn after 5 minutes. Serve immediately.

MUSHROOM SQUARES

This cross between an omelet and a creamy custard will hit the spot at snack time but could be served for lunch.

Total Preparation Time: 27 to 30 minutes
Microwave Time: 7 to 9 minutes
Yield: 8 servings

---

4 ounces Cheddar cheese, chilled, cut to fit feed tube
8 ounces mushrooms
2 large sprigs watercress or parsley
1 small onion, peeled, cut into 1-inch pieces
1 green onion and top, cut into 1-inch pieces
1 package (3 ounces) cream cheese, cut into quarters, softened
3 eggs
2 tablespoons flour
2 teaspoons dry sherry
1 teaspoon drained capers
2 dashes Worcestershire sauce
¼ teaspoon salt
⅛ teaspoon white pepper

Shred (Shredding Disc) Cheddar cheese; remove. Slice (Slicing Disc) mushrooms; remove. Process watercress using on/off technique until minced. Add onions, cream cheese, eggs, flour, sherry, capers, Worcestershire sauce, salt, and pepper to bowl; process (Steel Knife) until mixture is smooth. Add shredded cheese; process using on/off technique until blended.

Arrange mushrooms in 12″ × 8″ glass baking dish; pour egg mixture over. Microwave uncovered at High 4 minutes, rotating dish ¼ turn every 2 minutes. Shield corners of pan with aluminum foil; microwave uncovered at High until mixture is almost set, 3 to 5 minutes, rotating dish ¼ turn every 2 minutes. Let stand loosely covered 5 minutes. Cut into squares; serve hot.

TWICE-BAKED POTATO SKINS

An absolutely habit-forming treat—either a high-calorie hazard or an economical source of nutrition, depending on your point of view! Count on this crisp yet creamy novelty to launch an informal party.

Total Preparation Time: 33 to 35 minutes
Microwave Time: 22 to 25 minutes
Yield: 4 servings

---

3 medium Idaho potatoes
3 slices bacon
¼ cup butter or margarine
½ teaspoon Dill Salt (see Index) or salt
1 to 2 dashes red pepper sauce
2 ounces Swiss or Cheddar cheese, chilled, cut to fit feed tube
½ small onion, peeled, cut into 1-inch pieces
¼ green pepper, seeded, cut into 1-inch pieces
¼ red or green pepper, seeded, cut into 1-inch pieces

Pierce potatoes several times with fork. Microwave on paper toweling at High until tender, 8 to 9 minutes. Let stand 5 minutes. Microwave bacon in glass baking dish, covered with paper toweling, at High until crisp, about 3 minutes; drain and crumble.

Cut potatoes lengthwise into quarters to make wedges. Carefully cut out potato, leaving ¼ inch potato on skins (reserve cutout potato for other use). Microwave butter in small glass bowl at High until melted; stir in salt and pepper sauce. Brush butter mixture on both sides of potato skins. Place skin sides up on paper toweling in glass baking dish; microwave uncovered at High 8 minutes, rotating dish ½ turn after 4 minutes.

Shred (Shredding Disc) cheese; remove. Process (Steel Knife) onion and peppers using on/off technique until chopped. Turn potato skins over; sprinkle with cheese. Top with chopped vegetables and bacon. Microwave uncovered at High until cheese is melted, about 2 minutes. Serve hot.

Tips: Remove cutout potato in large pieces for use in French-Style Vegetable Puree (see Index). Two medium potatoes will yield the amount of peeled, cooked potato required for the puree.

If you are preparing baked potatoes for another use that does not require the skins, you can freeze the skins for use in this recipe. Remove the potato as directed above. Freeze skins on a baking sheet until firm; then transfer to a plastic bag, seal, and freeze up to 3 months.

CONTINUOUS CHEESE CROCK

The best-tasting way to save pieces of leftover cheese. Use any combination of firm cheeses, nuts, herbs, and spices, and renew the blend weekly or monthly, as bits of cheese accumulate.

Total Preparation Time: 9 to 12 minutes
Microwave Time: 1 to 3 minutes
Yield: 1½ cups spread

---

4 ounces cheese (Swiss, Cheddar, Monterey Jack, mozzarella, etc.), cut into 1-inch pieces
1 package (3 ounces) cream cheese, cut into quarters, softened
½ cup nuts (almonds, walnuts, pecans, hazelnuts, cashews, etc.)
2 tablespoons butter or margarine
½ teaspoon Basil Salt (optional; see Index)
1 to 2 tablespoons brandy, cognac, or dry sherry
Crackers, toast triangles, zucchini and cucumber slices, medium mushroom caps

Process (Steel Knife) cheeses, nuts, butter, Basil Salt, and brandy until smooth, scraping side of bowl with rubber spatula if necessary. Spread cheese mixture generously on crackers or toast, spoon onto vegetable slices, or fill mushroom caps. Microwave on glass serving plate, uncovered, at High until cheese is hot and beginning to melt, 1 minute for 12 crackers or vegetable slices, about 3 minutes for 12 mushroom caps. Serve hot.

Tip: Refrigerate cheese blend in a tightly covered container; add any cheeses, nuts, or herbs, as desired. If the flavor of the mixture becomes too sharp, add cream cheese or butter. To add to the cheese crock, microwave mixture in glass bowl at 50% (Medium) just until softened; transfer to food processor bowl. Add new ingredients and process as directed above. To keep the renewed cheese crock longer than 2 months, add 1 to 2 tablespoons brandy, cognac, or sherry every 6 to 8 weeks.

HONEY FRUIT SNACK MIX

Superior munching, without the additives or cost of packaged mixtures. Equally satisfying for late-night snacks, picnics, and impromptu parties.

Total Preparation Time: 20 to 22 minutes
Microwave Time: 16 to 18 minutes
Yield: 4 cups

---

1 cup dry whole wheat or rye Bread
   Crumbs (see Index)
½ cup walnuts
½ cup dried apricots
½ cup pitted prunes
1½ cups uncooked quick oats
⅓ cup shredded coconut
1 teaspoon ground cinnamon
¼ cup butter or margarine
¼ cup honey
2 tablespoons maple syrup or honey
⅓ cup golden raisins

Make bread crumbs. Process (Steel Knife) walnuts until coarsely chopped; remove. Process (Steel Knife) apricots and prunes until coarsely chopped.

Microwave oats in 12″ × 8″ glass baking dish, uncovered, at High 2 minutes, stirring after 1 minute. Stir in bread crumbs, walnuts, coconut, and cinnamon; mix well. Microwave butter in small glass dish at High until melted; stir butter, honey, and maple syrup into oatmeal mixture. Microwave uncovered at 70% (Medium High) 7 minutes, stirring every 2 minutes. Stir in apricots, prunes, and raisins; microwave uncovered at 70% (Medium High) 2 minutes. Cool to room temperature. Store at room temperature in airtight container up to 2 weeks.

FOOD PROCESSOR NUT BUTTERS AND VARIATIONS

Not a microwave recipe, but a formula for every food processor owner. Even if you don't love peanut butter, consider the quick gift convenience of a jar of Spiced Date or Chutney Nut Butter. They're elegant when made with cashews or pecans and extraordinary with macadamia nuts. However, don't substitute almonds; you won't get the same creamy consistency.

Total Preparation Time: 4 to 6 minutes
Yield: 1 cup

---

2 cups peanuts, walnuts, cashews,
   macadamia nuts, or pecans

Process (Steel Knife) nuts until smooth butter is formed, 3 to 4 minutes, scraping bowl with rubber spatula if necessary. For chunky nut butter, add ½ cup more nuts and process (Steel Knife) using on/off technique until chopped. Refrigerate covered.

Tip: If you are making chunky nut butter, you may wish to toast the additional ½ cup nuts before processing. Microwave in glass pie plate, uncovered, at High until toasted, about 2 minutes.

VARIATIONS

MAPLE OR HONEY: Make nut butter with desired nuts as above, adding 1 to 2 tablespoons maple syrup or honey.

SPICED DATE: Make nut butter with desired nuts as above, adding ¼ teaspoon ground cinnamon and a dash of ground nutmeg. Add ⅓ cup pitted dates; process (Steel Knife) using on/off technique until chopped.

DILL: Make nut butter with desired nuts as above, adding 1 teaspoon dried dillweed.

CHUTNEY: Make nut butter with desired nuts as above, adding 2 to 4 tablespoons chutney.

COCONUT: Make nut butter with desired nuts as above. Add ¼ cup shredded coconut; process (Steel Knife) using on/off technique until blended.

CURRY: Make nut butter with desired nuts as above, adding ¼ to ½ teaspoon curry powder.

14 Sauces and
Do-Ahead Mixes

FRESH TOMATO SAUCE

This sauce is so useful, both alone and as an ingredient in other recipes, that you might want to make an extra batch for the freezer when tomatoes are lush and ripe.

Total Preparation Time: 30 to 33 minutes
Microwave Time: 20 to 23 minutes
Yield: 2 cups

4 sprigs parsley
1 clove garlic, peeled
2 green onions and tops, cut into 1-inch pieces
2 pounds tomatoes, seeded, cut into 1-inch pieces
2 tablespoons tomato paste
2 teaspoons light brown sugar
¼ teaspoon dried tarragon leaves
⅛ teaspoon dried thyme leaves
¼ teaspoon salt
⅛ teaspoon white pepper

Process (Steel Knife) parsley until minced. With machine running, drop garlic through feed tube; process using on/off technique until minced. Add onions and tomatoes to bowl; process using on/off technique until chopped. Transfer mixture to 1-quart glass casserole; stir in remaining ingredients. Microwave uncovered at High until sauce has thickened, about 20 minutes, stirring every 5 minutes.

Tips: To seed tomatoes, cut them into halves crosswise and squeeze halves gently. Ripen tomatoes at room temperature, stem ends up, away from direct sunlight.

To avoid spattering, lay a sheet of waxed paper over the casserole.

HOT SALSA

An essential sauce for Mexican food, but also a source of seasoning excitement for grilled poultry, meat, or seafood.

Total Preparation Time: 19 to 21 minutes
Microwave Time: 11 to 13 minutes
Yield: about 2 cups

2 sprigs fresh coriander or ½ teaspoon dried coriander leaves
1 clove garlic, peeled
2 medium onions, peeled, cut into 1-inch pieces
2 to 3 jalapeño peppers, seeded, cut into 1-inch pieces
2 tablespoons vegetable oil
1 pound tomatoes, seeded, cut into 1-inch pieces
½ teaspoon sugar
⅛ to ¼ teaspoon cayenne pepper
¼ teaspoon salt
2 dashes red pepper sauce

Process (Steel Knife) coriander using on/off technique until minced. With machine running, drop garlic through feed tube, processing until minced. Add onions and peppers to bowl; process using on/off technique until coarsely chopped. Microwave onion mixture and oil in 1½-quart glass casserole, uncovered, at High 3 minutes, stirring after 1½ minutes.

Process (Steel Knife) tomatoes using on/off technique until coarsely chopped. Stir tomatoes, sugar, pepper, salt, and pepper sauce into onion mixture. Microwave uncovered at High 8 to 10 minutes, until thickened, stirring every 4 minutes.

Tips: If full-flavored tomatoes are not available, 1 can (28 ounces) tomatoes, well drained, can be substituted.

Be careful not to touch your eyes when handling hot peppers, as the juice can cause irritation.

HORSERADISH COCKTAIL SAUCE

Serve hot or chilled with shrimp, other seafood, and grilled meats.

Total Preparation Time: 8 to 10 minutes
Microwave Time: 4 to 5 minutes
Yield: about 1¼ cups

½ medium onion, peeled, cut into 1-inch
    pieces
2 teaspoons cider vinegar
1 medium dill pickle, cut into 1-inch pieces
1 cup chili sauce
1 tablespoon horseradish
2 teaspoons Worcestershire sauce
1 teaspoon Dijon-style mustard
⅛ teaspoon pepper
2 to 3 dashes red pepper sauce

Process (Steel Knife) onion and vinegar using on/off technique until chopped; remove Steel Knife. Microwave onion mixture in food processor bowl, covered with plastic wrap, at High 2 minutes. Insert Steel Knife and add pickle to bowl; process using on/off technique until finely chopped. Add remaining ingredients to bowl; process (Steel Knife) until smooth. Microwave in glass serving bowl, covered, at High until hot, about 2 minutes.

CHILI STEAK SAUCE

A sauce well worth the careful stirring required to heat it. It is superb with grilled beef or chicken.

Total Preparation Time: 7 to 9 minutes
Microwave Time: 3 to 4 minutes
Yield: about 1 cup

2 green onions and tops, cut into 1-inch
    pieces
½ cup mayonnaise or salad dressing
½ cup chili sauce
1 egg white
1 tablespoon Worcestershire sauce
1 to 2 teaspoons prepared horseradish
1 tablespoon chili powder
½ teaspoon curry powder
½ teaspoon salt

Process (Steel Knife) green onions using on/off technique until finely chopped. Add remaining ingredients to bowl; process using on/off technique until blended. Microwave in 2-cup glass measure, uncovered, at 50% (Medium) just until hot, 3 to 4 minutes, stirring with whisk every 30 seconds (do not overcook or mixture will separate). Serve hot.

HOLLANDAISE SAUCE

Not only fast, but fail-safe. You can make this hollandaise up to 2 days in advance, refrigerate it, and reheat it. It is blended and cooked in the food processor bowl; so if the sauce starts to curdle or separate, you can reinsert the Steel Knife and process it until smooth. The elegance of asparagus hollandaise or eggs benedict couldn't be made easier!

Total Preparation Time: 4 to 5 minutes
Microwave Time: 2 to 3 minutes
Yield: about 1 cup

½ cup cold butter, cut into pieces
2 tablespoons lemon juice
½ teaspoon Dijon-style mustard (optional)
2 dashes red pepper sauce
2 egg yolks, room temperature

Arrange butter pieces around bottom of food processor bowl without Steel Knife; microwave uncovered at High until butter is soft, but not melted, about 1 minute. Insert Steel Knife; add lemon juice, mustard, and pepper sauce to bowl. Process until mixture is blended. With machine running, add yolks through feed tube 1 at a time, processing 30 seconds after each addition.

Remove Steel Knife; microwave uncovered at 50% (Medium) until thickened, about 1½ minutes, stirring after 1 minute. Stir and serve.

Tips: For Lime Hollandaise, substitute lime juice for the lemon juice and omit the mustard.

Whole eggs or 1 egg and 1 egg yolk can

be substituted for the yolks; sauce made with whole eggs will require about 15 seconds more cooking time. It is important that the eggs be at room temperature. To bring them to room temperature quickly, place them in a bowl of warm water and let stand 5 minutes.

If a fluffier sauce is desired, sauce can be processed with Steel Knife halfway through cooking time and again at the end.

If sauce should separate or curdle during cooking, process with Steel Knife until smooth.

Sauce can be made up to 30 minutes in advance and left in the food processor bowl, covered, at room temperature. To reheat, microwave as above about 1 minute, stirring after 30 seconds. If sauce thickens too much upon standing, process with Steel Knife until smooth; with machine running, add 1 tablespoon warm water through feed tube before reheating.

Sauce can be refrigerated covered up to 2 days. Before reheating, process (Steel Knife) to blend; with machine running, add 1 tablespoon warm water through feed tube. Remove Steel Knife; scrape down side of bowl. Microwave uncovered at 50% (Medium) 1½ minutes, stirring after 30 seconds.

BÉARNAISE SAUCE

This more assertive, tarragon-seasoned relative of hollandaise is just as easy to make and tastes fabulous with grilled steaks, poached salmon, and roast beef.

Total Preparation Time: 10 to 11 minutes
Microwave Time: 3 to 4 minutes
Yield: about 1 cup

1 shallot or ½ small white onion, peeled, cut into 1-inch pieces
1½ tablespoons white tarragon vinegar

1½ tablespoons dry white wine
1 tablespoon dried tarragon leaves
½ cup cold butter, cut into pieces
2 egg yolks, room temperature

With machine running (Steel Knife), drop shallot through feed tube, processing until minced. Add vinegar, wine, and tarragon to bowl; process until blended.

Remove Steel Knife; scrape down sides of bowl. Microwave covered at High 1 minute. Arrange butter pieces evenly around bottom of bowl; microwave uncovered at 50% (Medium) until butter is soft but not melted, about 1 minute. Cool to room temperature.

Insert Steel Knife. With machine running, add yolks through feed tube one at a time, processing 30 seconds after each addition. Remove Steel Knife; microwave uncovered at 50% (Medium) until thickened, about 1½ minutes, stirring after 30 seconds. Stir and serve.

Tip: See cooking and storage tips for Hollandaise Sauce (previous recipe).

BUTTER SAUCE

A suitably simple accent for broiled fish, Three-Vegetable Terrine, or Tomato Timbales (see Index). The softened butter added at the end, through the food processor feed tube, produces a light, fluffy consistency.

Total Preparation Time: 7 to 9 minutes
Microwave Time: 4 to 5 minutes
Yield: about 1½ cups

¼ cup butter or margarine
2 tablespoons flour
1 cup chicken broth
1 to 3 teaspoons lemon juice
Salt
2 to 3 tablespoons butter or margarine, softened

Microwave ¼ cup butter in 2-cup glass measure, uncovered, at High until melted; stir in flour. Microwave uncovered at High 30 seconds. Stir in chicken broth; microwave at High until mixture boils and thickens, 2 to 3 minutes, stirring after 1 minute. Stir in lemon juice and salt to taste.

Insert Steel Knife in food processor bowl. Transfer butter mixture to bowl. With machine running, add remaining butter, ½ tablespoon at a time, through feed tube, until blended.

GARLIC SAUCE

For those who like garlic, an irresistible fragrance! Serve it with fish or chicken. When cooked, the whole cloves of garlic become mild and delicious.

Total Preparation Time: 22 to 24 minutes
Microwave Time: 10 to 12 minutes
Yield: ¾ cup

2 heads garlic
1 small onion, peeled, cut into 1-inch peces
⅔ cup butter or margarine

Peel cloves of garlic. With machine running (Steel Knife), drop half the cloves through feed tube, processing until minced. Add onion to bowl; process using on/off technique until minced.

Microwave minced garlic mixture and butter in 1-quart glass casserole, covered, at 50% (Medium), 5 minutes, stirring after 2½ minutes. Stir in whole garlic cloves; microwave covered at 50% (Medium) just until turning golden, 5 to 7 minutes, stirring every 2½ minutes (do not overcook as garlic can burn easily).

Tips: To make Garlic Butter, increase butter to 2 cups and proceed as above. Strain the butter and keep it refrigerated. It has hundreds of uses. It will gently season mushrooms, onions, green beans, spinach, and other vegetables sautéed in it, and it's an excellent basting sauce for grilled, roast, or broiled lamb and poultry.

If you wish, you can add the cooked whole cloves of garlic to the eggplant when you are processing Spicy Eggplant Dip (see Index).

FRESH PINEAPPLE–CRANBERRY SAUCE

A fresher-tasting cranberry relish for holiday poultry and ham. Any surplus sauce will freeze well in covered container.

Total Preparation Time: 28 to 30 minutes
Microwave Time: 18 to 20 minutes
Yield: 4 cups

¾ cup pecans
1 large pineapple (2 to 2½ pounds), peeled, cored, cut into 1-inch pieces
12 ounces fresh or frozen, thawed cranberries
1½ cups packed light brown sugar
3 whole allspice
1 stick cinnamon
2 tablespoons cornstarch
¼ cup cold water

Process (Steel Knife) pecans; reserve. Process (Steel Knife) pineapple until coarsely chopped. Process (Steel Knife) half the cranberries until chopped. Mix all ingredients except pecans, cornstarch, and water in 2-quart glass measure; microwave uncovered at High 15 minutes, stirring every 5 minutes. Stir in combined cornstarch and water; microwave uncovered at High until thickened, about 3 minutes, stirring after 1½ minutes. Stir in pecans.

TWICE–AS–FAST SAUCE MIX

This basic mixture provides quick thickening for microwave-smooth sauces, soups, and gravies. Keep a supply in the refrigerator for use in the following sauces as well as other recipes in this book.

Total Preparation Time: 5 to 6 minutes
Microwave Time: ½ to 1 minute
Yield: about 1¾ cups

---

1 cup butter or margarine, cut into pieces
1 cup all-purpose flour
1½ teaspoons salt
1 teaspoon chicken-flavor instant bouillon

Arrange butter in bottom of food processor bowl without Steel Knife; microwave at High until butter is soft, about 30 seconds. Insert Steel Knife; add flour, salt, and bouillon. Process until thoroughly blended. Refrigerate in covered container.

Tips: Salt and bouillon can be omitted.
Recipe preparation times assume that you have Twice-As-Fast Sauce Mix already made. If you don't, you can combine equal parts of butter and flour to make amount of sauce mix specified in recipe.

MUSHROOM SAUCE

Total Preparation Time: 12 to 13 minutes
Microwave Time: 6 to 7 minutes
Yield: 1¼ cups

---

3 tablespoons Twice-As-Fast Sauce Mix (previous recipe)
2 ounces mushrooms
1 cup milk
1 teaspoon Worcestershire sauce
¼ teaspoon white pepper
2 ounces Gruyère cheese, cut to fit feed tube

Microwave sauce mix in 4-cup glass measure, uncovered, at High 2 minutes. Process (Steel Knife) mushrooms until chopped;

stir into sauce mix. Microwave uncovered at High 1 minute. Stir in milk, Worcestershire sauce, and pepper. Microwave uncovered at High until sauce boils and thickens, 3 to 3½ minutes, stirring with whisk every minute. Shred (Shredding Disc) cheese; stir into sauce until melted. Serve with cooked vegetables or meats.

CALVADOS SAUCE

Total Preparation Time: 9 to 11 minutes
Microwave Time: 6 to 8 minutes
Yield: about 1½ cups

---

2 cloves garlic, peeled
2 large shallots, peeled, or ¼ small onion, peeled, cut into 1-inch pieces
2 tablespoons chicken or pork pan drippings or butter or margarine
3 tablespoons Twice-As-Fast Sauce Mix (see Index)
1 cup whipping cream or half-and-half
3 to 4 tablespoons Calvados or brandy

With machine running (Steel Knife), drop garlic and shallots through feed tube, processing until minced. Microwave garlic mixture and pan drippings in 4-cup glass measure, uncovered, at High 2 minutes. Stir in sauce mix; microwave 1 minute. Stir in cream; microwave uncovered at 50% (Medium) until just boiling, 3 to 5 minutes, stirring with whisk every minute. Stir in Calvados; serve hot sauce with pork or chicken.

SHERRY BEEF SAUCE

Total Preparation Time: 9 to 10 minutes
Microwave Time: 7 to 8 minutes
Yield: about 1¼ cups

---

3 tablespoons Twice-As-Fast Sauce Mix (see
   Index)
½ clove garlic, peeled
¼ medium onion, peeled, cut into 1-inch
   pieces
1 cup beef broth
½ teaspoon dried chervil leaves
½ teaspoon Worcestershire sauce
1 egg yolk
1 tablespoon dry sherry or vermouth

Microwave sauce mix in 4-cup glass
measure, uncovered, at High 2 minutes.
Process (Steel Knife) garlic and onion using
on/off technique until minced; stir into sauce
mix. Microwave uncovered at High 1 minute.
Stir in beef broth, chervil, and Worcestershire
sauce. Microwave uncovered at High until
mixture thickens and boils, 3 to 3½ minutes,
stirring with whisk every minute. Stir about ¼
cup mixture into egg yolk; stir yolk mixture
into sauce. Microwave uncovered at High 1
minute, stirring after 30 seconds; stir in
sherry. Serve with beef and game.

SOUR CREAM–GREEN ONION
SAUCE

Total Preparation Time: 9 to 10 minutes
Microwave Time: 6 to 7 minutes
Yield: about 1 cup

3 tablespoons Twice-As-Fast Sauce Mix (see
   Index)
2 green onions and tops, cut into 1-inch
   pieces
¾ cup milk
1 teaspoon teriyaki sauce
½ teaspoon prepared mustard
½ teaspoon dried savory leaves
⅛ teaspoon white pepper
¼ to ⅓ cup sour cream

Microwave sauce mix in 4-cup glass
measure, uncovered, at High 2 minutes.
Process (Steel Knife) onions using on/off
technique until finely chopped; stir into sauce
mix. Microwave uncovered at High 1 minute.

Stir in milk, teriyaki sauce, mustard, savory,
and pepper. Microwave uncovered at High
until sauce boils and thickens, 3 to 3½ minutes,
stirring with whisk every minute. Stir in sour
cream until blended. Serve over cooked
vegetables or poultry.

DILL SAUCE

Total Preparation Time: 7 to 8 minutes
Microwave Time: 5 to 6 minutes
Yield: about 1½ cups

3 tablespoons Twice-As-Fast Sauce Mix (see
   Index)
1⅓ cups milk
1 teaspoon Dijon-style mustard
¾ teaspoon dried chives
¾ teaspoon dried dillweed or 1½ teaspoons
   snipped fresh dill
⅛ teaspoon white pepper

Microwave sauce mix in 4-cup glass
measure, uncovered, at High 2 minutes. Stir in
milk and remaining ingredients; microwave at
High until mixture boils and thickens, 3 to 3½
minutes, stirring with whisk every minute.
Serve over fish, poultry, and vegetables.

SWEET–SOUR SAUCE

Total Preparation Time: 10 to 11 minutes
Microwave Time: 6 to 7 minutes
Yield: about 1¼ cups

3 tablespoons Twice-As-Fast Sauce Mix (see
   Index)
¼ medium onion, peeled, cut into 1-inch
   pieces
¼ green pepper, seeded, cut into 1-inch
   pieces
1 cup orange juice
2 tablespoons light brown sugar
2 tablespoons cider vinegar

Microwave sauce mix in 4-cup glass measure, uncovered, at High 2 minutes. Process (Steel Knife) onion and pepper using on/off technique until finely chopped; stir into sauce mix. Microwave uncovered at High 1 minute. Stir in orange juice, sugar, and vinegar; microwave uncovered until mixture boils and thickens, 3 to 3½ minutes, stirring with whisk every minute. Serve over vegetables, fish, poultry, duck, and pork.

FOOD PROCESSOR MAYONNAISE AND VARIATIONS

Homemade mayonnaise is worlds apart in taste and texture from commercial blends. Not only does it lighten chicken, seafood, ham, and egg salads but it also serves as a beautiful sauce for cold meats, poultry, and fish. Choose among the variations for "instant" dips and accompaniments. Try the Walnut Mayonnaise with cold chicken, the Green Mayonnaise with cold poached fish, the Sesame Mayonnaise as a dip with crisp vegetables, and the Horseradish Mayonnaise on turkey sandwiches. Cream-enriched Chantilly Mayonnaise is heavenly with cold roast beef or lamb. Unless the recipe specifies otherwise, you can use either homemade or commercial mayonnaise in the recipes in this book but the food processor blend will always yield finer results.

Total Preparation Time: 3 to 4 minutes
Yield: about 1½ cups

---

2 egg yolks, room temperature
1 tablespoon lemon juice
1 tablespoon white wine vinegar
1 teaspoon Dijon-style mustard
¼ teaspoon salt
⅛ teaspoon white pepper
1¼ cups vegetable oil

Process (Steel Knife) egg yolks, lemon juice, vinegar, mustard, salt, and pepper until blended. With machine running, slowly pour oil through feed tube, pouring more quickly as mayonnaise in bowl thickens. Refrigerate in covered container up to 10 days.

VARIATIONS

WALNUT: Substitute ¼ cup walnut oil for ¼ cup of the vegetable oil; make recipe as above. If desired, process (Steel Knife) ½ cup toasted walnuts until chopped prior to making mayonnaise and reserve; stir into mayonnaise. The same substitutions can be made with almond oil and slivered almonds.

SESAME: Substitute 1 tablespoon to ¼ cup sesame oil (amount depends upon intensity of flavor, as Oriental sesame oil is very intense) for 1 tablespoon to ¼ cup vegetable oil; make recipe as above. Microwave 1 to 2 tablespoons sesame seeds in glass pie plate, uncovered, at High until toasted, 2 to 3 minutes, stirring after every minute; cool and stir into mayonnaise.

THOUSAND ISLAND: Make mayonnaise as above. Add ⅓ cup catsup; 2 sweet pickles, cut into 1-inch pieces; 1 hard-cooked egg, cut into quarters; and ½ to 1 teaspoon prepared horseradish to bowl. Process (Steel Knife) using on/off technique until egg is coarsely chopped. Served chilled or hot. To heat, microwave in 2-cup glass measure, uncovered, at 10% (Low) until hot through, 2½ to 3 minutes, stirring with whisk after 1½ minutes (do not overcook, or mayonnaise will separate).

SHALLOT: With machine running (Steel Knife), drop 2 shallots through feed tube, processing until minced. Proceed with recipe as above, substituting red wine or champagne vinegar for the white wine vinegar.

GREEN: Process (Steel Knife) 3 sprigs parsley, 2 sprigs coriander, and 4 to 6 spinach leaves until minced; reserve. Make mayonnaise as above; stir in minced herbs and spinach.

CUCUMBER: Process (Steel Knife) ½ medium cucumber, pared, seeded, and cut into 1-inch pieces, using on/off technique, until chopped; reserve. Make mayonnaise as above; stir in cucumber and ½ teaspoon dried dillweed or 1½ teaspoons snipped fresh dill.

GARLIC: With machine running (Steel Knife), drop garlic through feed tube, processing until minced. Proceed with mayonnaise recipe as above.

HORSERADISH: Make mayonnaise as above; add ½ cup currant jelly and 1 to 2 tablespoons prepared horseradish to bowl; process (Steel Knife) using on/off technique until blended.

CHANTILLY: Process (Steel Knife) 1 cup whipping cream until thick; reserve. Make mayonnaise as above; fold in cream.

Tips: To ensure good results, start with all ingredients at room temperature.

When adding oil through feed tube, pour very slowly at first—only a few drops at a time—until mixture begins to thicken. If mayonnaise fails to thicken, pour it into a 2-cup measure and use this quick "rescue" technique: Process (Steel Knife) an additional egg yolk until beaten. With the machine running, slowly pour the mayonnaise mixture through the feed tube and process until thickened.

FOOD PROCESSOR BUTTER AND VARIATIONS

The most delicious butter is easily "churned" in the food processor. Mimic the fresh taste, if you wish, by blending purchased butter with sour cream. Either way, you can add sweet or savory seasonings to make great toppings for vegetables, meats, pancakes, toast, and dinner rolls.

Total Preparation Time: 5 to 8 minutes
Yield: about ⅔ cup

---

2 cups whipping cream

Process (Steel Knife) cream until mixture becomes grainy in appearance and water begins to separate; continue processing until mixture returns to a smooth consistency and becomes pale yellow in color, 8 to 10 minutes. Rinse in cold water; drain in strainer. Pack butter into covered container and refrigerate.

VARIATIONS

MOCK FOOD PROCESSOR BUTTER: Process (Steel Knife) ⅔ cup unsalted butter, slightly softened, and 1 tablespoon sour cream until fluffy; pack into covered container and refrigerate.

STRAWBERRY BUTTER: Process (Steel Knife) ⅔ cup butter, 3 ounces cream cheese, ½ cup hulled fresh strawberries, 3 tablespoons honey, and 2 teaspoons grated lemon rind until fluffy. Serve with baked potatoes, pancakes, or French toast.

CHUTNEY BUTTER: Process (Steel Knife) ⅔ cup butter, 2 tablespoons chutney, 1 teaspoon yogurt, and ¼ teaspoon curry powder until fluffy; add ¼ cup peanuts and process (Steel Knife) using on/off technique until peanuts are chopped. Serve with baked sweet potatoes; roast lamb, pork, or chicken; steamed asparagus, acorn squash, or carrots.

PARMESAN–GARLIC BUTTER: Process (Steel Knife) 2 large sprigs parsley using on/off technique until minced. With machine running, drop ½ ounce cubed Parmesan cheese and 1 clove garlic through feed tube, processing until finely grated. Add ⅔ cup butter, 1 tablespoon sour cream, ¼ teaspon dried marjoram leaves, ⅛ teaspoon dried oregano leaves, and ⅛ teaspoon dried thyme leaves to bowl; process (Steel Knife) until smooth. Serve with baked potatoes, cooked green vegetables, or grilled meats.

CLARIFIED BUTTER AND VARIATION

It's much easier to clarify or brown butter without burning it in the microwave oven. Some cooks prefer Clarified Butter for sauces, and most agree that it yields the best fillo pastries. The toasted taste of Brown Butter will highlight any plain, cooked vegetable.

Total Preparation Time: 3 to 4 minutes
Microwave Time: 2 to 3 minutes
Yield: about ¾ cup

Microwave 1 cup butter in glass measure at High until melted and bubbly. Let stand several minutes for milk solids to collect at bottom. Skim foam from top and pour clear butter into container; discard milk solids.

VARIATION

BROWN BUTTER: Microwave clarified butter in glass measure at High until butter turns brown in color, 2 to 3 minutes. Serve over cooked vegetables.

GARLIC SALT AND VARIATIONS

Sprinkle these seasoning salts on meats and vegetables—and wrap up extra jars as gifts for friends who cook.

Total Preparation Time: 12 to 14 minutes (plus refrigeration time)
Microwave Time: 3 minutes
Yield: 1 cup

2 cloves garlic, peeled
1 cup coarse (Kosher) salt

With machine running (Steel Knife), drop garlic through feed tube, processing until minced. Add salt to bowl; process using on/off technique until mixture is very finely ground. Refrigerate covered overnight.

Pour salt mixture into glass pie plate; microwave uncovered at High 3 minutes, stirring every minute. Cool to room temperature; process (Steel Knife) until smooth. Store in airtight container at room temperature.

VARIATIONS

DILL: Follow above recipe, substituting ¾ teaspoon dried dillweed for the garlic; add dillweed to food processor bowl with salt.

BASIL: Follow above recipe, substituting 1 teaspoon dried basil leaves, ½ teaspoon paprika, and ¹⁄₁₆ teaspoon turmeric for the garlic; add basil, paprika, and turmeric to food processor bowl with salt.

MUSTARD: Follow above recipe, substituting ½ teaspoon dry mustard for the garlic; add mustard to food processor bowl with salt.

BREAD CRUMBS AND VARIATIONS

Fresh and dried bread crumbs can do so much so fast that no kitchen should be without a supply of the best quality crumbs. Make these with any kind of leftover bread. The yield will vary, depending on the type of bread.

Total Preparation Time: 8 to 11 minutes
Microwave Time: 3 to 4 minutes
Yield: about 2 to 2½ cups fresh crumbs, 1 to 1¼ cups dry crumbs

4 ounces French or Italian bread, torn into pieces

Process (Steel Knife) bread using on/off technique until fine crumbs are formed. Refrigerate fresh crumbs in airtight container up to 1 month.

To make dry crumbs, spread fresh crumbs in thin layer in 12″ × 8″ glass baking dish. Microwave uncovered at High until dry, 3 to 4 minutes, stirring after 2 minutes; cool. If desired, process (Steel Knife) to finer texture. Store dry crumbs in airtight container at room temperature up to 2 months.

VARIATIONS

WHEAT AND WALNUT: Process (Steel Knife) 4 large sprigs parsley until minced; add 4 ounces whole wheat bread, torn into pieces, to bowl. Process as above. Add ¼ cup uncooked oats, ¼ cup walnuts, ⅛ teaspoon ground cinnamon, 1/16 teaspoon ground mace, and 1/16 teaspoon ground nutmeg to bowl. Process 2 seconds. Store fresh crumbs or make dry crumbs as above.

RAISIN: Process (Steel Knife) 4 ounces raisin bread, torn into pieces, ⅓ cup pecans, ⅛ teaspoon ground allspice, and pinch cloves using on/off technique as above. Store fresh crumbs or make dry crumbs as above.

GARLIC–HERB: With machine running (Steel Knife), drop 1 clove peeled garlic through feed tube, processing until minced. Add 4 ounces French or Italian bread, torn into pieces, to bowl; add 1 teaspoon dried chives, ½ teaspoon dried basil leaves, ¼ teaspoon dried oregano leaves, and ⅛ teaspoon dried marjoram leaves to bowl. Process as above; store fresh crumbs or make dry crumbs as above.

HOT SPICY RYE: Process (Steel Knife) 1 small green onion, cut into 1-inch pieces, using on/off technique until chopped. Add 4 ounces rye bread, torn into pieces, ⅛ to ¼ teaspoon cayenne pepper, ⅛ teaspoon ground cumin, and ⅛ teaspoon paprika to bowl. Process as above; store fresh crumbs or make dry crumbs as above.

PARMESAN: With machine running (Steel Knife), drop 1 ounce Parmesan cheese, cut into 1-inch pieces, through feed tube, processing until finely grated. Add 4 ounces whole wheat bread, torn into pieces, and ½ teaspoon dried tarragon leaves to bowl; process as above. Store fresh crumbs or make dry crumbs as above.

SESAME: Process (Steel Knife) 3 large sprigs parsley using on/off technique until minced. Add 4 ounces French or Italian bread, torn into pieces, to bowl; process as above. Add 2 tablespoons sesame seeds and ½ teaspoon chervil to bowl; process 2 seconds. Store fresh crumbs or make dry crumbs as above.

BREAD VARIATIONS: The above recipes can be made with French, Italian, whole wheat, rye, or pumpernickel bread. Raisin bread can be used to make the plain or Wheat and Walnut variation.

CROUTONS AND VARIATIONS

For casseroles, soups, salads, and stuffings— the superior flavor and economy of homemade croutons.

Total Preparation Time: 12 to 15 minutes
Microwave Time: 5 to 7 minutes
Yield: 3 cups

¼ cup butter or margarine
6 sprigs parsley
4 ounces day-old or French bread, cut into scant ½-inch cubes (about 3 cups)

Microwave butter in 12″ × 8″ glass baking dish at High until melted. Process (Steel Knife) parsley using on/off technique until minced; stir into butter. Add bread cubes to baking dish, tossing to coat with butter mixture. Microwave uncovered at High until lightly browned and dry, 3 to 4 minutes, stirring every 2 minutes. Cool to room temperature (croutons become more crisp as they cool); store in airtight container at room temperature up to 1 week or freeze up to 2 months.

VARIATIONS

GARLIC: With machine running (Steel Knife), drop 1 large clove peeled garlic through feed tube, processing until minced. Mix with melted butter and bread cubes and microwave as above.

HERB: Mix 1 teaspoon minced fresh or ½ teaspoon dried herbs with melted butter and bread cubes and microwave as above. Use any favorite herb or combination of herbs including tarragon, basil, dillweed, oregano, chervil, marjoram, rosemary, or coriander.

SWEET OR SAVORY: Mix ¼ to ½ teaspoon ground spices with melted butter and bread cubes and microwave as above. Use cinnamon, nutmeg, mace, chili powder, or allspice.

PARMESAN: With machine running (Steel Knife), drop ½ ounce Parmesan cheese through feed tube, processing until grated. Toss warm croutons with cheese; cool as above.

BREAD VARIATIONS: Croutons can be made with any kind of bread. Rye, whole wheat, and pumpernickel are excellent for garlic, herb, or savory croutons; raisin bread can be used for basic or sweet croutons.

BAKING MIX

It makes no sense to buy baking mix when you can blend your own in seconds and store it without chemical preservatives. Use it to make Poppy Seed Biscuits, Cheese Twists, and Fresh Fruit Cobbler (see Index), as well as your own recipes. Substitute half whole wheat flour or enrich the mix by substituting ½ cup wheat germ for ½ cup flour.

Total Preparation Time: 3 to 4 minutes
Yield: 4 cups mix

---

4 cups unbleached flour
1½ tablespoons baking powder
2 teaspoons sugar

½ teaspoon baking soda
½ teaspoon salt
¼ teaspoon vegetable shortening

Process (Steel Knife) all ingredients using on/off technique until mixture is blended. Refrigerate in airtight container.

CHICKEN BROTH

There is no comparison between the flavor of homemade broths and stocks and commercial mixtures. But quantities of such liquids should be cooked conventionally. You may want to microwave this relatively fast chicken broth, however, if you are caught short of stock-making time or if you don't want to heat up the kitchen. Chop and add whatever fresh greens you have available, whether parsley, dill, celery leaves, or carrot tops; these will enhance the flavor immeasurably.

Total Preparation Time: 40 to 70 minutes
Microwave Time: 30 to 60 minutes
Yield: about 1 quart

---

1 medium carrot, pared, cut to fit feed tube
1 rib celery, cut to fit feed tube
1 medium onion, peeled, cut to fit feed tube
1 pound chicken parts (wings, backs, necks)
6 cups water
2 bay leaves
Pinch dried thyme leaves

Slice (Slicing Disc) carrot, celery, and onion. Microwave vegetables and remaining ingredients in 3-quart glass casserole, uncovered, at High 30 to 60 minutes, depending upon desired strength of flavor.

Strain; discard chicken pieces and vegetables. Cool to room temperature; refrigerate broth up to 4 days or freeze up to 2 months.

Onion Cornbread
Poppy Seed Biscuits
Sour Cream Scones
Walnut Streusel Coffee Cake
Zucchini Muffins
Date-Nut Casserole Bread
Cheese Twists
Herbed-Wheat Crackers
Garlic-Herb Toast
Onion-Walnut Loaf
Oatmeal Bread
Three-Grain Bread

15 Breads

ONION CORN BREAD

A fast supper menu-maker when the main course is a hearty soup or leftover meat. For an outstanding brunch bread, stir two or three strips of crumbled, cooked bacon into the batter.

Total Preparation Time: 20 to 22 minutes
Microwave Time: 5 to 7 minutes
Yield: 6 servings

2 ounces Cheddar cheese, chilled, cut to fit feed tube
½ medium onion, peeled, cut into 1-inch pieces
2 tablespoons butter or margarine
1 cup buttermilk
2 eggs
2 tablespoons sugar
1 tablespoon vegetable oil
1 cup cornmeal
1 cup all-purpose flour
1½ teaspoons baking powder
½ teaspoon salt

Shred (Shredding Disc) cheese; reserve. Process (Steel Knife) onion using on/off technique until chopped. Microwave onion and butter in 2-cup glass measure, uncovered, at High until onion is golden, 2 to 4 minutes, stirring after 2 minutes.

Process (Steel Knife) buttermilk, eggs, sugar, and oil until smooth. Sprinkle onion mixture, cornmeal, flour, baking powder, and salt over ingredients in bowl; process using on/off technique just until blended. Spoon batter into greased 9-inch square glass baking dish; microwave uncovered at High until mixture is set and springs back when touched, 3 to 5 minutes, rotating dish ¼ turn every 2 minutes.

Sprinkle reserved cheese over corn bread; let stand uncovered 5 minutes. Cut into squares; serve warm.

Tip: Don't overprocess the batter. A few on/off turns should be sufficient to blend in the dry ingredients. Scrape down the side of the bowl as needed.

POPPY SEED BISCUITS

The warm reassurance of a "made from scratch" bread in almost no time at all. These biscuits are a natural accompaniment to gravy-rich entrées and "downhome" breakfasts.

Total Preparation Time: 16 to 18 minutes
Microwave Time: 4 to 6 minutes
Yield: 1 dozen

2 cups Baking Mix (see Index)
½ cup milk
1 tablespoon butter or margarine
2 tablespoons dry Bread Crumbs (see Index)
½ teaspoon poppy seeds

Place Baking Mix in food processor bowl with Steel Knife; with machine running, pour milk through feed tube until ingredients form ball of dough. Let dough spin around bowl 5 times.

Pat dough on lightly floured surface to ½-inch thickness; cut biscuits with 2-inch round cutter. Microwave butter in small custard cup at High until melted. Brush tops of biscuits with butter; sprinkle with combined bread crumbs and poppy seeds.

Place biscuits on 2 plates lined with paper toweling. Microwave 1 plate at a time uncovered at High until biscuits have risen and are slightly dry on top, 2 to 3 minutes, rotating plate ¼ turn every minute. Serve warm.

Tips: If you have a browning dish, check the manufacturer's instructions for cooking biscuits; if biscuits are browned on the dish, bread crumbs and poppy seeds may be omitted.

You may wish to keep honey-butter on hand for breakfast. Process (Steel Knife) honey and butter until fluffy; refrigerate tightly covered up to 1 month. Use 1 part honey to 3 parts butter or equal parts of honey and butter, depending on desired sweetness.

Strawberry Butter (see Index) is another fine spread for hot biscuits.

SOUR CREAM SCONES

The British favorite, baked extra tender with sour cream, invites a cup of tea anytime but really shines at an American-style brunch.

Total Preparation Time: 20 to 21 minutes
Microwave Time: 5 to 6 minutes
Yield: 1 dozen

2 cups all-purpose flour
2 tablespoons sugar
1 tablespoon baking powder
¼ teaspoon baking soda
1 teaspoon salt
¼ cup cold butter or margarine, cut into pieces
¼ cup whipping cream or half-and-half
½ cup sour cream
1 egg
1 tablespoon sugar
⅛ teaspoon ground cinnamon
Dash ground mace
Dash ground nutmeg
Butter or margarine
Orange marmalade

Process (Steel Knife) flour, 2 tablespoons sugar, the baking powder, baking soda, salt, and ¼ cup butter using on/off technique until mixture resembles coarse crumbs. Add cream, sour cream, and egg to bowl; process using on/off technique just until mixed (dough will be soft).

Divide dough in half. Pat each half on lightly floured surface into 6-inch circle; cut each circle into 6 wedges. Mix 1 tablespoon sugar, the cinnamon, mace, and nutmeg; sprinkle over scones.

Place 6 scones in circle with pointed ends toward center on plate lined with paper toweling. Microwave uncovered at High 2½ to 3 minutes, or until no longer doughy; let stand 2 minutes. Repeat with remaining scones.

Serve warm with butter and marmalade.

Tip: Sour Cream Scones can be frozen, wrapped in aluminum foil, up to 3 months. To reheat, microwave on paper toweling at High, 30 seconds per scone.

WALNUT STREUSEL COFFEE CAKE

If you're not careful, this walnut-laced cake will disappear as quickly as it's baked!

Total Preparation Time: 27 to 29 minutes
Microwave Time: 7 to 9 minutes
Yield: 6 to 8 servings

1 cup walnuts
2 tablespoons light brown sugar
1 tablespoon flour
½ teaspoon ground cinnamon
⅛ teaspoon ground mace
½ cup cold butter or margarine, cut into pieces
¾ cup granulated sugar
¾ cup sour cream
1 egg
1 teaspoon vanilla
1½ cups all-purpose flour
1 teaspoon baking powder
1 teaspoon baking soda

Process (Steel Knife) walnuts, brown sugar, 1 tablespoon flour, the cinnamon, and mace using on/off technique until nuts are finely chopped; remove.

Process (Steel Knife) butter and granulated sugar until smooth and fluffy. Add sour cream, egg, and vanilla to bowl; process until smooth. Sprinkle 1½ cups flour, the baking powder, and soda over ingredients in bowl; process using on/off technique just until blended.

Spoon half the batter into ungreased 6-cup glass or plastic ring mold. Sprinkle with half the nut mixture. Repeat with remaining batter and nuts. Microwave on inverted saucer, uncovered, at 50% (Medium) 5 minutes, rotating mold ¼ turn every minute. Microwave uncovered at High until cake springs back when touched, 2 to 4 minutes, rotating mold ¼ turn every minute (cake may have moist spots on the top). Let stand on counter top 10 minutes. Serve warm.

Tips: Cake can be baked 1 day in advance; store covered at room temperature. The texture

*will become denser as the cake stands, and
you may prefer it this way. If you bake
the cake in a 2-quart casserole, with a
glass placed open end up in the center,
you can remove it more easily for freezing.
Let it stand at least 4 hours after baking;
then remove, wrap in aluminum foil and
freeze. To reheat, microwave slices on
paper toweling at High 30 seconds.*

*For most efficient processing, scrape
down the side of the workbowl once or
twice when combining butter and sugar. It
is not necessary to combine dry
ingredients before adding them to the food
processor bowl; just sprinkle them over the
ingredients in the bowl.*

*To make a delicious filling for baked
apples, follow the first step of the above
recipe. Prepare apples by coring and
paring a strip of skin from the top of each
apple. Place apples in glass baking dish
or custard cups. Spoon walnut mixture
into centers and top each with a thin pat
of butter. Microwave covered with waxed
paper at High 2 to 3 minutes per apple;
let stand 3 minutes. Extra walnut
mixture can be refrigerated covered up to
1 month.*

ZUCCHINI MUFFINS

An excellent muffin by any standard—
unusually moist and well spiced. But the food
processor adds to the enticement by removing
any second thoughts about shredding zucchini,
and the microwave oven excels at this type of
batter bread.

Total Preparation Time: 26 to 29 minutes
Microwave Time: 6 to 8 minutes
Yield: 1 dozen

¾ cup pecans or walnuts
1 small zucchini, cut to fit feed tube (about
   4 ounces)
⅓ cup granulated sugar

⅓ cup packed light brown sugar
3 tablespoons vegetable oil
2 tablespoons cold butter or margarine
1 egg
¼ teaspoon vanilla
⅔ cup all-purpose flour
½ teaspoon ground cinnamon
½ teaspoon baking soda
⅛ teaspoon baking powder
¹⁄₁₆ teaspoon ground allspice
¹⁄₁₆ teaspoon ground nutmeg
¼ teaspoon salt

Process (Steel Knife) pecans using on/off
technique until finely chopped; remove. Shred
(Shredding Disc) zucchini; remove. Process
(Steel Knife) sugars, the oil, and butter until
very soft and fluffy. Add egg and vanilla to
bowl; process using on/off technique until
blended. Add ¼ cup of the pecans and the
zucchini to the bowl; process using on/off
technique just until blended. Sprinkle flour,
cinnamon, baking soda, baking powder,
allspice, nutmeg, and salt over ingredients in
bowl; process using on/off technique just until
flour disappears.

Place 6 paper liners in microwave muffin
pan. Spoon about 2 tablespoons mixture into
each liner (about half full). Microwave
uncovered at High 2 minutes, rotating pan ¼
turn after 1 minute. Microwave uncovered at
50% (Medium) until toothpick inserted in
center of muffins comes out clean, about 1
minute (tops of muffins will look very moist).
Let muffins stand on counter top 5 minutes.
Repeat with remaining batter. Dip tops of
muffins in remaining chopped nuts.

*Tip: If you don't have a plastic microwave
   muffin pan, batter can be spooned into 6
   paper-lined custard cups. Arrange cups in
   a circle in the oven and proceed as above,
   rearranging cups after 1 minute.*

DATE–NUT CASSEROLE BREAD

Spread thin wedges or half-slices of this

round loaf with cream cheese and savor it with fruit salads or morning coffee.

Total Preparation Time: 43 to 45 minutes
Microwave Time: 13 to 15 minutes
Yield: 1 loaf

---

1 cup pitted dates
⅓ cup granulated sugar
⅓ cup packed light brown sugar
1 cup walnuts
⅔ cup water
1 teaspoon baking soda
¼ cup butter or margarine
1 egg
1 teaspoon vanilla
2 cups all-purpose flour
1 teaspoon baking powder
¼ teaspoon ground nutmeg
¼ teaspoon ground allspice
½ teaspoon salt

Process (Steel Knife) dates and sugars using on/off technique until coarsely chopped. Add walnuts to bowl; process using on/off technique until coarsely chopped. Microwave water in 1-cup glass measure at High until boiling. Add water and baking soda to bowl; process (Steel Knife) 2 seconds using on/off technique. Let stand 10 minutes.

Microwave butter in 1-cup glass measure at High until melted; add butter, egg, and vanilla to bowl. Process (Steel Knife) using on/off technique, 3 seconds. Sprinkle flour, baking powder, nutmeg, allspice, and salt over ingredients in bowl. Process (Steel Knife) using on/off technique just until flour is blended into mixture.

Cut 5-inch circle of waxed paper and place in bottom of 1½-quart glass casserole; spoon batter into casserole, smoothing top. Microwave uncovered at 50% (Medium) 8 minutes, rotating casserole ¼ turn every 2 minutes. Microwave uncovered at High until moistness is almost gone from center of bread, 2 to 4 minutes. Let stand on counter top 10 minutes. Remove from casserole and remove waxed paper. Cool on wire rack. Makes 1 loaf.

Tip: One cup of mixed dried fruit or raisins can be substituted for the dates.

CHEESE TWISTS

Set out for predinner nibbling, these twists are just rich enough to soothe appetites without spoiling them. They are also superb with soups and entrée salads.

Total Preparation Time: 26 to 28 minutes
Microwave Time: 6 to 8 minutes
Yield: 1½ dozen

---

2 ounces Swiss cheese, chilled, cut to fit feed tube
1 sprig parsley
¼ ounce Parmesan cheese
1¼ cups Baking Mix (see Index)
2 tablespoons butter or margarine
⅛ teaspoon cayenne pepper
4 to 5 tablespoons ice water
Paprika

Shred (Shredding Disc) Swiss Cheese; remove. Process (Steel Knife) parsley using on/off technique until minced. With machine running, drop Parmesan cheese through feed tube; process until minced. Add Swiss cheese, Baking Mix, butter, and cayenne pepper to bowl; process (Steel Knife) until mixture resembles coarse crumbs. With machine running, add water through feed tube until ingredients form ball of dough.

Roll dough on lightly floured surface into rectangle ¼ inch thick. Cut into strips 5″ × ½″. Twist strips. Microwave 6 strips at a time in 12″ × 8″ glass baking dish, uncovered, at High until crisp, 2 to 2½ minutes, rotating dish ¼ turn after 1 minute. Sprinkle with paprika; let cool on wire rack (twists become crisper as they cool).

Tip: Cheese Twists can be made 2 days in advance; store in a tightly covered container at room temperature. To recrisp

*them, microwave on paper toweling,
uncovered, at High until warm, about 30
seconds to 1 minute, and cool on wire rack.
For most effective heating, arrange twists
in a spoke pattern.*

HERBED-WHEAT CRACKERS

Not as dry as packaged crackers, these
fragile squares make good light nibbling
unadorned or with a soft cheese, such as ripe
Camembert or Boursin.

Total Preparation Time: 26 to 28 minutes
Microwave Time: 6 to 8 minutes
Yield: about 3 dozen

---

4 sprigs parsley
1 clove garlic, peeled
½ cup all-purpose flour
½ cup whole wheat flour
½ teaspoon dried savory leaves
¹⁄₁₆ teaspoon dried thyme leaves
½ teaspoon salt
6 tablespoon cold butter or margarine, cut
   into pieces
3 to 4 tablespoons ice water

Process (Steel Knife) parsley using on/off
technique until minced. With machine running
(Steel Knife), drop garlic through feed tube,
processing until minced. Add flours, savory,
thyme, and salt to food processor bowl; process
(Steel Knife) until mixed. Add butter to bowl;
process using on/off technique until mixture is
crumbly. With machine running, add water
through feed tube until mixture holds together
but is not sticky (dough will not form a ball).
Roll dough on floured surface into rectangle
16″ × 10″; cut into 2-inch squares. Place 10
crackers in greased 12″ × 8″ glass baking dish;
microwave uncovered at High until crisp,
about 2 minutes. Cool on wire rack; crackers
will become crisper as they cool. Repeat with
remaining crackers. Store at room temperature
in airtight container.

GARLIC-HERB TOAST

This very easy Melba-type toast makes good
use of leftover bread and saves the cost of
purchased crackers. It goes well with spreads,
cheeses, salads, and soups. Try it with Double-
Dressed Chicken Salad or Continuous Cheese
Crock (see Index).

Total Preparation Time: 24 to 33 minutes
Microwave Time: 15 to 18 minutes
Yield: 18 pieces

---

2 large sprigs parsley
1 clove garlic, peeled
½ cup cold butter or margarine, cut into
   pieces
½ teaspoon dried basil leaves
¼ teaspoon oregano leaves
⅛ teaspoon dried marjoram leaves
18 thin slices Italian bread (¼ inch thick)

Process (Steel Knife) parsley using on/off
technique until minced. With machine running,
drop garlic through feed tube; process until
minced. Add butter, basil, oregano, and
marjoram to bowl; process until smooth.
Microwave butter mixture in glass custard cup
at High until melted. Lightly brush butter
mixture on one side of bread slices. Microwave
6 bread slices on microwave roasting rack,
uncovered, at High until bread is completely
dry, and beginning to brown, 4 to 7 minutes,
turning bread slices over and rotating rack ¼
turn every 2 minutes. Cool on wire rack (bread
will become crisper as it cools). Store at room
temperature in airtight container up to 1 week.

*Tip: To make plain Melba toast, omit herbs and
proceed as above.*

ONION-WALNUT LOAF

An unusual pizza-style loaf—flat, puffy, and
smothered with onion and walnuts. The shape
and toppings disguise the purchased dough,

but the convenience is unmistakable. Serve it with plain entrées or soups, or as a snack.

Total Preparation Time: 76 to 77 minutes (plus 20 more, if needed)
Microwave Time: 31 to 32 minutes (plus 10 more, if needed)
Yield: 1 loaf

---

1 loaf frozen white bread dough
¾ cup walnuts
1 large onion, peeled, cut to fit feed tube
¼ cup butter or margarine
1 teaspoon Worcestershire sauce
½ teaspoon dried sage leaves
Cornmeal

Place frozen dough in an 8½″ × 4½″ glass loaf pan; place pan in glass baking dish; fill baking dish halfway with warm water. Microwave loosely covered at 50% (Medium) 2 minutes, rotating dish ¼ turn after 1 minute. Turn dough over in loaf pan; microwave loosely covered at 50% (Medium) 2 minutes, rotating dish ¼ turn after 1 minute. Let loaf pan stand in baking dish, loosely covered, 10 minutes, or until thawed.

Place baking dish in oven. Microwave dough loosely covered at 10% (Low) 10 minutes. Repeat procedure, if necessary, until dough has doubled in bulk.

Process (Steel Knife) walnuts using on/off technique until coarsely chopped; remove. Slice (Slicing Disc) onion. Microwave butter in 1-quart glass casserole at High until melted; stir in onion. Microwave uncovered at High 10 minutes, or until onion is golden, stirring every 4 minutes. Stir in walnuts, Worcestershire sauce, and sage.

Roll dough on lightly floured surface into 10-inch round; place in 10-inch glass quiche pan sprinkled lightly with cornmeal. Spoon onion mixture over top of bread; let stand lightly covered 15 minutes. Make indentations in bread at 2-inch intervals, using handle of wooden spoon. Microwave uncovered at 70% (Medium High) until dough springs back when touched, 6 to 7 minutes, rotating pan ¼ turn every 2 minutes. Let stand on counter top 5

minutes; remove from pan and cool on wire rack.

Tips: Whole wheat or rye bread dough can be substituted for the white bread dough.

The toppings can be varied. For an appetizer bread, substitute ½ cup ripe olives and two sweet red pimientos, cut into quarters, for the walnuts; add 1 ounce Parmesan cheese, cut into 1-inch pieces. With machine running (Steel Knife), drop cheese through feed tube, processing until grated. Chop (Steel Knife) the pimientos; drain well. Slice (Slicing Disc) the olives. Proceed as above; cut loaf into squares.

OATMEAL BREAD

One loaf of this oat-enriched bread, with butter and jam, will not go very far! But if you don't consume it all straight from the oven, you'll have the perfect bread for all kinds of cheese sandwiches.

Total Preparation Time: 68 to 72 minutes (plus 20 more, if needed)
Microwave Time: 28 to 30 minutes (plus 10 more, if needed)
Yield: 1 loaf

---

1 package (¼ ounce) active dry yeast
2 tablespoons sugar
¼ cup warm water (110° F)
¾ cup milk
⅓ cup uncooked quick oats
2¼ cups all-purpose flour
¼ cup whole wheat flour
½ teaspoon baking soda
1 teaspoon salt
2 tablespoons cold butter or margarine
2 to 3 tablespoons cold water
Milk
Uncooked quick oats

Stir yeast and sugar into ¼ cup warm water in small bowl; let stand 5 minutes. Microwave ¾ cup milk in 2-cup glass measure at High just until boiling; stir in ⅓ cup oats and cool to room temperature.

Measure flours, baking soda, salt, and butter into food processor bowl; process (Steel Knife) until mixture resembles coarse crumbs. Add yeast mixture and oat mixture to bowl; process (Steel Knife) using on/off technique until mixed. With machine running, add 2 to 3 tablespoons cold water through feed tube for dough to form ball; let ball of dough spin around bowl 12 to 15 times. Remove Steel Knife; cover food processor bowl with plastic wrap.

Place food processor bowl in glass baking dish; fill baking dish halfway with warm water. Microwave at 10% (Low) 10 minutes; let stand covered 10 minutes. Repeat procedure, if necessary, until dough has doubled in bulk. Punch down dough.

Grease 8½″ × 4½″ loaf pan; coat with oats. Shape dough into loaf; place in pan. Place loaf pan in glass baking dish with warm water. Microwave uncovered at 10% (Low) 10 minutes; let stand 10 minutes. Repeat procedure, if necessary, until bread has doubled in bulk. Remove loaf pan from baking dish.

Brush top of loaf lightly with milk; sprinkle with oats. Microwave uncovered at 70% (Medium High) until bread springs back when touched lightly, about 7 minutes, rotating pan ¼ turn after 4 minutes. Remove bread from pan immediately; cool upside down on wire rack (bottom and sides of loaf may be a little sticky, but will dry upon standing).

Tips: For deeper color, toast the oats in a 9-inch glass dish or pie plate. Microwave uncovered at High 3 minutes, rotating the dish ¼ turn halfway through.

Add water to dough cautiously; you need only enough water for dough to form a ball. If dough is too sticky to form a ball, add all-purpose flour, 1 tablespoon at a time; sprinkle flour over dough and process until mixed. If your food processor slows down, indicating that it cannot handle the full quantity, divide

dough in half; process each half until it forms a ball and recombine dough by hand.

Oatmeal Bread will not form a crust in the microwave oven. You can let the dough rise in the oven, as above, and bake it conventionally. Bake in preheated 400° F oven until top starts to brown and bread sounds hollow when tapped, about 25 minutes.

Dough can be frozen up to 1 month; punch down dough after first rising, shape into loaf, and wrap tightly. To thaw and continue rising, place frozen dough in greased, oat-coated loaf pan and follow the first two paragraphs of Onion-Walnut Loaf (previous recipe).

THREE-GRAIN BREAD

A dense, chewy whole grain loaf dotted with caraway seeds. Bake it conventionally, if you wish, to add crustiness to the Old World flavor.

Total Preparation Time: 72 to 76 minutes (plus 20 more, if needed)
Microwave Time: 28 to 30 minutes (plus 20 more, if needed)
Yield: 1 large loaf

---

1 package (¼ ounce) active dry yeast
½ cup warm water (110° F)
⅓ cup dark corn syrup
1⅓ cups all-purpose flour
1 cup whole wheat flour
⅔ cup rye flour
2 teaspoons caraway seeds
1 tablespoon grated orange rind
1½ teaspoons salt
¼ cup cold butter or margarine, cut into 4 pieces
¼ to ½ cup warm water (110° F)
Cornmeal or flour
1 tablespoon butter or margarine
½ teaspoon caraway seeds

Mix yeast, ½ cup water, and the corn syrup in small bowl; let stand 5 minutes. Process (Steel Knife) flours, 2 teaspoons caraway seeds, the orange rind, and salt until blended; add ¼ cup butter to bowl. Process (Steel Knife) using on/off technique until butter is cut into flour and mixture resembles coarse crumbs. Add yeast mixture to bowl; process using on/off technique until blended. With machine running, add ¼ to ½ cup water through feed tube for dough to form a ball; let ball of dough spin around bowl 15 times. Remove Steel Knife; cover food processor bowl with plastic wrap.

Place food processor bowl on shallow baking dish; fill baking dish halfway with warm water. Microwave at 10% (Low) for 10 minutes; let stand covered 10 minutes. Repeat procedure, if necessary, until dough has doubled in bulk. Punch down dough; form into ring about 9 inches in diameter with 3-inch hole in the center. Place dough on paper toweling lightly coated with cornmeal; place on glass plate. Microwave uncovered at 10% (Low) 10 minutes; let stand uncovered 10 minutes. Repeat procedure, if necessary, until dough has doubled in bulk.

Microwave 1 tablespoon butter in small glass custard cup at High until melted. Brush top of dough with butter; sprinkle with ½ teaspoon caraway seeds. Microwave uncovered at 70% (Medium High) until top of bread springs back lightly when touched, about 8 minutes, rotating loaf ¼ turn after 4 minutes. Transfer to wire rack; let stand at least 5 minutes before serving.

Tips: See previous recipe for mixing and kneading tips.

To bake Three-Grain Bread conventionally, let rise as above. Transfer dough to greased baking sheet coated with cornmeal. Brush with butter and sprinkle with seeds as above. Bake in preheated 400° F oven until loaf is golden and sounds hollow when tapped, about 25 minutes.

16 Desserts

PINEAPPLE–CASHEW SQUARES

A rich, crumbly bar cookie glazed with preserves.

Total Preparation Time: 28 to 31 minutes
Microwave Time: 9 to 10 minutes
Yield: 2 dozen

⅓ cup cashews
½ cup cold butter or margarine, cut into pieces
⅓ cup granulated sugar
⅓ cup packed light brown sugar
½ teaspoon vanilla
1 cup all-purpose flour
¾ cup uncooked quick oats
1 teaspoon baking powder
¼ teaspoon ground allspice
⅛ teaspoon ground mace
Dash ground ginger
½ cup pineapple preserves
1 teaspoon lemon juice

Process (Steel Knife) cashews using on/off technique until finely chopped; reserve. Process (Steel Knife) butter, sugars, and vanilla until mixture is fluffy. Sprinkle cashews, flour, oats, baking powder, allspice, mace, and ginger over ingredients in bowl; process using on/off technique until blended (mixture will be crumbly). Pat mixture evenly on bottom of greased 9-inch square glass baking dish. Microwave uncovered at 50% (Medium) until crust is set and springs back when touched lightly, 6 to 7 minutes, shielding corners with aluminum foil and rotating dish ¼ turn after 3 minutes. Let stand on counter top 10 minutes.

Mix preserves and lemon juice; spread over crust. Microwave uncovered at 50% (Medium) 3 minutes. Cool on wire rack; cut into squares.

Tips: Scrape down bowl at least once when processing butter and sugars to ensure smooth consistency.

It is not necessary to combine dry ingredients before adding them to the food processor bowl; just sprinkle them over the ingredients in the bowl.

CHOCOLATE CHERRY BROWNIES

Cherries make double-chocolate brownies even chewier. To add to the baking temptation, the chocolate is melted and all ingredients are mixed in the food processor bowl. These bars are wonderful served warm with a scoop of ice cream.

Total Preparation Time: 46 to 47 minutes
Microwave Time: 10 to 11 minutes
Yield: 12 servings

⅓ cup blanched almonds
⅓ cup maraschino cherries, very well drained
2 ounces unsweetened chocolate, broken into pieces
⅓ cup cold butter or margarine, cut into pieces
½ cup granulated sugar
½ cup packed light brown sugar
2 eggs
½ teaspoon vanilla
⅔ cup all-purpose flour
¼ teaspoon baking powder
½ teaspoon salt
1 cup semisweet chocolate morsels
6 maraschino cherries, drained, cut into halves

Process (Steel Knife) almonds and ⅓ cup cherries using on/off technique until finely chopped; reserve. Remove Steel Knife; place 2 ounces chocolate and the butter in food processor bowl. Microwave uncovered at High until chocolate and butter are soft, but not melted, 2 to 3 minutes. Insert Steel Knife; add sugars, eggs, and vanilla to bowl. Process until ingredients are blended. Add reserved almonds and cherries to bowl; process using on/off technique until blended. Sprinkle flour, baking powder, and salt evenly over chocolate mixture; process using on/off technique just until blended.

Grease bottom of 8-inch square glass baking dish; spread batter in dish. Microwave uncovered at High just until center is dry, about 6 minutes, shielding corners with aluminum foil and rotating dish ¼ turn after 3 minutes. Let stand on counter top 20 minutes. Sprinkle chocolate morsels evenly over brownies; microwave at High until chocolate is soft, about 2 minutes. Spread chocolate evenly over brownies with spatula; garnish with cherry halves.

Tip: Test for doneness by inserting a toothpick into the center of the brownies. Be careful not to overcook; brownies will become firmer during standing time.

APRICOT-DATE BARS

Fruit, chocolate, and nuts sandwiched between a crisp cookie crust and a quick streusel topping. Get a head start by using a cake mix and blending the crust in the baking dish.

Total Preparation Time: 37 to 40 minutes
Microwave Time: 25 to 26 minutes
Yield: 3 dozen

½ cup butter or margarine
1 package (18.5 ounces) yellow cake mix
1 cup uncooked quick oats
1 egg, beaten
½ cup walnuts
2 cups pitted whole dates
1 cup dried apricots
¼ cup sugar
1½ cups water
1½ ounces semisweet chocolate

Microwave butter in 12″ × 8″ glass baking dish at High until melted. Stir in cake mix and oats until blended; reserve 1 cup crumb mixture. Add egg to mixture in baking dish and mix; press evenly on bottom of dish. Microwave uncovered at High until set, 5 to 6 minutes, rotating dish ¼ turn every 2 minutes. Process (Steel Knife) walnuts using on/off technique until chopped; reserve. Process (Steel

Knife) dates, apricots, and sugar using on/off technique until chopped. Microwave date mixture, water, and chocolate in 2-quart glass measure, covered with plastic wrap, at High 5 minutes; stir after 2½ minutes. Microwave uncovered at High for 3 minutes, stirring twice. Cool to room temperature.

Spread cooled date mixture over crust; sprinkle with reserved walnuts and crumb mixture. Microwave uncovered at High 10 minutes, rotating dish ¼ turn every 2 minutes. Cool on wire rack; cut into bars.

Tip: Apricot-Date Bars can be frozen, wrapped in aluminum foil, up to 3 months.

CHOCOLATE SHORTBREAD COOKIES

Flecks of chocolate and chopped pecans in a traditional, buttery shortbread.

Total Preparation Time: 30 to 32 minutes
Microwave Time: 8 to 10 minutes
Yield: 40

---

2 ounces semisweet chocolate, broken into pieces
⅔ cup pecans
2⅔ cups all-purpose flour
¾ cup powdered sugar
1 cup cold butter or margarine, cut into pieces
1 tablespoon vanilla
Cocoa or powdered sugar

Process (Steel Knife) chocolate using on/off technique until finely chopped. Add pecans to bowl; process using on/off technique until finely chopped. Add flour, ¾ cup powdered sugar, the butter, and vanilla to bowl; process using on/off technique just until mixed and smooth (chocolate pieces will be visible in dough).

Divide dough into quarters; divide each quarter into 10 equal pieces. Roll 10 pieces into balls; place around edge of waxed paper-lined 9-inch glass quiche dish or glass baking dish. Flatten cookies with bottom of glass. Microwave uncovered at High until crisp, 2 to 2½ minutes, rotating dish ¼ turn after 1 minute. Let stand 5 minutes; remove and cool on wire rack (cookies will become crisper as they cool). Repeat with remaining dough. Sprinkle cookies with cocoa or powdered sugar. Store at room temperature in airtight container.

Tips: Don't overprocess the dough; bits of chocolate should remain visible.

Chocolate shortbread dough, divided into quarters and wrapped in aluminum foil, can be frozen up to 2 months. For maximum convenience, freeze cookie-size balls of dough in a single layer on a baking sheet until firm; then transfer to a plastic bag and seal. Thaw dough balls on waxed paper in quiche dish and proceed as above.

⅛ teaspoon ground nutmeg
1¼ cups Baking Mix (see Index)
2 tablespoons butter or margarine
¼ cup packed light brown sugar
¼ cup milk
1 tablespoon granulated sugar
¼ teaspoon ground cinnamon

Slice (Slicing Disc) apples; place in 9-inch square glass baking dish. Toss apples with lemon juice, raisins, orange rind, ¼ cup granulated and ¼ cup brown sugar, the allspice, nutmeg, and ¼ cup of the Baking Mix.

Microwave apple mixture uncovered at High until apples are crisp-tender, 6 to 8 minutes, rotating dish ¼ turn after 3 minutes.

Process (Steel Knife) remaining 1 cup Baking Mix, the butter, and ¼ cup brown sugar until mixture is crumbly. Add milk to bowl; process using on/off technique just until blended. Spoon batter around edges of glass baking dish; microwave uncovered at High until topping has baked, 4 to 6 minutes, rotating dish ¼ turn after 3 minutes. Sprinkle with combined 1 tablespoon granulated sugar and the cinnamon. Serve warm.

FRESH FRUIT COBBLER

Keep Baking Mix on hand to assemble this all-seasons fresh fruit dessert in a matter of minutes.

Total Preparation Time: 23 to 28 minutes
Microwave Time: 10 to 14 minutes
Yield: 6 to 8 servings

2 pounds tart cooking apples or fresh peaches, pared, cored, cut to fit feed tube
2 tablespoons lemon juice
⅓ cup dark raisins
1 teaspoon grated orange or lemon rind
¼ cup granulated sugar
¼ cup packed light brown sugar
⅛ teaspoon ground allspice

APPLE PRALINE BUNDT CAKE

A moist, old-fashioned cake indulged with a touch of glamour. The mock praline topping takes only a few minutes to make but adds irresistible crunchiness.

Total Preparation Time: 51 to 53 minutes
Microwave Time: 18 to 20 minutes
Yield: 12 servings

Graham cracker crumbs
⅔ cup walnuts
1 pound apples (about 3 medium), pared, cored, cut to fit feed tube
¾ cup granulated sugar
¾ cup packed light brown sugar

1 cup vegetable oil
4 eggs
1½ cups all-purpose flour
1½ teaspoons baking powder
1 teaspoon baking soda
2 teaspoons ground cinnamon
¼ teaspoon ground nutmeg
¼ teaspoon ground allspice
Praline Glaze (recipe follows)

Grease 12-cup plastic fluted cake pan; coat with graham cracker crumbs. Process (Steel Knife) walnuts using on/off technique until coarsely chopped; remove. Shred (Shredding Disc) apples to make 2 cups; remove. Process (Steel Knife) sugars and oil until smooth; add eggs and process until smooth. Sprinkle flour, baking powder, baking soda, cinnamon, nutmeg, and allspice evenly over sugar mixture. Process (Steel Knife) using on/off technique just until blended. Add ½ cup of the walnuts and the apples to bowl; process using on/off technique just until blended into batter. Pour batter into prepared cake pan. Microwave elevated on microwave roasting rack, uncovered, at 50% (Medium) 12 minutes, rotating pan ¼ turn every 5 minutes. Microwave uncovered at High until cake springs back when touched lightly (cake may have moist spots on surface), 4 to 6 minutes, rotating pan ¼ turn after 2 minutes. Let stand on counter top 15 minutes; invert onto serving plate.

Make Praline Glaze. Pierce cake with long-tined fork; spoon glaze over warm cake. Sprinkle with remaining walnuts.

Praline Glaze

Yield: ¾ cup

3 tablespoons butter or margarine
⅓ cup packed light brown sugar
2 tablespoons brandy
2 tablespoons water

Microwave butter in 2-cup glass measure at High until melted; stir in sugar, brandy, and

water. Microwave uncovered at High until boiling; boil 30 seconds. Stir until sugar is dissolved.

Tips: Apple Praline Bundt Cake gets even better if you let it stand overnight, because the syrup will continue to soak into the cake.

To make graham cracker crumbs, break 2½-inch-square crackers into pieces; process (Steel Knife) using on/off technique until finely ground. Store crumbs in airtight container at room temperature up to 2 months. Three crackers will yield sufficient crumbs to coat cake pan.

Cake can be baked in a 3-quart glass casserole with a glass placed open end up in the center. Prepare casserole as above; grease glass.

CINNAMON APPLESAUCE

You may never purchase applesauce again! Homemade is incomparably better, and this recipe is much, much faster than most. Serve it for dessert, with plain cookies, or to accompany roast lamb or poultry.

Total Preparation Time: 17 to 19 minutes
Microwave Time: 8 to 10 minutes
Yield: about 3 cups

2½ pounds tart cooking apples, pared, cored, cut to fit feed tube
¼ cup water
¼ cup sugar
1 tablespoon brandy (optional)
½ teaspoon ground cinnamon
⅛ teaspoon ground mace
¹⁄₁₆ teaspoon ground nutmeg

Slice (Slicing Disc) apples. Microwave apples and water in 2½-quart glass casserole, covered, at High until apples are tender, about 8 minutes, stirring after 4 minutes. Process (Steel Knife) apple mixture, sugar, brandy, cinnamon, mace, and nutmeg until smooth. Cool to room temperature; refrigerate.

Tips: When the autumn harvest arrives, you may wish to make several batches of Cinnamon Applesauce and freeze or can the surplus. It can be kept frozen in covered containers up to 6 months. To can the sauce, pack it into sterilized canning jars and process in a water-bath canner according to the manufacturer's or USDA guidelines; never try to can food in the microwave oven.

Cinnamon Applesauce is delicious served in individual-portion Ginger Crumb Crusts. Make crumb mixture according to recipe (see Index) and press into bottoms of six 4-inch ceramic tart pans or 10-ounce custard cups; microwave according to recipe, rearranging pans after 1 minute. Cool and spoon applesauce into crusts. Make extra crumb mixture to sprinkle over sauce or garnish with thin slices of lemon.

CITRUS FREEZE

A most refreshing sherbet, and a delightful source of vitamin C. Serve it fancy with Apricot-Date Bars (see Index) for company, or keep it around for warm-weather snacks.

Total Preparation Time: 37 to 41 minutes (plus freezing time)
Microwave Time: 6 to 7 minutes
Yield: 8 servings (½ cup each)

1¼ cups sugar
1 cup water
4 to 6 oranges
4 to 5 large lemons, peeled, cut into quarters
¼ cup orange-flavored liqueur
Fresh mint sprigs (optional)

Mix sugar and water in 4-cup glass measure. Microwave uncovered at High until mixture boils, about 5 minutes; continue microwaving 1 minute, or until sugar is dissolved. Cool to room temperature. Grate rind from 1 orange; stir into sugar syrup.

Peel oranges and cut into quarters. Process (Steel Knife) oranges until all juice is extracted; strain and discard pith and seeds. Measure 2 cups orange juice. Process (Steel Knife) lemons until all juice is extracted; strain and discard pith and seeds. Measure 1 cup lemon juice.

Stir orange and lemon juice into sugar syrup; stir in liqueur. Pour mixture into 2 ice cube trays; freeze. Remove cubes from ice cube trays; store in plastic bag in freezer.

To serve, process (Steel Knife) 6 to 8 cubes at a time until smooth. Serve immediately in small bowls.

Tips: You can crush the citrus cubes effectively in the food processor because they do not freeze hard.

Citrus Freeze is tangy enough to serve as a palate-refresher between rich dinner courses.

One large pineapple, pared, cored, and cut into 1-inch pieces can be substituted for the lemons; adjust sugar according to the sweetness of the pineapple.

LEMON BOSTON CREAM PIE

A tall, regal cake—well worth the time investment for a special celebration. The top glistens with chocolate glaze and the custard filling is smooth and lemony.

Total Preparation Time: 45 to 50 minutes (plus chilling time)
Microwave Time: 19 to 22 minutes
Yield: 12 servings

Lemon Filling (recipe follows)
½ cup cold butter or margarine, cut into
   pieces
1½ cups sugar
2 eggs
1 cup milk
1 teaspoon vanilla
2¼ cups all-purpose flour
2 tablespoons cornstarch
1 tablespoon baking powder
½ teaspoon salt
Chocolate Cream Glaze (recipe follows)

Make Lemon Filling.

Process (Steel Knife) butter and sugar until very fluffy, about 1 minute, scraping side of bowl with rubber spatula after 30 seconds. Add eggs to bowl; process 1 minute. Add milk and vanilla to bowl; process just until blended. Sprinkle flour, cornstarch, baking powder, and salt evenly over ingredients in bowl; process using on/off technique just until flour disappears (do not overprocess).

Line bottom of 9-inch round glass or plastic cake pan with waxed paper; spoon in half the batter. Microwave uncovered at 50% (medium) 6 minutes; rotating pan ¼ turn every 2 minutes. Microwave at High until cake springs back when touched lightly, 2 to 3 minutes, (center of cake will still look moist and unbaked). Let cake stand on counter top 5 minutes; remove from pan and cool on wire rack. Repeat with remaining batter.

Make Chocolate Cream Glaze. Place 1 cake layer on serving plate; spread with Lemon Filling. Place second cake layer on filling; spread top of cake with Chocolate Cream Glaze. Refrigerate until serving time.

Lemon Filling

Yield: about 1¼ cups

⅓ cup sugar
2 tablespoons cornstarch
⅛ teaspoon salt
¾ cup water
1 egg yolk, beaten

3 tablespoons fresh lemon juice
2 teaspoons grated lemon rind
1 tablespoon butter or margarine

Mix sugar, cornstarch, and salt in 4-cup glass measure; stir in water. Microwave uncovered at High until very thick, 2 to 3 minutes, stirring every minute. Stir about 3 tablespoons cornstarch mixture into egg yolk; stir yolk mixture into cornstarch mixture. Microwave uncovered at 50% (Medium) 1 minute. Stir in lemon juice, lemon rind, and butter until butter is melted. Cover surface of mixture with plastic wrap; refrigerate until chilled, about 2 hours.

Chocolate Cream Glaze

Yield: about ¾ cup

1 ounce unsweetened chocolate
1 tablespoon butter or margarine
½ package (3-ounce size) cream cheese
½ teaspoon vanilla
¾ to 1 cup powdered sugar

Microwave chocolate, butter, and cream cheese in food processor bowl (without Steel Knife) uncovered at High until chocolate is softened, 1 to 2 minutes. Insert Steel Knife; process chocolate mixture and vanilla until smooth and fluffy, scraping side of bowl with spatula if necessary. Add half the sugar to bowl; process (Steel Knife) until sugar is blended into mixture. Add remaining sugar a few tablespoons at a time, processing until sugar is blended into mixture and mixture is of spreadable consistency.

Tips: Lemon Filling can be made 1 day in advance; refrigerate covered. Cake layers can be baked 1 day in advance; store at room temperature covered with plastic wrap.

Cake layers can also be baked conventionally, in 2 greased, floured 9-inch pans. Bake in preheated 375° F oven until toothpick inserted in center comes out clean, about 25 minutes.

WHIPPED CREAM
RICE PUDDING

Not only the creamiest, but also an extremely attractive rice pudding. Unmold it and garnish with fresh berries or peeled, sliced orange. Spoon some raspberry sauce (see Tip below) over the top, if you wish, and pass the rest separately.

Total Preparation Time: 45 to 48 minutes (plus chilling time)
Microwave Time: 28 to 31 minutes
Yield: 10 to 12 servings

---

1 cup uncooked long-grain rice
2½ cups milk
6 egg yolks
¾ cup granulated sugar
1½ cups half-and-half
1 tablespoon orange-flavored liqueur (optional)
2 teaspoons vanilla
2 packages (¼ ounce each) unflavored gelatin
½ cup water
½ cup blanched hazelnuts or almonds
2 cups whipping cream
⅓ cup powdered sugar

Microwave rice and milk in 2-quart glass casserole, covered, at High until rice is tender and milk is absorbed, about 15 minutes.

Process (Steel Knife) egg yolks and granulated sugar until thick and lemon colored, 1½ to 2 minutes. Microwave half-and-half in 4-cup glass measure uncovered at High just until boiling. With machine running, pour about ½ cup half-and-half through feed tube; stir egg mixture into half-and-half. Microwave uncovered at 50% (Medium) until thickened, 8 to 10 minutes, stirring every 2 minutes. Stir in liqueur and vanilla.

Stir gelatin into water in 1-cup glass measure; microwave uncovered at High until gelatin is dissolved, 30 to 45 seconds. Stir gelatin mixture into custard; stir custard mixture into rice. Refrigerate until chilled but not set, 45 minutes to 1 hour.

Process (Steel Knife) hazelnuts using on/off technique until chopped. Microwave nuts in

glass pie plate, uncovered, at High until toasted, 2 to 3 minutes, stirring every minute.

Process (Steel Knife) cream and powdered sugar until thick. Fold cream mixture and nuts into rice mixture; spoon into lightly greased 2-quart mold. Refrigerate until set, about 4 hours. Loosen edge of mold with tip of knife; dip mold briefly in warm water. Unmold on serving plate.

Tip: To make raspberry sauce, process (Steel Knife) one 10-ounce package partially thawed raspberries with 1 tablespoon sugar (optional) until smooth.

ORANGE 'N' SPICE
STEAMED PUDDING

If you look forward to steamed pudding at holiday time but dread the chopping and long steaming ritual, you'll appreciate this "unsteamed" pudding both for its speed and its fruity taste. Serve with Brandy Sauce (see following recipe), if you wish, and make extras for holiday gifts.

Total Preparation Time: 35 to 40 minutes
Microwave Time: 18 to 22 minutes
Yield: 8 to 10 servings

---

1 cup mixed dried fruit
½ cup currants or dark raisins
⅔ cup sugar
1 cup orange juice
½ cup dark corn syrup
2 tablespoons butter or margarine
1 egg
1 tablespoon grated orange rind
1 tablespoon orange-flavored liqueur or orange juice
½ teaspoon vanilla
½ cup dry bread crumbs
½ teaspoon ground cinnamon
1/16 teaspoon ground mace
1/16 teaspoon ground nutmeg
1 cup all-purpose flour
1 teaspoon baking soda
½ teaspoon salt
Whipped cream

Process (Steel Knife) fruit, currants, and 2 tablespoons of the sugar using on/off technique until fruit is finely chopped. Microwave fruit mixture and orange juice in 2-quart glass casserole, covered, at High until fruit is softened, 6 to 8 minutes, stirring after 3 minutes.

Process (Steel Knife) remaining sugar, the corn syrup, butter, egg, and orange rind until blended. Sprinkle remaining ingredients except whipped cream over mixture in bowl; process using on/off technique until blended. Add fruit mixture to bowl; process using on/off technique until blended. Spoon batter into greased 6-cup plastic or glass ring mold or 2-quart glass casserole with glass placed open end up in center. Microwave covered with plastic wrap at 50% (Medium) until set and toothpick inserted in center comes out clean, 12 to 14 minutes, rotating mold ¼ turn every 5 minutes. Let stand covered on counter top 10 minutes. Unmold on serving plate. Serve warm with whipped cream.

Tips: To make traditional hard sauce, process (Steel Knife) ½ cup softened butter with 2½ cups powdered sugar and ¼ cup brandy until smooth, scraping down side of bowl once or twice.

Orange 'N' Spice Steamed Pudding can be made 2 weeks in advance; refrigerate wrapped in aluminum foil. To reheat, microwave covered with plastic wrap at 50% (Medium) until warm, about 5 minutes.

RAISIN BREAD PUDDING WITH BRANDY SAUCE

Apple contributes to the ideal, moist texture of this pudding and pecans enhance the spices. Benefit twice from your microwave oven—once in the quick cooking and again in carefree reheating. Unlike conventional ovens, the microwave oven will warm bread pudding without drying it out.

Total Preparation Time: 36 to 41 minutes
Microwave Time: 14 to 17 minutes
Yield: 8 servings

2 tablespoons butter or margarine
4 slices raisin bread, cut into ½-inch cubes (about 2 cups)
½ teaspoon ground cinnamon
Pinch ground allspice
Pinch ground cloves
½ cup pecans
1 large apple, pared, cored, cut into 1-inch pieces
1 cup evaporated milk
3 eggs
⅔ cup packed light brown sugar
1 teaspoon vanilla
1 teaspoon grated orange rind
Brandy Sauce (recipe follows)

Microwave butter in 1½-quart glass casserole, uncovered, at High until melted; add bread cubes and toss. Sprinkle bread cubes with cinnamon, allspice, and cloves; toss. Microwave uncovered at High until bread cubes are crisp, 3 to 4 minutes, stirring after 2 minutes.

Process (Steel Knife) pecans and apple separately, using on/off technique, until coarsely chopped; add to bread cube mixture. Process (Steel Knife) remaining ingredients except Brandy Sauce until smooth; pour over bread cube mixture and toss. Microwave covered at High until set, 5 to 7 minutes, rotating casserole ¼ turn after 3 minutes. Let stand 10 minutes.

Make Brandy Sauce; serve with warm pudding.

Brandy Sauce

Yield: about 1 cup

⅓ cup butter or margarine
¼ cup granulated sugar
¼ cup packed light brown sugar
½ cup whipping cream or half-and-half
2 egg yolks, beaten
2 tablespoons brandy

Microwave butter in 4-cup glass measure at High until melted, about 2 minutes. Stir in sugars, cream, and egg yolks, Microwave uncovered at High 3 minutes, or until thickened, stirring with whisk every 30 seconds. Stir in brandy.

Tips: Substitute rye bread for the raisin bread, if you wish. The pudding can be served with whipped cream instead of Brandy Sauce.

The pudding can be refrigerated, covered, up to 2 days. To reheat, microwave covered at 50% (Medium) until warm.

BUTTERED CRUMB CRUST AND VARIATIONS

The fastest pie crust is the first step to fabulous Chocolate Mousse Pie, Lemon Cheesecake with Raspberry Sauce, and Apricot-Glazed Fruit Tart. Vary the type of crumb to match the filling and use with your favorite pudding or custard fillings, too. The Sesame and Poppy Seed variations are especially good for fruit and fruit-flavored fillings.

Total Preparation Time: 9 to 11 minutes
Microwave Time: 3 to 5 minutes
Yield: 1 pie crust (about 1⅓ cups crumbs)

---

22 graham crackers (2½ inches square), broken into pieces
2 to 3 tablespoons sugar
6 tablespoons butter or margarine

Process (Steel Knife) graham crackers and sugar using on/off technique until finely ground. Microwave butter in glass pie plate, uncovered, at High until melted; stir in crumb mixture and blend well. Press mixture on bottom and side of pie plate. Microwave

uncovered at High 1½ minutes, rotating pie plate ¼ turn after 1 minute. Cool on wire rack.

Tips: Melt butter in the baking dish that the crumb crust will bake in, whether it is a glass pie plate, glass quiche dish, or glass or plastic cake pan.

For an almost-instant dessert, fill the crumb crust with your favorite ice cream, softened, and freeze until firm. Spoon pureed raspberries or melted chocolate over each portion at serving time. To soften ice cream, microwave it in a glass bowl, uncovered, at 10% (Low).

VARIATIONS

GINGER: Substitute 12 gingersnaps (2½ ounces), broken into halves, for half the graham crackers; if desired, 25 gingersnaps can be substituted for the graham crackers.

VANILLA: Substitute 5½ ounces vanilla cookie wafers, broken into halves, for the graham crackers; omit sugar.

CHOCOLATE: Substitute 5½ ounces chocolate cookie wafers, broken into halves, for the graham crackers; omit sugar.

CRAZY MIXED-UP: Use 5½ ounces of any combination of above crumbs in place of the graham crackers; reduce sugar according to proportion of vanilla or chocolate cookies used.

TOASTED NUT: Microwave ½ cup desired nuts in glass pie plate, uncovered, at High until toasted, about 3 minutes, stirring after 1½ minutes. Substitute nuts for 7 graham crackers in above recipe.

SESAME SEED: Microwave 2 tablespoons sesame seeds in glass pie plate, uncovered, at High until toasted, about 2 minutes, stirring after 1 minute. Add butter to pie plate and proceed as above.

POPPY SEED: Stir 2 tablespoons poppy seeds into crumb mixture.

LEMON CHEESECAKE WITH RASPBERRY SAUCE

Processor blending and microwaves produce a fluffy cheesecake that's delectable with pureed raspberries.

Total Preparation Time: 24 to 25 minutes (plus chilling time)
Microwave Time: 12 to 13 minutes
Yield: 12 servings

Ginger Crumb Crust (see Index)
2 packages (8 ounces each) cream cheese, cut into quarters, softened
1 cup sugar
2 eggs
2 tablespoons lemon juice
1 teaspoon finely grated lemon rind
1 cup sour cream
3 tablespoons sugar
1 lemon, ends trimmed, cut to fit feed tube
1 package (10 ounces) frozen raspberries, slightly thawed
1 tablespoon sugar (optional)

Make Ginger Crumb Crust, pressing crumb mixture onto bottom and 1 inch up side of 9-inch round glass or plastic cake pan. Microwave at High 1½ minutes, rotating dish ¼ turn after 1 minute. Cool on wire rack.

Process (Steel Knife) cream cheese, 1 cup sugar, the eggs, lemon juice, and rind until smooth and fluffy, scraping bowl with rubber spatula if necessary. Spread mixture in crumb crust. Microwave uncovered at High until set, 7 to 8 minutes, rotating dish ¼ turn every 2 minutes. Combine sour cream and 3 tablespoons sugar; spread over cheesecake. Place cake pan on an inverted saucer. Microwave uncovered at 70% (Medium High) 3 minutes, rotating dish ¼ turn after 1½ minutes. Cool to room temperature; refrigerate until chilled, about 2 hours.

Slice (Slicing Disc) lemon; remove. Process (Steel Knife) raspberries and 1 tablespoon sugar until smooth. Cut cheesecake into wedges; garnish with lemon slices. Serve with raspberry sauce.

Tips: Elevating the cake pan on an inverted saucer or microwave roasting rack for the last 3 minutes of baking ensures that the center will cook evenly.

To get the most juice from a lemon or other citrus fruit, microwave at High 15 seconds. To soften cream cheese, remove from metallic wrapping, place on glass plate, and cut blocks of cheese into quarters; microwave uncovered at High just until softened.

To make Chocolate Cheesecake, process ½ cup cocoa with cream cheese mixture. Substitute 2 tablespoons orange juice for the lemon juice; substitute orange for the lemon rind and slices. Stir 2 tablespoons cocoa into sour cream mixture. Follow above recipe to make cheesecake, substituting Chocolate or Toasted Nut Crumb Crust (recipe above), if desired.

CHOCOLATE MOUSSE PIE

Some people call this a French silk pie, because the filling is as smooth as silk. The sugar dissolves as the pie stands; so refrigerate overnight for smoothest texture.

Total Preparation Time: 22 to 24 minutes (plus chilling time)
Microwave Time: 4 to 6 minutes
Yield: 8 servings

Buttered Crumb Crust or Chocolate Crumb Crust (see previous page)
3 ounces unsweetened chocolate, broken into pieces
½ cup cold butter or margarine, cut into pieces
½ cup granulated sugar
¼ cup packed light brown sugar
1 teaspoon vanilla
3 eggs
1 cup whipping cream

Make Buttered Crumb Crust using 9-inch glass pie plate.

Arrange chocolate pieces evenly in food processor bowl without Steel Knife. Microwave uncovered at High until chocolate is very soft, 2 to 3 minutes. Insert Steel Knife. Add butter and sugars to bowl; process until mixture is light and fluffy, about 15 seconds, scraping side of bowl with rubber spatula if necessary. Add vanilla to bowl. With machine running, add eggs one at a time through feed tube, blending well after each addition (sugar will not be dissolved). Spoon mixture into crust. Refrigerate until filling is set, 4 to 6 hours, or overnight. (Sugar will dissolve and filling will become smooth.)

Process (Steel Knife) cream until stiff. Garnish pie with whipped cream.

Tip: If desired, shred (Shredding Disc) 1 ounce chocolate and sprinkle over pie as garnish.

APRICOT–GLAZED FRUIT TART

A beautifully smooth pastry cream is the key to this elegant tart. Make the crust and the cream days in advance, if you wish. But slice the fruit and assemble the tart just before you sit down to dinner.

Total Preparation Time: 35 to 42 minutes (plus chilling time)
Microwave Time: 9 to 12 minutes
Yield: 12 servings

Pastry Cream (recipe follows)
Toasted Nut Crumb Crust (see Index)
¼ **medium pineapple, pared, cored, cut to fit feed tube**
¼ **medium cantaloupe or honeydew melon, pared, seeded, cut to fit feed tube**
½ **pint strawberries, hulled**
1 **banana, peeled, cut to fit feed tube**
¼ **cup apricot preserves**

Make Pastry Cream.
Make Toasted Nut Crumb Crust; pat onto 10-inch glass serving plate or in bottom of 10-inch

quiche dish. Do not bake; refrigerate until ready to assemble tart.

Spread Pastry Cream in crust. Slice (Slicing Disc) fruits separately; arrange decoratively over custard. Microwave preserves in 1-cup glass measure, uncovered, at High until melted, about 1 minute; brush preserves over fruit. Refrigerate tart until serving time.

Pastry Cream

Yield: about 3 cups

1 **cup sugar**
⅔ **cup all-purpose flour**
6 **egg yolks**
1 **cup half-and-half**
1 **cup whipping cream**
3 **tablespoons almond or orange-flavored liqueur**
1 **teaspoon vanilla**

Process (Steel Knife) sugar and flour using on/off technique until almost powdered. Add egg yolks to bowl; process until mixture is thick and lemon colored, scraping side of bowl with spatula if necessary. Microwave half-and-half and cream in 8-cup glass measure, uncovered, at High just until boiling, 2 to 4 minutes. With machine running, slowly pour half the cream mixture through feed tube into egg mixture, processing until blended. Stir egg mixture into remaining cream mixture. Microwave uncovered at 70% (Medium High) until thickened, 6 to 8 minutes, stirring with whisk every 2 minutes. Stir in liqueur and vanilla. Cool to room temperature. Refrigerate until ready to use.

Tips: Flavor will be best if tart is assembled as close to serving time as possible.

Other soft fruits, such as sliced peaches, sliced kiwi, raspberries, or blueberries can be substituted. Arrange fruit for maximum color contrast; concentric circles will yield a portion of all fruits in each slice, but a pinwheel of 8 sections is very attractive also.

When slicing strawberries, arrange them sideways in the feed tube for long, attractive slices.

INDIVIDUAL FRUIT TARTS

A very pretty alternative to a large fruit tart. The individual tarts are easier to serve than slices when the filling is whole blueberries or raspberries.

Total Preparation Time: 25 to 55 minutes (plus chilling time)
Microwave Time: Depends on pastry used
Yield: 6 servings

½ recipe Pastry Cream (previous recipe)
Toasted Nut Crumb Crust, Fillo Pastry Shells, or Tart Shells (see Index)
Assorted fresh fruit (melon, peaches, pineapple, kiwi, strawberries, bananas, etc.)
¾ **cup peach or apricot preserves**

Make Pastry Cream.
Make desired crust for tarts. If making crumb crust, press crumb mixture in bottoms of six 4-inch tartlet pans. Do not bake; refrigerate until ready to assemble tarts. Follow recipe directions for other crusts.
Select desired fruit. Peel, seed, core, or hull fruit as necessary; cut fruit to fit feed tube. Slice (Slicing Disc) fruit. Spoon Pastry Cream into tart crusts; arrange fruit decoratively over tops of tarts. Microwave preserves in 1-cup glass measure, uncovered, at High until melted, about 1 minute; brush preserves over fruit. Refrigerate tarts until serving time.

Tip: Flavor will be best if tarts are assembled as close to serving time as possible.

PIE PASTRY AND VARIATIONS

Microwave pastry is reliably tender and there is no need to fear overmixing or toughening the dough in the food processor. However, the pastry remains pale; so add the food coloring, if you wish. Use the Sesame, Cheese, and Herb variations with quiches. The Citrus variation is sensational for Coconut-Banana Cream Pie or individual Fruit Tarts (see Index).

Total Preparation Time: 13 to 17 minutes (plus chilling time)
Microwave Time: 5 to 7 minutes
Yield: 1 pastry shell

1½ **cups all-purpose flour**
6 **tablespoons frozen butter or margarine, cut into pieces**
3 **tablespoons chilled vegetable shortening**
2 **tablespoons sugar**
Few drops yellow food color (optional)
4 **to 5 tablespoons ice water**

Process (Steel Knife) flour, butter, shortening, and sugar using on/off technique until mixture resembles coarse meal. With machine running, add food color and water through feed tube until ingredients form ball of dough. Refrigerate dough covered 30 minutes.
Roll dough on lightly floured surface into round 1-inch larger than inverted glass pie plate; ease pastry into pie plate. Flute and trim pastry; pierce bottom with tines of fork. Microwave uncovered at High until pastry is beginning to brown, 5 to 7 minutes, rotating plate ¼ turn every 3 minutes. Cool on wire rack.

TART SHELLS: Make pastry as above. Roll pastry on lightly floured surface into round ⅛ inch thick. Invert six 10-ounce glass custard cups on dough; cut around custard cups to make rounds of dough. Shape pastry rounds on bottoms of custard cups; microwave as above. Remove shells from custard cups and cool on wire rack.

Tip: Refrigerating the dough makes it easier to roll; so does flouring the rolling pin.

VARIATIONS

SESAME: Add 1 tablespoon toasted sesame seeds to flour; make pastry as above.

NUT: Process (Steel Knife) the flour with ¼ cup nuts using on/off technique until nuts are finely chopped before adding other ingredients to the bowl. Make pastry as above.

CHEESE: Add ¼ cup shredded Cheddar or Swiss cheese to flour; omit sugar. Make pastry as above.

CITRUS: Add 1 tablespoon finely grated lemon, orange, or lime rind to flour; make pastry as above.

HERB: Add ½ teaspoon desired dried herbs to flour; omit sugar. Make pastry as above.

TOFFEE PIE

A sinfully good party pie, easily flavored with processor-chopped toffee bars. As long as you're indulging, you might want to make it with Nut Pastry.

Total Preparation Time: 35 to 37 minutes (plus chilling time)
Microwave Time: 9 to 13 minutes
Yield: 10 to 12 servings

---

1 Pie Pastry (previous recipe)
1 envelope (¼ ounce) unflavored gelatin
¼ cup cold milk
2 egg yolks
1 cup half-and-half
2 tablespoons sugar
1 teaspoon vanilla
⅛ teaspoon salt
4 chocolate-covered toffee candy bars (⅞ ounce each), broken into 1-inch pieces
1 cup whipping cream
2 tablespoons sugar

Make Pie Pastry using 9-inch glass pie plate.
Stir gelatin into milk in 1-cup glass measure. Microwave uncovered at High until gelatin is dissolved, 30 to 45 seconds.

Process (Steel Knife) egg yolks until thick and lemon colored, about 2 minutes. Combine beaten yolks, half-and-half, and 2 tablespoons sugar in 4-cup glass measure. Microwave uncovered at High until thickened, 4 to 6 minutes, stirring with whisk every 2 minutes. Stir in vanilla, salt, and gelatin mixture. Refrigerate until chilled, but not set, 1½ to 2 hours.
Process (Steel Knife) candy bars using on/off technique until finely chopped; remove. Process (Steel Knife) cream and 2 tablespoons sugar until thick; fold into gelatin mixture. Fold candy into gelatin mixture; spoon into pastry shell. Refrigerate until set, about 4 hours.

COCONUT–BANANA CREAM PIE

The best of two flavors for those who love delicate cream pies. If you wish to use freshly grated coconut, see Index for preparation tip.

Total Preparation Time: 47 to 52 minutes (plus chilling time)
Microwave Time: 19 to 22 minutes
Yield: 8 servings

Pastry Cream (see Index)
3 tablespoons coconut- or banana-flavored liqueur or 1 teaspoon vanilla
Pie Pastry (see Index)
¾ cup flaked coconut
2 medium bananas, peeled

Make Pastry Cream, substituting coconut-flavored liqueur for the almond-flavored liqueur. Refrigerate until chilled.
Make Pie Pastry, using 9-inch glass pie plate. Microwave coconut in glass pie plate, uncovered, at High until toasted, 3 to 4 minutes, stirring every minute.
Slice (Slicing Disc) 1 banana; arrange in bottom of pastry. Spoon Pastry Cream over banana; garnish edge of Pastry Cream with coconut. Refrigerate until serving time.
At serving time, slice (Slicing Disc) remaining banana; garnish top of pie.

BAKLAVA

Bake this famous Greek pastry in small triangles for maximum crispness. Then pour hot honey syrup over the dessert at serving time to meld the wonderful flavors of spiced walnut filling and flaky pastry.

Total Preparation Time: 31 to 32 minutes
Microwave Time: 8 to 10 minutes
Yield: 8 servings

¾ **cup walnuts**
¼ **cup dry bread crumbs (see Index)**
3 **tablespoons sugar**
½ **teaspoon ground cinnamon**
1⁄16 **teaspoon ground cloves**
⅓ **cup butter or margarine**
8 **sheets fillo pastry**
⅓ **cup honey**
⅓ **cup sugar**
⅓ **cup water**
1 **teaspoon grated orange rind**

Process (Steel Knife) walnuts using on/off technique until finely chopped; add bread crumbs, 3 tablespoons sugar, the cinnamon, and cloves to bowl. Process (Steel Knife) until very finely chopped.

Microwave butter in small glass bowl, uncovered, at High until melted. Cut sheets of fillo lengthwise into 4 equal strips. Brush 1 strip with butter; top with second strip and brush with butter. Sprinkle 1 tablespoon nut mixture over pastry; fold short end of pastry strip to side, forming triangle. Continue folding, flag-style. Repeat with remaining fillo, butter, and nut mixture.

Place 8 pastries seam sides down in circle in glass quiche dish or plate; microwave uncovered at High 2 minutes, turning pastries over after 1 minute. Repeat with remaining 8 pastries. Cool on wire rack (pastries will become crisper as they cool). Store in airtight container at room temperature.

At serving time, microwave honey, ⅓ cup sugar, the water, and orange rind in 2-cup glass measure, uncovered, at High until boiling. Place pastries in shallow glass baking dish; pour syrup over and let stand 5 minutes.

(Do not let stand longer or pastries will become soggy.) Serve immediately.

Tips: Fillo pastry, which is very similar to strudel dough, can be found in the frozen food cases of large supermarkets and both German and Middle Eastern groceries. Thaw fillo completely, according to package directions, before using; unused portions can be tightly wrapped and refrozen. When working with strips of fillo, keep remaining pieces covered with a damp dish towel to prevent them from drying out. This precaution is important, as the paper-thin dough can very quickly dry out and become too brittle to work with.

To fold Baklava triangles (illustration):

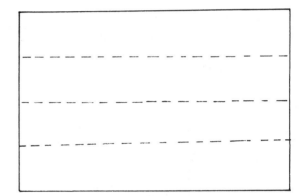

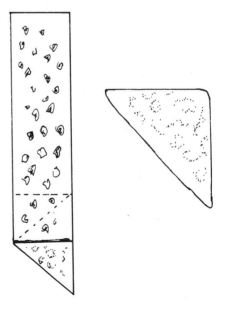

Unbaked Baklava can be frozen, tightly wrapped, up to 3 months.

FILLO PASTRY SHELLS

These crisp pastry shells are enormously versatile. Fill them with ice cream or Pastry Cream and Fresh Fruit. Substitute them for pie pastry to make individual Coconut-Banana Cream Pies. And use them to highlight entrées, such as Chicken and Shrimp in Fillo Shells, or your favorite seafood salad. (See Index for recipes.)

Total Preparation Time: 23 to 25 minutes
Microwave Time: 4 to 5 minutes
Yield: 6 shells

---

5 to 8 sheets fillo pastry
¼ cup butter or margarine

Cut fillo into thirty 4½-inch squares. Microwave butter in glass custard cup, uncovered, at High until melted. Brush 1 square fillo with butter; top with 1 square fillo. Repeat with butter and 3 more squares fillo; shape around bottom of inverted 10-ounce glass custard cup. Repeat with remaining fillo and butter to make 5 more shells. Place three custard cups in oven; microwave uncovered at High until crisp, 1 to 1½ minutes (pastry should NOT turn brown). Let stand 2 minutes; remove shells from custard cups and cool on wire rack. Repeat with remaining 3 shells. Store at room temperature in airtight container.

Tips: See previous recipe for tips on handling fillo pastry.

To cut squares of fillo, leave the sheets in a stack and cut straight down through the layers with a sharp slicing or serrated knife (don't drag the knife or you will risk tearing the pastry). You can also cut pastry with kitchen shears.

VIENNESE CHOCOLATE

The world's most luxurious sipping—a custom imported from European pastry shops. Serve it with cookies or all by itself, after dinner or at teatime. Drizzle a small amount of chocolate or coffee liqueur into each mug, if you wish.

Total Preparation Time: 16 to 18 minutes
Microwave Time: 5 to 7 minutes
Yield: 6 servings (about 4 ounces each)

---

1 cup whipping cream
2 ounces semisweet chocolate, broken into pieces
2 cups milk
2 tablespoons sugar
1 teaspoon vanilla
Freshly grated nutmeg

Process (Steel Knife) cream until stiff; transfer to small bowl. Place chocolate in food processor bowl without Steel Knife; microwave uncovered at High until chocolate is soft but not melted, about 2 minutes, stirring after 1 minute. Insert Steel Knife. Microwave milk, sugar, and vanilla in 4-cup glass measure, uncovered, at High just until boiling. With machine running (Steel Knife), pour milk mixture through feed tube, processing until completely mixed with chocolate. Add whipped cream to bowl; process using on/off technique just until blended. Serve in small mugs; sprinkle with nutmeg.

Tip: Cream will whip more quickly if the food processor workbowl and Steel Knife are both chilled before processing.

FLAVORED COFFEES

For convenient brewing, process instant coffee with sugar and spices and keep the mixture on hand. All of these coffees can be served over ice or laced with a complementary liqueur.

NEW ORLEANS COFFEE

Total Preparation Time: 5 to 7 minutes
Microwave Time: 1 to 2 minutes
Yield: 12 servings

¾ **cup instant coffee crystals**
¼ **cup packed light brown sugar**
¼ **teaspoon ground cardamom**
Water
Whipping cream (optional)
Cinnamon sticks (optional)

Process (Steel Knife) coffee, sugar, and cardamom until mixed; store in airtight container. For each cup coffee, measure ⅔ cup water into coffee cup; microwave uncovered at High until boiling; stir in scant 1½ tablespoons coffee mixture. Process (Steel Knife) cream until stiff. Garnish coffee with dollop of cream; serve with cinnamon stick stirrer.

COFFEE MOCHA

Total Preparation Time: 8 to 9 minutes
Microwave Time: 1 to 2 minutes
Yield: 12 servings

¾ **cup instant coffee crystals**
½ **cup sugar**
¼ **cup cocoa**
1½ **teaspoons ground cinnamon**
⅛ **to ¼ teaspoon ground nutmeg**
Milk
Water

Semisweet chocolate (optional)
Whipping cream (optional)

Process (Steel Knife) coffee, sugar, cocoa, cinnamon, and nutmeg until mixed; store in airtight container. For each cup coffee, measure ⅓ cup milk and ⅓ cup water into coffee cup; microwave uncovered at High until boiling; stir in 2 tablespoons coffee mixture. Shred (Shredding Disc) chocolate; remove. Process (Steel Knife) cream until stiff. Garnish coffee with dollop of cream; sprinkle with chocolate.

ORANGE SPICED COFFEE

Total Preparation Time: 6 to 8 minutes
Microwave Time: 1 to 2 minutes
Yield: 12 servings

¾ **cup instant coffee crystals**
¼ **cup sugar**
2 **tablespoons presweetened orange drink mix**
¾ **teaspoon ground allspice**
¼ **teaspoon ground cloves**
Milk
Water
1 **small orange, cut to fit feed tube (optional)**

Process (Steel Knife) coffee, sugar, drink mix, allspice, and cloves until mixed; store in airtight container. For each cup coffee, measure ⅓ cup milk and ⅓ cup water into coffee cup; microwave uncovered at High until boiling; stir in 1½ tablespoons coffee mixture. Slice (Slicing Disc) orange; garnish each cup of coffee with orange slice.

Chocolate Peanut Butter Cups
Chocolate Rum Truffles
Coconut Pecan Caramels
Caramel Corn Snack Mix
Candied Walnuts
New England Mincemeat
Peach Chutney
Jalapẽno Pepper Jelly
Vegetable Antipasto
Bread and Butter Pickles
Orange Flowerpot Breads

17 Candies and Food Gifts

CHOCOLATE PEANUT BUTTER CUPS

The best of gifts, the worst temptation! If anything, these divine chocolate, peanutty candies are too easy to make!

Total Preparation Time: 32 to 34 minutes (plus
freezing time)
Microwave Time: 2 to 4 minutes
Yield: 1½ dozen

---

12 ounces semisweet chocolate
3 tablespoons butter or margarine
1 cup cocktail peanuts
1½ teaspoons honey
½ cup powdered sugar
3 tablespoons butter or margarine, softened
Assorted preserves (any flavor)

Microwave chocolate and 3 tablespoons butter in 4-cup glass measure, uncovered, at High until melted, 2 to 4 minutes; stir well. Spread chocolate on sides and bottoms of 18 mini-muffin papers with small spatula or brush (you should have 2 to 3 tablespoons chocolate left over); place in freezer until firm, about 10 minutes.

Process (Steel Knife) peanuts until smooth butter is formed, 5 to 6 minutes, scraping bowl with rubber spatula if necessary. Add honey, half the sugar, and 3 tablespoons softened butter to bowl; process (Steel Knife) until smooth. Add remaining sugar; process until smooth.

Spoon a generous teaspoon of desired preserves in bottom of each chocolate cup; fill each almost to top with peanut butter mixture. Brush remaining chocolate over each cup to seal in filling; freeze until firm, about 10 minutes. Carefully peel off paper. Store in airtight container at room temperature.

CHOCOLATE RUM TRUFFLES

An elegant chocolate almost entirely prepared right in the food processor bowl. A grand menu finale, these make a terrific gift for a dinner host or hostess.

Total Preparation Time: 19 to 22 minutes (plus
chilling time)
Microwave Time: 4 to 6 minutes
Yield: about 3 dozen

---

1 cup blanched almonds
8 graham crackers (2½-inch squares), broken into pieces
8 gingersnaps, broken into halves
2 tablespoons light rum
1 cup semisweet chocolate morsels
½ cup cold butter or margarine, cut into pieces
½ cup powdered sugar
½ teaspoon vanilla
⅓ cup whipping cream

Process (Steel Knife) almonds until finely chopped. Microwave almonds in glass pie plate uncovered at High until toasted, about 3 minutes, stirring after 1½ minutes; reserve.

Process (Steel Knife) graham crackers and gingersnaps using on/off technique until finely ground. Add rum to bowl; process using on/off technique until blended. Add chocolate, butter, sugar, and vanilla to bowl. Microwave cream in 1-cup glass measure, uncovered, at High until boiling; with machine running (Steel Knife), add boiling cream through feed tube, processing until mixture is smooth and scraping bowl with rubber spatula if necessary. Refrigerate mixture in food processor bowl until firm enough to hold shape.

Spoon chocolate mixture into pastry bag fitted with medium plain tip. Pipe mixture in ½-inch mounds onto cookie sheet; refrigerate until firm. Roll candies in chopped almonds. If candies become too soft at room temperature, refrigerate in covered container.

Tips: *The chocolate morsels will melt when you pour the boiling cream through the food processor feed tube with the machine running.*

You can spoon the chocolate mixture onto the cookie sheet instead of piping it through a pastry bag, if you wish.

COCONUT PECAN CARAMELS

The ideal creamy caramel, with the chewiness of coconut and the crunch of pecans.

Total Preparation Time: 41 to 46 minutes
Microwave Time: 31 to 34 minutes
Yield: 4 dozen pieces

½ cup shredded coconut
1 cup pecans
1 cup granulated sugar
1 cup packed light brown sugar
¾ cup light corn syrup
⅓ cup butter or margarine
2 cups whipping cream
⅛ teaspoon salt
1 teaspoon vanilla

Microwave coconut in glass pie plate, uncovered, at High until toasted, 1½ to 2 minutes, stirring every 30 seconds. Process (Steel Knife) pecans using on/off technique until finely chopped. Microwave pecans in glass pie plate, uncovered, at High until toasted, about 3 minutes, stirring after 1½ minutes.

Combine sugars, corn syrup, butter, 1 cup of the cream, and the salt in 4-quart glass bowl. Microwave uncovered at High 10 minutes, stirring twice. Gradually stir in remaining cream. Microwave uncovered at High until mixture registers 250° F on candy thermometer, 16 to 19 minutes; stir 3 times during first 12 minutes of cooking time and every minute thereafter, checking temperature every minute. Stir in coconut, pecans, and vanilla; pour into greased 8-inch square pan. Cool; cut into squares.

Tips: Do not leave the thermometer in the candy mixture unless it is specially designed for microwave ovens. It is very important to check the temperature every minute toward the end of cooking time, as the temperature can increase suddenly; if the mixture gets too hot, it will become brittle. It is possible, but quite inconvenient, to make caramels without a thermometer. If you do not have a thermometer, use the water test: Drop a little of the syrup into a cup of cold water; it should form a firm ball that does not flatten upon removal from the water.

For easier cleanup after candy making, add water to the cooking bowl and microwave at High to dissolve the sugar mixture, scraping the sides of the bowl occasionally.

CARAMEL CORN SNACK MIX

Shake and bake this favorite snack mix in a brown paper bag. No mess, and no candy thermometer needed.

Total Preparation Time: 17 to 20 minutes
Microwave Time: 7 to 8 minutes
Yield: about 4 quarts

1 cup pitted dates
8 ounces walnuts
3 cups miniature pretzels
3 quarts popped corn
½ cup butter or margarine
¼ cup dark corn syrup
1 cup packed light brown sugar
½ teaspoon baking soda
1 teaspoon vanilla

Process (Steel Knife) dates and walnuts separately, using on/off technique, until coarsely chopped. Combine dates, walnuts, pretzels, and popped corn in large, heavy, brown paper grocery bag.

Microwave butter, corn syrup, and sugar in 8-cup glass measure, uncovered, at High 5 minutes, stirring every 2 minutes. Stir in baking soda and vanilla. Pour mixture over popped corn mixture in bag; close bag (fold top of bag down twice to close securely) and shake well. Microwave at High 2 minutes, shaking bag every minute. Microwave at High 30 seconds; shake bag and pour mixture into serving bowl; let cool.

Tips: Consult the manufacturer's manual to determine whether you can make popped corn in your oven; if not recommended, make popped corn conventionally. Do not make popped corn in a paper bag.

The paper bag ensures that each grain of popcorn will be evenly coated with the caramel mixture. If you prefer to cook the snack mix in serving bowls, divide the popped corn mixture between 2 heatproof 3-quart glass bowls. Make caramel mixture as above and pour half the mixture into each bowl; toss well. Microwave 1 bowl at a time, as above, stirring every minute.

To make plain caramel corn, omit dates, walnuts, and pretzels; use 4 quarts of popped corn.

Caramel Corn Snack Mix can be stored at room temperature in airtight containers up to 1 month.

CANDIED WALNUTS

An afterdinner confection or snack for those who like things not-too-sweet.

Total Preparation Time: 15 to 20 minutes
Microwave Time: 8 to 12 minutes
Yield: about 2½ cups

2½ cups walnut halves
2 egg whites
2 tablespoons water
¼ cup powdered sugar
⅛ teaspoon cream of tartar
¼ teaspoon ground cinnamon

Microwave walnuts in 12″ × 8″ glass baking dish, uncovered, at High until toasted, about 3 minutes, stirring after 1½ minutes. Cool to room temperature.
Process (Steel Knife) egg whites, water, sugar, and cream of tartar until egg whites form stiff peaks. Add cinnamon to bowl; process using on/off technique until blended. Fold egg whites into walnuts in baking dish until nuts are evenly coated with egg mixture.

Microwave uncovered at High until nuts are glazed, 5 to 7 minutes, stirring every 1½ minutes (nuts will be sticky). Cool to room temperature. (Nuts will become dry. If not completely dry, microwave uncovered at High 1 to 2 minutes longer.) Store in airtight container.

NEW ENGLAND MINCEMEAT

This well-calculated investment in holiday pie baking will last from one season to the next. Purchased mincemeat can't compare in depth of flavor.

Total Preparation Time: 110 to 120 minutes
Microwave Time: 90 to 92 minutes
Yield: 2 quarts

---

1 cup pecans
2½ cups golden raisins
2 cups sugar
1 cup currants
1½ teaspoons ground cinnamon
½ teaspoon ground nutmeg
½ teaspoon ground allspice
¼ teaspoon ground cloves
⅛ teaspoon salt
1/16 teaspoon pepper
1 pound lean boneless beef, cut into 1-inch pieces
4 ounces beef suet, chilled, cut into 1-inch pieces
1 can (16 ounces) tart cherries, undrained
1½ pounds tart apples, pared, cored, cut into quarters
1 cup apple juice
¼ cup lemon juice
Grated rind from 1 lemon
Grated rind from 1 orange
¼ to ½ cup brandy

Process (Steel Knife) pecans using on/off technique until finely chopped; transfer to 3½-quart glass bowl. Process (Steel Knife) raisins and 1 cup of the sugar using on/off technique until finely chopped; add to nuts in bowl. Stir in currants, remaining sugar, the cinnamon, nutmeg, allspice, cloves, salt, and pepper. Process (Steel Knife) beef and suet separately, using on/off technique, until finely chopped; add to fruit mixture. Process (Steel Knife) cherries and juice using on/off technique until chopped; add to fruit mixture. Process (Steel Knife) apples using on/off technique until chopped; stir into fruit mixture with remaining ingredients except brandy, mixing thoroughly.

Microwave mixture uncovered at High 1½ hours, stirring every 15 minutes. Cool to room temperature; stir in brandy. Refrigerate in covered containers up to 1 year. Stir every 3 to 4 weeks, adding more brandy, if desired.

Tip: Unless you have a large-model food processor, chop no more than ½ pound of beef at a time.

PEACH CHUTNEY

It's so easy to processor-chop and microwave your own chutney that there's little reason to settle for the inferior taste of commercial products. To keep up with the seasons, substitute other fruit when the peaches aren't ripe. Serve chutney with poultry, lamb, or ham, as well as Indian curries.

Total Preparation Time: 32 to 39 minutes
Microwave Time: 20 to 25 minutes
Yield: about 1½ cups

---

1 **clove garlic, peeled**
4 **medium peaches, pared, pitted, cut into 1-inch pieces**
1 **green pepper, seeded, cut into 1-inch pieces**
1 **small onion, peeled, cut into 1-inch pieces**
1 **jalapeño or hot pepper, seeded, cut into 1-inch pieces**
¾ **cup packed light brown sugar**
½ **cup dark raisins**

½ **cup cider vinegar**
2 **tablespoons lime juice**
1 **teaspoon ground ginger**
½ **teaspoon dry mustard**
½ **teaspoon salt**

With machine running (Steel Knife), drop garlic through feed tube, processing until minced. Add peaches, green pepper, onion, and hot pepper to bowl; process using on/off technique until coarsely chopped.

Combine peach mixture and remaining ingredients in 1½-quart glass casserole. Microwave uncovered at High until thickened, 20 to 25 minutes, stirring every 10 minutes. Spoon into sterilized jar; cool to room temperature. Cover and refrigerate up to 1 month.

Tips: See following recipe for instructions on sterilizing jars. For longer storage, process jars in a water-bath canner according to USDA or manufacturer's instructions. Do not attempt to can food in the microwave oven. Peach Chutney can also be frozen tightly covered up to 6 months.

Four medium pears or one small cantaloupe or honeydew melon can be substituted for the peaches; pare, core or seed, and cut fruit into 1-inch pieces.

JALAPEÑO PEPPER JELLY

There's just a hint of chili heat in this scrumptious jelly. Mostly it tastes very fresh and mildly sweet—unlike any other kind of preserve. Serve it as an hors d'oeuvre with crackers and softened cream cheese; it won't overwhelm dinner appetites.

Total Preparation Time: 20 to 25 minutes
Microwave Time: 12 to 13 minutes
Yield: about 3 pints

---

1 medium fresh jalapeño or poblano
  pepper, seeded, cut into 1-inch pieces
4 medium fresh or canned jalapeño
  peppers, seeded, cut into 1-inch pieces
1 medium green pepper, seeded, cut into 1-
  inch pieces
⅔ cup distilled white vinegar
⅔ cup cider vinegar
5½ cups sugar
¼ teaspoon crushed dried red pepper
1 to 2 dashes red pepper sauce
2 packets (3 ounces each) liquid fruit pectin

Process (Steel Knife) jalapeño and green
peppers using on/off technique until finely
chopped. Combine peppers and remaining
ingredients, except pectin, in 8-cup glass
measure. Microwave uncovered at High until
mixture boils, about 8 minutes. Let mixture
boil 3 minutes. Stir in pectin. Microwave
uncovered at High until mixture boils; boil 1
minute. Skim off foam; pour into sterilized
jars. Cool to room temperature. Cover and
refrigerate up to 3 months.

*Tips: For best flavor, use at least one fresh chili
pepper in this recipe; the rest can be
canned. If you use canned chilies, rinse
and drain them thoroughly. Be careful not
to touch eyes when removing seeds and
veins, as the juice can cause irritation.*

*To sterilize jars, stand them in a large
kettle, add water to cover and heat to
boiling conventionally; boil, covered, for
10 minutes and leave jars immersed in
the hot water until you are ready to use
them. There is no reason to use the
microwave oven for this purpose.*

VEGETABLE ANTIPASTO

Low-calorie hors d'oeuvres, great picnic fare,
and a bright garnish for platters of cold meats
and cheese are all packed in colorful jars of
Vegetable Antipasto. The mixture comes

together so quickly that you may want to make
several batches, especially when there's a good
supply of ripe peppers.

Total Preparation Time: 24 to 26 minutes
Microwave Time: 9 to 11 minutes
Yield: 1 quart

---

2 medium carrots, pared, cut to fit feed
  tube
1 cup cauliflowerets
¼ cup water
2 medium red or green peppers, seeded, cut
  to fit feed tube
4 ounces mushrooms
¾ cup pitted ripe olives
⅔ cup olive oil
½ cup water
½ cup white wine vinegar
¼ cup lemon juice
1 teaspoon dry mustard
12 peppercorns
1 teaspoon dried tarragon leaves
¼ teaspoon dried thyme leaves
1 bay leaf, crumbled
⅛ teaspoon crushed dried red peppers

Slice (Slicing Disc) carrots and
cauliflowerets; microwave in 2 separate bowls
with 2 tablespoons water, covered with plastic
wrap, at High until crisp-tender, about 4
minutes. Drain. Slice (Slicing Disc) fresh
peppers, mushrooms, and olives separately.
Layer vegetables in sterilized 1-quart glass jar.
Microwave oil and remaining ingredients in
4-cup glass measure, uncovered, at High until
boiling, about 5 minutes. Pour over vegetables.
Cool to room temperature; cover and
refrigerate up to 1 month.

BREAD AND BUTTER PICKLES

Treat all sandwich platters to these tangy
slices and honor a good cucumber harvest by
presenting extra jars as gifts.

Total Preparation Time: 30 to 35 minutes (plus standing time)
Microwave Time: 15 to 20 minutes
Yield: about 3 pints

2　pounds cucumbers, ends trimmed, cut to fit feed tube
2　medium onions, peeled, cut to fit feed tube
½　cup salt
5　cups water
1　cup cider vinegar
1　cup sugar
1　teaspoon mustard seeds
½　teaspoon dill seeds
½　teaspoon ground turmeric
¼　teaspoon ground allspice

Slice (Slicing Disc) cucumbers and onions; transfer to 3-quart bowl. Sprinkle with salt; pour in 4 cups of the water. Let stand 2 hours. Drain and rinse thoroughly.

Microwave remaining 1 cup water, the cucumber mixture, and remaining ingredients in 3-quart glass casserole, covered, at High until vegetables are crisp-tender, 15 to 20 minutes, stirring after 8 minutes. Spoon pickles into sterilized jars; cool to room temperature. Cover and refrigerate up to 1 month.

Tips: To sterilize jars and to can pickles for longer storage, see recipes for Jalapeño Pepper Jelly and Peach Chutney (see Index).

The above recipe can easily be doubled, but don't microwave more than 3 pints at a time.

ORANGE FLOWERPOT BREADS

An adorable way to present individual loaves of a rich, raisin-pecan bread. Wrap them as gifts or "plant" at brunchtime tablesettings.

Total Preparation Time: 69 to 73 minutes
Microwave Time: 26 to 27 minutes
Yield: 8 loaves

¼　cup orange juice
1　package (¼ ounce) active dry yeast
3　tablespoons granulated sugar
2　cups unbleached flour
1　teaspoon salt
⅓　cup frozen butter or margarine, cut into pieces
¼　cup pecans
¼　cup dark raisins
1　teaspoon grated orange rind
2　eggs
⅓　cup powdered sugar
⅛　teaspoon vanilla
1　to 2 teaspoons orange juice
3　teaspoons grated orange rind

Microwave ¼ cup orange juice in 1-cup glass measure until warm (110° F); stir in yeast and granulated sugar. Let stand 5 minutes. Insert Steel Knife in food processor bowl. Measure flour and salt into bowl; add butter, pecans, raisins, and 1 teaspoon orange rind. Process using on/off technique until butter is incorporated into the flour. Add eggs to bowl; process until dough forms a ball. Let ball of dough spin around bowl 5 times. (If dough is too moist, sprinkle 1 to 2 tablespoons flour over dough and process until blended.) Remove Steel Knife; cover food processor bowl with plastic wrap.

Place food processor bowl in shallow glass baking dish; fill baking dish halfway with warm water. Microwave at 10% (Low) 10 minutes; let stand covered 10 minutes. Shape dough into 8 equal-sized balls. Generously grease 8 clean clay flowerpots, 2½″ × 2½″. Place dough in flowerpots; cover loosely with plastic wrap. Place flowerpots in a circle in the oven; place 2 small custard cups filled with warm water in diagonal corners of oven. Microwave at 10% (Low) 10 minutes; let stand covered 10 minutes or until doubled in bulk. Remove plastic wrap and custard cups; rearrange flowerpots. Microwave uncovered at 50%

(Medium) until tops of breads are no longer
moist, 5 to 6 minutes, rearranging flowerpots
after 3 minutes. Let stand on counter top 5
minutes.

Mix powdered sugar, vanilla, and 1 to 2
teaspoons orange juice to make glaze
consistency. Spoon glaze over breads; sprinkle
with 3 teaspoons orange rind.

Tips: *Make sure orange juice is no warmer
than 110° F when you stir in the yeast.
Scrape down side of bowl, as necessary,
when processing the dough.*

*Breads can be baked in 8 greased, 3-
ounce custard cups, if desired; proceed as
above.*

Index

C.1

641.589 Spitler, Sue.
S
            Twice as fast